1936 3-

Edith R. [illegible]

April 1937.

This book was dirty like this when I bought it! Why didn't I send it back to Macy's?

A BOOK OF MENUS WITH RECIPES

A BOOK OF MENUS WITH RECIPES

BY
DELLA T. LUTES

BREAKFAST
LUNCHEON
DINNER
BUFFET SUPPER

G·P·PUTNAM'S SONS
New York
1936

Printed in the United States of America
VAN REES PRESS, NEW YORK

CONTENTS

To My Fellow Sufferers in Meal Planning

ALL the years of my life—at least all of those years which have been linked with homemaking—and they have been many, I have had to plan meals for a family to eat. And most of that time I have cooked them as well. Never once has there been an obsequious butler or even an obstreperous housekeeper to take the menu from my hand and execute it. I have always had to do my own executing. Moreover, there has never been a time when, with a flourish of my pen I could write down porter-house steak one day and crown roasts the next (especially during the last hard-pressed years) with strawberries in January, cucumbers in February and green peas in March. I thought I was doing pretty well by the family if I gave them a cucumber in their salad on Easter with strawberry shortcake for dessert. Even that was a long way ahead of the way we had to do it when I was a little girl on a farm in Southern Michigan. Then we waited for the seasons to deliver their treasures in rote and made the best of it.

So, because I like my food of good flavor even if it must be plain, and because a reasonably well balanced diet was cheaper to manage in the long run than doctors' bills, or irritated people, the planning of meals took on new interest and became more or less of a game. Housework has to be made a game if you are not going to let it get the best of you.

How to cook inexpensive meals so they would not all taste alike; how to combine meats, vegetables and fruits to get the best in flavor and appearance; in short, how to set a table for an average, middle class family that would give them something to look forward to, and to remember with pleasure, was the game—or the problem, whichever way you want to look at it.

This is no easy task, as all who read will agree, and although throughout the years when homemaking was my first and only interest, I knew that all my neighbor women were struggling with the same problem, I did not wholly realize that meal planning was the biggest bug-bear in every homemaking woman's life until I took a job where women all over the country were my neighbors. Then, when letters began to pour in by the thousands asking for help in menu making, I realized that here, perhaps, was an opportunity for a real service.

There is an abundance of food of all kinds to be had in these days and we do not have to wait for the seasons to roll around to get a variety. Most of it, too, is easily prepared. Too easily prepared, sometimes, to stimulate interest and imagination or to encourage either originality in preparation or even that personal care that gives distinction to a dish. Even the "prepared" dishes can usually be doctored up a little to please individual taste, and quite a little study can be given to the combination of foods with no harm to any one.

There is still, for most of us, the matter of economy and the consequent danger of monotony. Hamburg steak *is* cheap, not only because it is low in price but because it is nutritious and contains no waste. So we have Hamburg twice a week anyway, prepared always in the same way until we ought to be ashamed to look a meat grinder in the face. A little thought and imagination—and study—will help to disguise it at least part of the time.

And so, because I have sometimes had imagination to spare as well as oceans of experience in economy, I have collected together a good many of the dishes resulting from both, and some others, and made them up into menus that may keep you from tearing your hair and walking the floor in that daily mad struggle with the question, "What *shall* I have for dinner today?" I thought that you might, instead, like to twirl the pages of this book back and forth until your eye lights upon something that just hits the spot, if it is no more than a dish you have had some time or other and had forgotten.

No claim is made for entire originality in these recipes. Most of them I have either made up, as the children say, out of my own head, or adapted; others have been contributed by friends, and heaven knows where *they* got them. Some have generously been contributed by such commercial companies as maintain entire departments for the sole purpose of developing recipes. But all of them have been tried—most of them in my own kitchen, and pronounced good. Not every one will like all of them, for I may like parsnips and you detest them. But there is a sufficiently wide choice so that I may have my parsnips and you may pass them by and find something you do like.

What I have done that seems to me the greater value, is to select not only dishes that taste well, but ingredients and foods that are not expensive, and then combine them with other appetizing foods making menus reasonably well balanced and easy to prepare.

These menus are not always complete as they stand. I have wanted to save space for the more important things and so I have left it to you to put in such things as bread (if you want it), potatoes when I did not have room for potatoes and the vegetables that I thought ought to be mentioned. Occasionally no first course is given. It has been my experience that sometimes the first course is left out of the menu after it gets on the table. And it is easy enough to put in a soup or an appetizer if it is wanted. All you have to remember is that with a hearty dinner, a thin soup or a fruit cocktail is better than a cream soup. That if you have a fruit salad you do not want a fruit cocktail; and that with a dinner in which there is fat, a sharp first course is better than a sweet or a heavy soup. So, I have mentioned enough first courses to take care of the company and left it to you to take care of the family.

Another thing that I have tried to bear in mind is the appeal to the eye. I suppose it wouldn't matter much to a blind man whether there was any parsley alongside his fish or not, but to those of us who are blessed with sight, there is huge satisfaction in the beauty of the food placed before us. One might think, from the frequency with which parsley is recommended in all food recipes of the day (or nearly all) that there was some tremendous if subtle propaganda afoot, but so far as I know most of the parsley grows in somebody's garden or comes out of the butcher's refrigerator. Parsley, to be sure, was once renowned for other purposes than garnishing. Hercules had a crown made of it after killing the Nemean Lion. And Horace used it to decorate his banquet halls. But we use it to decorate the plate of ham and eggs, and a thousand other things.

If you give it a moment's thought you can see how flat and unappealing would be a dinner of fish with white sauce, a dish of mashed potatoes, another of cauliflower. But, with some radish roses, a few sprigs of parsley, slices of carrot or lemon, a stuffed olive here and there, the whole scene changes and the digestive juices begin to respond. So, if you see radish roses, slices of cucumber and carrot, small beets, cauliflowerlets, and radishes mentioned over and over as garnishes, you won't think I am just filling space, but realize that this is just a little prodding so that you will go me a step further and think up something your own self that will beautify—and glorify—the food on your table, plain and unassuming though it is.

For most of the dishes here given are plain. Of course there is a turkey dinner, and a goose dinner and a fricasseed duck and things like that—even planked steak and planked fish which look very swanky but which in reality save dishes. But in the main the food is what we call good plain cooking. And that, I believe, is what we need most to learn.

To my way of thinking it is far better that a young wife should know just how to prepare and cook a stew with dumplings than how to stodge up some kind of a sweet mess that no man would want to eat and that would give him indigestion if he did. How to cook a pork chop to perfection and make a good milk gravy afterward will endear a girl to an honest man more than all the whipped cream and marshmallow confections she can muster. Or else I'm mistaken.

How to broil a steak, how to make a chicken pie, what to serve with both or either are vital things in home life. You cannot get around the fact that life depends on food. So does, in great measure, happiness. So, certainly does a great deal of our pleasure. A handsomely dressed, properly set, well furnished table supplied with good food perfectly cooked, and a few congenial souls around it is one of the most satisfying things in life. But no amount of lovely linen, solid silver or crystal can make up for underdone veal, soggy biscuit or "paste" masquerading as white sauce. As for a good apple pie—words fail me. The art of making a good apple pie is, if not already lost, fast receding into that dim and lovely past where home-made bread and sugar cookies and buckwheat cakes long since disappeared. If somebody could think up a contest so that all the housewives in the country would began to vie with each other in the making of apple pie, it would not matter whether we had a New Deal or no Deal at all. It would not matter who was President or whether we lived by the Alphabet or the Roman numerals. For then the American Home would be restored, and the *home* would rule the country.

LUNCHEON MENUS

NEW ENGLAND CLAM CHOWDER
STUFFED TOMATOES
FIG TART

THE luncheon menus which follow are simply planned and with no claim to elaborate detail. We think them especially suitable for family use, or for informal entertaining. Occasionally we have slipped in a dish that might, perhaps, cause a little flurry in the bridge club, but in the main the menu is intended as a solution to the commoner problem of what to have to eat when you have a house guest, or when you want to entertain one of the girls who is home on a visit. First courses are not always given, since, with the main dish a reasonably light one and a not too heavy dessert, it does not matter so much whether a soup, a cocktail or a salad precedes the meal. Cream soups are frequently suggested because they contribute weight to the meal—a consideration which prohibits them from the heavier dinner. And cream soups as well as chowders, are too delicious not to be often included somewhere in our diet.

New England Clam Chowder

1 pt. clams
2 onions
6 large crackers
1 tbsp. butter
1 pt. milk
3 potatoes (medium)
¼ lb. lean salt pork
Salt, pepper

Cut pork into very small pieces and fry out the fat. Slice the onions, dice the raw potatoes. Fry both onion and potato in fat until nearly tender. Chop the clams and put in saucepan with the vegetables and just enough water to cover. Let simmer thirty minutes, adding water as it boils away. At the end of that time add hot milk, butter, seasonings. Pour over crackers and serve very hot.

When clams are left over from a steamed clam feast, add clam broth instead of water to sautéd potatoes, simmer as before, add already cooked and chopped clams; then add milk and seasonings. The use of clam broth is really preferable as it makes a better flavored chowder.

Stuffed Tomatoes

Firm ripe tomatoes
Salt, pepper, sugar
Butter
Left-over meat
Bread crumbs
Grated cheese
Toast

Slice the tops from as many firm good sized tomatoes as there are servings. Remove pulp from center and sprinkle with salt and pepper. Put a small piece of butter in the bottom of each. Fill with finely chopped and well seasoned cold cooked meat mixed with a fourth its quantity of tomato pulp also well seasoned. Sprinkle thickly with buttered bread crumbs. Set in a buttered glass baking dish which has been sprinkled with bread crumbs, and set in a moderate oven until tomatoes are tender. Just before they are done, sprinkle grated cheese over and remove from oven when cheese is melted and crumbs are brown.

Fig Tart

1 cup cooked raisins
1 cup cooked figs
1 egg
1 cup sugar
Juice and grated rind of 1 lemon

Chop fruit, add sugar, lemon and beaten egg. Fill cooked pastry shell almost full and place thin strip of pastry across top and bake 20 or 25 minutes at 350 degrees.

GRAPE-FRUIT—JELLY CENTER

HAM LOAF

LEMON SOUFFLÉ

To make menus intelligently, some knowledge of nutritional fundamentals is necessary but it does not require a doctor's degree to accomplish this feat. One should remember, for one thing, that variety *is* the spice of life, and that this is as true of daily meals as anywhere else. And that without variety, the process of providing three meals a day becomes a monotonous routine, and the consumption of them, while taking a shorter time, even worse. There should be variety in appearance—for the eye eats first and waits on neither appetite nor manners; in flavor, for no matter how "good for you" a food may be, if it doesn't taste good, eating it will be like taking any bitter medicine. It should have variety in texture: an all-soft menu is for the young toothless, the aged ditto and those of the same distemper who are in the process of getting fitted up with substitute teeth. Neither do we want all hard-tack at a meal. Surprise to the palate is as stimulating as to the eyes. Besides, the teeth need exercise.

Grape-fruit—Jelly Center

Select well-weighted, bright yellow or rust-yellow grapefruit. Cut squarely across the center. With either a very sharp pointed knife or a curved grapefruit knife, separate the pulp from the skin by running it around between pulp and white fibrous lines. Then cut down both sides of each dividing membrane to loosen the pulp. Remove the core with a grapefruit corer. Sprinkle each half with one tablespoonful of confectioners' sugar, and set away to chill. When ready to serve, fill the center cavity with a cube of any sweet jelly or orange marmalade.

Ham Loaf

1½ lbs. uncooked ham
1 cup bread crumbs
½ cup chili sauce or catsup
1 egg
⅛ tsp. pepper
3 hard cooked eggs
2 tbsp. water

Grind ham, add crumbs (which should be stale but not dry), chili sauce, water, slightly beaten egg and pepper. Mix thoroughly. Pack mixture into a greased loaf pan, arranging the hard cooked eggs end to end through the center. Bake in moderate oven. Chill and slice. Serve with cucumber sauce (page 203).

Lemon Soufflé

½ cup shortening
2 eggs
1 tsp. vanilla
1 cup sugar
⅔ cup milk
2 cups flour
3 tsp. baking powder

Cream shortening and sugar. Add egg. Beat thoroughly. Mix flour and baking powder. Add vanilla to milk. Add wet and dry ingredients alternately to shortening and sugar. Mix thoroughly. Spread batter into greased cake tin to ¼-inch thickness. Bake in moderate oven (350) twenty to twenty-five minutes. Leave cake in tin. Make filling as follows:

⅓ cup flour
⅔ cup sugar
2 egg yolks
1⅓ cups water
⅛ tsp. salt
Juice and rind 1 lemon

Mix sugar, salt and flour. Add water and cook until thick. Add egg yolks and beat thoroughly. Add juice and rind of lemon. Cool. Spread filling over cake after cake has cooled. Top with meringue, made from two egg whites, one-half teaspoon baking powder, and one-half cup granulated sugar. Put in low oven (325) to brown meringue. Cool and serve.

GINGER ALE SHERBET—WATERMELON BALLS
SHERRY-SHRIMP NEWBURG
BUTTERSCOTCH PARFAIT

In planning the menu a balance should be kept between sweets and acids. Neither an all-sweet nor an all-sour meal would be appetizing. Some sour, some sweet, and some neutral foods such as rice, macaroni, noodles, potato, and bread should be introduced to act as a combining agent. Not too many highly seasoned foods should be served at one meal. And yet a little high seasoning lends piquancy to the meal. Another consideration is the digestibility of food. Most foods properly cooked are reasonably digestible to the normal stomach, but some are more so than others. Pork, for instance, is not quite so easily taken care of as ripe beef, and should not be followed by a heavy pudding, but a light dessert instead.

Ginger Ale Sherbet—Watermelon Balls

1 tsp. gelatin
¼ cup lemon juice
4 tbsp. sugar
1 egg white
2 cups ginger ale

Soak gelatin in lemon juice and dissolve over hot water. Add sugar and ginger ale. Pour into freezing trays and place in refrigerator to set for 45 minutes; turn into a bowl, and beat. Add stiffly beaten egg white and return to trays. Freeze for four to five hours. Stir every half hour for first two hours. Cut balls from ripe watermelon with potato ball cutter or small spoon, and chill. When ready to serve, half fill good sized, tall stemmed glasses with the balls, and pile sherbet on top. Lay one ball and a mint leaf on top.

Sherry-Shrimp Newburg

1 tbsp. butter or margarine
1 cup lobster meat
1 cup crab or shrimp
1 cup light cream
2 eggs
¼ tsp. salt
⅛ tsp. cayenne
1 tbsp. lemon juice
2 tbsp. sherry or sherry flavoring

Melt the butter in the upper part of a double boiler or chafing dish, place this directly over the fire, add the seafood which has been cut into medium sized pieces and toss it about in the pan until butter is absorbed. Now add the cream, place over hot water and when thoroughly heated stir in the beaten eggs, and cook until mixture thickens like custard, but do not allow it to boil. Add the seasonings and last of all stir in the sherry. Blend thoroughly and serve on toast.

Butterscotch Parfait

1¼ cups brown sugar
½ cup water
1 tsp. vanilla
2 tbsp. butter
3 eggs
1½ cups cream
½ cup nut meats

Put in small saucepan the brown sugar and butter and stir and boil one minute. Add the water; stir until sugar is melted and boil without stirring to 238 degrees F. or until syrup forms a soft ball when tried in cold water. Pour slowly on to the egg yolks well beaten, and beat until cold and thick. Fold in the egg whites beaten stiff, the vanilla, the cream beaten stiff, and the nut meats broken in pieces. Put in paper cases, sprinkle with nut meats and place in can of ice cream freezer with waxed paper and cardboard between the layers. Surround can with ice and salt, allowing two quarts ice mixed with one quart salt, using more ice and salt mixture if necessary. Leave four hours or until frozen. Mixture may be frozen in small baking powder boxes or ice cream molds instead of in the paper cases.

CHICKEN SOUP WITH RICE
TOMATOES STUFFED WITH JELLIED VEGETABLES
BREAD CUSTARD

THE "groaning table" is no longer considered either necessary or even enticing. There is distinction between plenty and overloading. Of course the "times" and the general state of household budgets has had considerable to do with this, but it is not a passing greatly to be regretted, so long as there is enough on the table and that appetizing. The great desideratum is to have plenty of good, plain food so well cooked that no man could ask for more or better. What this country needs is no longer a good five cent cigar with which to top the meal, but women who consider it just as valuable, cultural and essential a part of their training for social life (which includes—or is made up of—homemaking) to understand both the nature and manipulation of food, as any other branch of education. It is pretty well agreed that men, when they do turn their attention to cookery, make better cooks than women. This not only because they may like food better than women do, but because they appreciate it more.

Chicken Soup with Rice

3 cups chicken broth
½ cup rice
½ cup minced chicken
3 cups milk
1 stalk celery
1 small onion
2 tbsp. butter
⅛ tsp. pepper
1 tsp. salt

Wash the rice and cook in chicken broth and milk about twenty to thirty minutes. When this reaches the boiling point add whole onion and celery. Cook until tender. Remove onion and celery and add the chicken and butter to the soup. Cook ten minutes longer and serve hot.

Tomatoes Stuffed with Jellied Vegetables

6 medium sized tomatoes
1 cup water
½ small onion
½ tsp. salt
1 tsp. sugar
½ tbsp. gelatin
1 tbsp. cold water
1 tbsp. vinegar
1 cup vegetables
Pepper

Remove skins from tomatoes, cut a slice from the stem end of each and scoop out the pulp. Sprinkle the inside of the tomato with salt and pepper, and invert to drain. To the tomato pulp add water, onion cut in small pieces, salt and sugar. Cook for fifteen minutes and rub through a sieve. There should be ¾ cup of liquid. Add water if necessary to make up this amount or cook longer to reduce it. Add gelatin which has been softened in cold water and when it is dissolved add the vinegar. Let stand until partially thickened and add the vegetables. Diced celery and cucumber with a little chopped green pepper or cabbage makes a good combination. Fill the tomato shells with the gelatin mixture and let stand until firm. Serve on lettuce with French Dressing or mayonnaise. (Page 195.)

Bread Custard

3 eggs
¼ tsp. salt
Vanilla
¼ cup sugar
1½ cups bottled or diluted evaporated milk
Slices of bread

Beat eggs, and sugar, and salt. Heat milk and add slowly to the eggs, stirring constantly. Cook in double boiler, continuing to stir until mixture thickens and a coating is formed on the spoon. If cooked too long, the custard will curdle. Flavor with vanilla. Cut slices of fresh bread one-fourth inch thick, remove crust, and shape in regular pieces. Soak in cold custard and fry in butter. Serve hot with hard sauce.

HOFFBRAU HAMBURG
PINEAPPLE-ENDIVE SALAD
SOUR CREAM PIE WITH HONEY

It is only our old American institution, to which somebody has given a German name. This recipe was originally called Hamburg Italienne, but as no legitimate reason for affiliating two nationalities that have little else in common, accompanied the dish, we took the liberty of covering the whole thing under one flag. It is a good dish and if you make it when mushrooms are plentiful, try a mushroom sauce over it. Cold, it is a good Sunday night supper dish and also adapts itself very well to a picnic. If some enterprising grower would offer a prize for the greatest number of uses to be made of canned pineapple the result would probably be almost equal to the number of words that could be contrived from the letters in Ringling's Greatest Show on Earth. We could contribute even more uses than will be found in this book, if we were induced.

Hoffbrau Hamburg

4 tbsp. cooking oil
1 small green pepper
1 small onion
½ cup canned corn
1 cup canned tomato soup
¼ cup grated cheese
¼ lb. hamburg steak (raw)
¼ lb. spaghetti (cooked)
Salt

Chop the pepper and the onion, mix all the ingredients and bake in a casserole in a moderate oven (350 degrees) for forty minutes.

Pineapple-Endive Salad

2 heads French endive
Lettuce
2 tbsp. Roquefort cheese
3 cakes cream cheese
Salt, pepper, paprika
1 can sliced pineapple
French Dressing

Separate the stalks from the heads of endive. Slip two or three stalks through a slice of pineapple and place on a crisp lettuce leaf. Combine the cream cheese and the Roquefort cheese, adding salt and pepper and a dash of paprika. Press through a coarse sieve or ricer and arrange a portion in tiny lettuce leaves in the center of the pineapple slice. Serve with French Dressing.

Sour Cream Pie with Honey

3 eggs
2 tbsp. flour
1 cup sour cream
⅓ cup honey
1 tsp. cinnamon
3 tbsp. honey

Separate the eggs and beat the yolks; add the honey which has been blended with the flour and cinnamon. Add the sour cream. One-third of a cup of chopped raisins or dates may be added. Cook until thick. Pour into a baked shell. Beat the egg whites to a stiff froth and add three tablespoonfuls of honey. Spread on top of the pie and brown lightly in a very slow oven.

CREAM OF CARROT SOUP
LOBSTER CUTLETS
EMILY'S PUDDING

THE three courses given in these menus may be supplemented as one chooses by such other accessories as hors d'œuvre preceding the soup—celery, radishes, olives, small pickles, or various kinds of crackers, croutons, Melba toast. With the main course nothing more, in our opinion is needed, unless it be potato chips. Fresh lobster is, of course, more expensive at certain times of year than others; but tinned lobster is fairly static in price and quite as satisfactory for use in such dishes as this, in Newburgs, or as salad material. A salad may accompany the cutlets or follow as a separate course according to the service one has. A simple and suitable salad to serve here would be hearts of lettuce with Thousand Island or Russian Dressing. With the salad a salty crisp cracker is best, or small hot tea biscuits, or corn muffins.

Cream of Carrot Soup

1 medium onion
3 tbsp. butter
¼ cup bread crumbs
2 cups white stock
⅛ tsp. white pepper
1 cup top milk
1 tbsp. flour
1½ cups carrot purée
½ tsp. salt

Cook carrots until tender and put through purée strainer. Slice onion and sauté until tender in one tablespoonful of butter. Do not brown. Add stock, bread crumbs, salt and pepper and simmer one hour. Strain through sieve. Mix flour with two tablespoonfuls of butter until smooth and stir this into the soup. Add milk and heat thoroughly. Then add carrot purée. Four servings in cream soup cups.

Lobster Cutlets

2 tbsp. butter
4 tbsp. flour
1 cup milk
½ tsp. salt
⅛ tsp. pepper
1 tsp. lemon juice
2 5-oz. cans lobster
1 egg yolk
Crumbs and egg

Make a thick white sauce of the butter, flour, milk, salt and pepper. Add egg yolk, lemon juice and finely minced lobster. Let stand until quite cold. Shape into chop shapes, dip in crumbs, egg, and again in crumbs and fry in deep fat. Insert a piece of macaroni in each pointed end to represent bone. Serve with Tartar Sauce. (Page 206.)

Emily's Pudding

1 cup milk
1 egg
½ cup sugar
1 tsp. gelatin
½ cup whipped cream
1 tsp. vanilla
Grated Chocolate

Cook milk, beaten egg and sugar in double boiler until slightly thickened. Add gelatin softened in one-fourth cup of water, and stir. Let cool but not to set, and add whipped cream and vanilla. Put in glass serving dish and cover with grated chocolate or chocolate shot.

LIVER WITH MUSHROOMS
BRIDGE MOLD SALAD
RHUBARB SHORT CAKE

THE Bridge Mold Salad has nothing to do with crossing the Rubicon. It simply means that you can find at any department store aluminum molds in the shape of hearts, diamonds, clubs and spades. If you have occasion to serve bridge enthusiasts a few cents spent on a set or two of these would be worth while. They are used for gelatin, mousses, aspics—even cakes. The rhubarb short cake introduces—or at least, can use another commercial produce—the individual two layer sponge cakes. These are probably not as good as can be made at home by a good sponge cake maker, but they are convenient and can be used for many different purposes, but we do *not* recommend them for a strawberry short cake. Nothing but either a good old-fashioned sour cream biscuit dough (which *nothing* can surpass for the purpose) or a rich, light baking powder biscuit dough should be allowed to figure as a strawberry short cake.

Liver with Mushrooms

1½ tbsp. flour
1 tbsp. butter
2 cups water
1 lb. calves' liver
Mushrooms

Brown flour in the cooking fat. Add water and cook until creamy. Cut liver in two-inch pieces. Pour boiling water over them and drain immediately. Drop pieces in brown sauce and cook slowly ten or twelve minutes. Have some mushrooms peeled; drop these into hot butter and simmer. Just before serving, add to the liver.

Bridge Mold Salad

1 cup boiling water
1 pkg. lemon gelatin
2 tbsp. lemon juice or vinegar
1 tsp. salt
1 cup crushed pineapple
2 tbsp. minced green pepper
2 heads lettuce
1 cup mayonnaise
2 cups diced cucumber

Pour the boiling water over the gelatin. When cool, add lemon juice, salt, cucumber, pineapple and green pepper. Pour into wet bridge molds and set in the refrigerator. At serving time, slice the heads of lettuce with a sharp knife into eight neat cross sections. Place the lettuce on plates and unmold the salad onto center of lettuce. Drop a spoonful of mayonnaise, colored green, on top of each diamond, heart, spade, or club salad.

Rhubarb Short Cake

This may be made in one large short cake, or in individual cakes by buying the small two-layer sponge cakes. Stew a quart of rhubarb and sweeten it rather more than for sauce. Let it cool but do not chill. If the individual sponge cakes are used put a layer of rhubarb (thick enough so it will not run) between two cakes and whipped cream on top. If a sponge cake is made at home, spread the rhubarb on top while the cake is warm, and cover with whipped cream.

CREAMED CHICKEN PATTIES
COLE SLAW—HONEY DRESSING
ORANGE TARTS

HONEY, we think, is too little appreciated as a flavor. In its concentrated form a little goes a long way, even with hot biscuits. But used in small quantities as a flavoring it lends a delicate and subtle hint of its own bland richness that is most pleasing. In a boiled salad dressing for certain fruits it is delicious, and even with some vegetables such as the cole slaw here given, or on a grated raw carrot it sends a mysterious challenge to the palate. The orange tarts may become lemon tarts by changing orange juice to lemon, and you may prefer whipped cream on them to the meringue. In that case, though, you will have to think up some use for the whites of three eggs. You might like to sprinkle them with cocoanut, or if you use whipped cream you could scatter chocolate shot on them, or a few chopped maraschino cherries. A strawberry to cap with would not be bad—these are versatile things and easily made. In this particular menu we recommend letting the meringue stand since there is whipped cream in the salad dressing.

Creamed Chicken Patties

2 tbsp. butter
2 tbsp. flour
1 cup rich milk
½ tsp. salt
Cayenne
1 cup cold chicken (cubed)
1 green pepper (chopped fine)

Melt butter, add flour, then the milk gradually, stirring carefully to keep smooth. Add seasonings, chicken, and pepper. When thoroughly heated, serve in patty shells. Do not fill the shells until ready to serve. Garnish with parsley.

Cole Slaw–Honey Dressing

Remove outer leaves from firm compact head of cabbage and shred very fine. Stand in ice water for half an hour; drain and shake dry in cheese-cloth; pour French dressing over and let stand one hour. Drain, and pour the following dressing over:

Honey Salad Dressing

3 egg yolks
1 tsp. mustard
1 tsp. salt
Butter size of walnut
⅓ cup vinegar
⅓ cup strained honey
1 cup whipped cream

Cook egg yolks, mustard, salt, butter, vinegar and honey together until thick, then set aside to cool, and just before serving stir into it one cup of whipped cream. This may be made the day before, omitting the cream which should not be added until ready to serve. More vinegar may be added if desired. Shred close-leafed white cabbage very fine and mix with dressing.

Orange Tarts

3 tbsp. corn starch
2 tbsp. flour
1 cup sugar
1 cup strained orange juice
1 cup water
3 eggs
Salt

Mix flour, corn starch, sugar and pinch of salt and sift. Add orange juice and water to this. Cook in double boiler over slow fire until thick, stirring. Cool and add beaten yolks of eggs. Cook about two minutes until eggs are set. Pour into individual shells of rich pastry already baked and cover with meringue made from egg whites and three tablespoonfuls of sugar. Brown in 350 oven.

EGG IN TOMATO WITH BACON
CREAMED SCALLIONS
PINEAPPLE TORTE

When the young onions first come in the spring they are too precious to cook because it takes quite a good many to serve even a small family. But as they grow more plentiful and cheaper this is a dish well worth trying. We find them every bit as much of a delicacy as asparagus. The young bottomed onions, too, when they are about half grown are delicious boiled and dressed with butter, pepper and salt. These are not often found in the market for the grower cannot afford to market them at that size, but if you are so fortunate as to have your own garden and the onions are pretty thick, try boiling some. In larger onions the Bermudas or Texas white onions are most delicate in flavor and best for boiling. For fried onions to bolster up a beefsteak the ordinary cooking onions are good. Beefsteak can stand real onion flavor. The red Italian onions, rather oblong in shape, are sweet and excellent for slicing with cucumber or in salad. The Spanish onion presents the best appearance in company with orange for that appetizing combination and its French Dressing.

Egg in Tomato with Bacon

Wipe clean and dry as many firm, not overripe tomatoes as you will want for two servings each. Cut them squarely across the center and scoop out centers, leaving a thick shell. Sprinkle with salt and pepper and put in a dot of butter. Set these in a shallow baking tin and carefully break into each a fresh egg. Sprinkle with salt, pepper and paprika and set in slow oven (350-375) until the egg is set.

Fry bacon strips according to number of servings. Garnish the platter with water cress or chicory centers and lay on a center of bacon strips with tomato and egg around edge. Serve with a wide knife.

Creamed Scallions

3 bunches green onions
1 cup white sauce (medium)
4 slices thin buttered toast
½ cup grated cheese

Boil onions very gently in a small amount of water until tender (onions should be cut in asparagus sized lengths). Place on buttered toast, cover with white sauce and sprinkle with grated cheese. Serve hot. (See Page 203 for White Sauce.)

Pineapple Torte

Crust for 2 pies
1 cup butter
2 cups flour
3 tbsp. sugar
2 egg yolks
Pinch salt

Mix all dry ingredients and rub butter into flour; moisten with egg yolks. Put this mass of dough into pie plates and fit to pan with hands as dough will not roll. Prick with fork and bake as you would pie shell at 425 until brown.

Filling (*2 Pies*)

1 small can grated pineapple
¾ cup granulated sugar
4 egg whites
Whipping cream

Bring to a boil and add two tablespoonfuls corn starch. Cook until thick. Remove from fire and add one cup shredded cocoanut. Beat four egg whites stiff and fold in. Fill baked shells and bake in moderate oven fifteen minutes like meringue. Cut in pieces like a pie, top with whipped cream. Fresh crushed strawberries can be used instead of pineapple.

FLUFFY OMELET—ONION SAUCE
POPOVERS
AVOCADO SALAD

HERE we are with our onions again. Now if you do like—or think you would like fluffy omelet, and do not like onions—just don't make the onion sauce, but put a layer of currant or raspberry jelly between the folds. Or maple sugar shavings and butter. Or try a parsley sauce (white sauce with minced parsley in it). Or minced ham. The Omelet need not be discarded by any means, just because of a little onion. But to those who do like onion—success. For baking popovers we have found two different types of baking utensils better than others. One is the heavy iron muffin tin, the other is the glass oven cups. Both are good. A popover requires a heavy cup, and it should be very hot and well greased when the batter is put in. Don't think we left the baking powder out because there should be none.

Fluffy Omelet

2 tbsp. tapioca
¾ tsp. salt
⅛ tsp. pepper
¾ cup milk
1 tbsp. butter
4 egg yolks beaten until thick and lemon-colored
4 egg whites, stiffly beaten

Combine tapioca, salt, pepper, and milk in top of double boiler. Place over rapidly boiling water, bring to scalding point (allow three to five minutes), and cook five minutes, stirring frequently. Add butter. Remove from boiling water; let cool slightly while beating eggs. Add egg yolks and mix well. Fold in egg whites. Pour into hot, buttered ten-inch frying pan. Cook over low flame three minutes. Then bake in moderate oven (350) fifteen minutes. Omelet is sufficiently cooked when a knife inserted comes out clean.

Onion Sauce

2 tbsp. butter
1 cup chopped onions
¼ cup water
1 tsp. flour
¼ tsp. salt
Dash of pepper

Melt butter; add onion and cook over low flame until onions are tender. Add flour and mix well; then add water and seasoning and cook five minutes. Place onion sauce between folded layers of omelet and serve at once.

Popovers

4 eggs
2 cups milk
2 cups flour
1 tsp. salt

Sift flour and salt together. Beat eggs thoroughly and add milk and flour alternately. Beat until light and frothy. Pour into very hot, greased iron or glass muffin pans and bake until they have puffed above the pan. Temperature 450 degrees for twenty-five minutes, 300 degrees for twenty minutes. Twelve popovers.

Avocado Salad

2 avocado pears
3 tomatoes
½ onion
1 tbsp. olive oil
½ cup vinegar
2 tbsp. prepared mustard
1 tsp. salt; pepper
Grated cheese

Peel pears, cut in halves, remove pits, and slice lengthwise. Peel tomatoes, cut in halves, then in quarters. Rub a salad bowl with garlic and line with watercress or white chicory leaves. Lay the sliced avocado and quartered tomato on the cress, alternating, and sprinkle finely minced onion over. To the half cup of vinegar add the mustard, salt, pepper, and mix thoroughly. Add the oil and blend. Pour over the salad. Sprinkle grated cheese over the top, and if you can get pomegranate seeds, top with a few of these. If not, scatter (in season) a few ripe currants over the top.

CREAM OF POTATO SOUP
LUNCHEON SALAD
BANANA PANCAKES

Cream of Potato Soup is a nourishing dish and, with either croutons or Melba Toast and with a simple salad, it makes a luncheon dish quite sufficient in itself for the normal child or the family which requires only a light meal at noon. The crisp toast or crouton furnishes the desirable contrast in texture. The salad, too, is a dish that, for average consumption, would require no further accompaniment than some kind of roll, biscuit or perhaps a slice of rye or orange bread. And the banana pancakes certainly are a meal in themselves. So, while we have provided a menu that, taken as it stands, is well balanced and not too hearty to offer a guest, it can be split in various ways to accommodate the appetite or the need.

Cream of Potato Soup

1½ cups riced potatoes
2 tbsp. butter
1 tbsp. minced onion
1 tbsp. flour
3 cups milk
½ cup cream (scalded)
1 tbsp. minced celery
Salt, pepper, paprika

Sauté the onion in melted butter, add the flour and blend with butter, browning slightly. Stir in the potatoes and milk alternately, stirring to smooth blend. Add celery, salt, pepper and stir until boiling point is reached and mixture is smooth. Add hot cream, sprinkle with paprika and serve at once.

Luncheon Salad

1 tbsp. gelatin
¼ cup cold water
½ cup boiling water
1 cup grapefruit juice (fresh or canned)
¼ cup sugar
12 stuffed olives sliced
¼ tsp. salt
½ cup evenly diced celery
Pecans

Soak gelatin in cold water for five minutes. Dissolve in the boiling water. Add grapefruit juice, sugar, salt, celery. Let cool. Prepare six small molds. Put one tablespoonful of the mixture in the bottom of each mold. Arrange the sliced olives and pecan meats on top of this in each mold and let it get firm. Then pour in the rest of the gelatin mixture. When ready to serve unmold on a lettuce leaf, put a tablespoonful of mayonnaise on each salad and another olive.

Banana Pancakes

3 tbsp. granulated sugar
6 tbsp. flour
¼ tsp. cinnamon
¼ tsp. salt
3 eggs
¾ pt. milk
3 ripe bananas

Crush bananas and add well beaten eggs, milk and dry ingredients sifted together. Let stand one to two hours. When ready to serve add to this:

Pancake Batter

2 cups flour
1½ tsp. soda
½ tsp. salt
1 tbsp. sugar
1 egg
2 cups sour milk
2 tbsp. melted butter (or other fat)

Mix and sift dry ingredients. Add well beaten egg mixed with the sour milk. Beat until smooth and add shortening.

FAMILY PLATE LUNCHEON DISH
UNUSUAL TOMATO SALAD
SOUR CREAM GINGERBREAD CHEESE WHIP

SPEAKING of naming things, this "Family Plate Luncheon" might have gone by some such name as "Glorified Chicken Soup," maybe, just because it has some mushrooms cooked in it. But while chicken soup is good and wholesome and nutritious, and mushrooms are always a luxury, we fail to see it as "glorified." It is not even a company dish, nor so recommended, but it does make a good honest family luncheon plate and so it goes. The "Unusual Tomato Salad" is just that. There are, in all probability, a thousand tomato combinations which make excellent salads, and perhaps this is not so unusual after all. Perhaps we should have just named it "A Good Tomato Salad." But then, there are hundreds, anyway, of good tomato salads. And because making this one up sandwich fashion seemed a little different to us we gave it a plain name that should call attention to it without letting any one down. The gingerbread masquerades under no name at all. Hiding gingerbread under some kind of befangled name would be, if anything could, a shade worse than painting the lily.

Family Plate Luncheon

1 can chicken soup
Flour
2 tbsp. milk
½ can mushrooms

To the chicken soup add the milk. Thicken with flour. Add the mushrooms. Arrange attractive slices of toast, pour mixture over and serve hot.

Unusual Tomato Salad

Tomatoes
Mayonnaise
Chopped green peppers
Chopped celery
Grated onion
Parsley

Peel smoothly uniform tomatoes and chill. Slice crosswise in thick slices. Spread each slice with firm mayonnaise and cover with finely chopped green peppers, celery and a little grated onion. Put together as a sandwich, permitting the filling to show at the edges. Top with a spoonful of mayonnaise flavored slightly with horseradish. Insert a sprig of watercress in each and serve very cold on lettuce leaves.

Sour-Cream Gingerbread Cheese Whip

3 cups flour
½ cup milk
½ cup shortening
1 tbsp. ginger
1½ cups molasses
1 tsp. soda
2 eggs
Pinch salt

Beat yolks of eggs and shortening together; add milk, molasses and soda; add flour, salt, and ginger. Beat egg whites to stiff froth, and fold into mixture. Bake in moderate oven (350-375) for forty-five minutes or until done.

For the "Whip," take a cake of cream cheese, mix with a tablespoonful or so of top milk and beat it until it is light and fluffy. Pile it on individual servings of warm gingerbread and garnish with a little preserved ginger or a cherry.

TOMATO SOUP WITH RICE
POTATO AND EGG SALAD
CANTALOUPE SUNDAE

A PURÉE sieve is another one of those things every well equipped kitchen ought to have. Of course any sieve will answer the purpose, but with an ordinary sieve you have to use your hand or a spoon to persuade the pulp through. The purée sieve or strainer has some kind of device for dressing which follows the contour of the sieve and forces the pulp through without effort. Now, a word about garlic. Every little while you will come across the phrase: "Put in a chilled salad bowl that has been rubbed with a garlic clove." Garlic is a member of the lily family which has been sort of kept under by the more aristocratic members of the clan. But he is a lusty relation—if humble, and is bound to be recognized sooner or later. We recommend sooner, for nothing so lends a touch of sophistication to a vegetable or meat salad, as a *suggestion* of garlic. No more than a suggestion. He *can* be objectionable if over encouraged. Rubbing the bowl with a toe from his cloven foot is one way to get what you want from him—and no more. Keeping a bottle of vinegar on hand in which a garlic clove reposes, is another.

Tomato Soup with Rice

2 cups strained tomatoes
1 cup rice
1 onion
2 tsp. salt
½ tsp. pepper
1 tbsp. butter
2 tbsp. flour
½ tsp. celery salt
6 cups boiling water

Wash rice and cook in boiling water with sliced onion until tender. Add tomatoes and press through purée sieve. Brown the flour in hot butter and add to rice and tomato. Season with salt, pepper, and celery salt. Serve hot with small toast squares.

Potato and Egg Salad

2 cups cold cooked diced potatoes
3 hard cooked eggs, chopped
1 tbsp. minced parsley
1 cup finely shredded cabbage
2 tbsp. chopped pickles
2 tbsp. chopped green pepper
Few drops onion juice

Moisten with mayonnaise and heap in a mound on bed of lettuce leaves.

Cantaloupe Sundae

½ tbsp. gelatin
2 tbsp. cold water
2 tbsp. finely cut candied ginger
½ cup boiling water
¼ cup whipped cream
3 cantaloupe halves

Soak gelatin in cold water about five minutes; dissolve in boiling water and chill until it begins to thicken. Then fold in whipped cream and candied ginger. Fill centers of small cantaloupes with mixture, chill until firm, then serve.

SPLIT PEA SOUP

STUFFED HAWAIIAN SWEETS   COLD BOILED BEEF

CABBAGE-CUCUMBER SALAD

One of the features in our campaign (if it is a campaign) for plain food well cooked, is an argument for plain names. Angels, goddesses and peris might find allurement in such appelations as "Heavenly Dessert," "Marshmallow Divinity," "Fairy Fluff," "Date Delight," "This and That Supreme," "Thus and So Surprise," and so on. As a usual thing the "Surprise" is the nearest to a proper description that such things come, and the surprise is that either it is just rice pudding under another name, or else that the vaunted dish is not as good as it ought to be considering its title. True, it does become a task to name all the "new"—or nearly allurement in such appellations as "Heavenly Dessert," "Marshmallow Divinity," no matter if it has whites of eggs in it, is, we feel, going too far. Why not, for a change, try our grandmother's method and if we happen on a new combination of ingredients that makes a special appeal to Uncle Joe, call it "Uncle Joe's Favorite Hoe Cake?" The cold boiled beef may well be any other cold meat.

Split Pea Soup

- 1½ cups split peas
- 3 qts. ham stock
- 2 tbsp. flour
- 1 tbsp. chopped celery
- 1 onion, chopped
- Seasonings

Put a ham bone (uncooked) in three quarts of cold water and bring to boil. Wash peas and soak overnight in water to cover. Drain and put in with the ham bone. Add the celery and onion and boil slowly and steadily for three hours, or until meat cleaves from bone. Strain and return to stove. Melt butter in frying pan, sauté the onion, then brown the flour in onion and fat; stir into this a few spoonfuls of the soup, stir well, then turn contents of frying pan into the soup. Cook about twenty minutes more. Serve with croutons. If a cooked ham bone is used it need not be boiled so long; only until peas are tender. There should be about three pints of liquid when done.

Stuffed Hawaiian Sweets

- 3 evenly sized sweet potatoes
- ½ tsp. salt
- ½ cup drained crushed Hawaiian Pineapple
- 1 tbsp. butter or margarine
- 1 tbsp. cream
- 6 marshmallows
- 2 tbsp. pineapple juice

Bake sweet potatoes, cut in halves and scoop out most of the contents. Mash thoroughly. Season with butter and salt. Add cream and pineapple. Fill shells. Slit the marshmallows and stuff with crushed pineapple. Place one on top of each half of sweet potato. Baste with pineapple juice which has been boiled rapidly for a moment. Brown under broiler flame.

Cabbage-Cucumber Salad

- 3 cups finely shredded cabbage
- 2 green peppers shredded
- 1½ cups diced cucumber
- 12 slices bacon
- 6 tbsp. French Dressing
- ¼ cup raisins
- Lettuce

Shred cabbage and pepper very fine and combine both with the cucumber. Fry the bacon to a crisp and cut in squares with scissors. Add bacon and salad dressing to the vegetables, put in salad bowl which has been lined with crisp lettuce leaves, and garnish with raisins.

DRIED BEEF RABBIT
FRIED CAULIFLOWER
APPLE-NUT SALAD

In general, the luncheon menus given in this book are planned as suitable for simple entertaining as they stand, or at least with some supplementary dish to precede or follow. Most of them will provide a still simpler luncheon menu for the family by eliminating one or two courses. Many of them would do very nicely as dinner menus with a little bolstering. The thing we have tried to do, here as in our dinner suggestions, is to stimulate the mind or memory of the menu maker, or to present an unusual dish easy to prepare and not expensive to produce. Sometimes, as in the case of the "Apple-Nut Salad" we have merely an old friend in new guise. This is not much more than a Waldorf Salad (given elsewhere) but in a new form and with a handful of raisins thrown in, gratis. Nevertheless, it is a good salad, popular, and a new way, or at least another way to present it. The cauliflower for frying should be very solid, compact and white. It will be found of very delicate flavor and a welcome change from the ordinary method of cooking.

Dried Beef Rabbit

2 tbsp. cooking fat
½ cup chipped dried beef
¼ cup chopped cheese
¾ cup canned or cooked tomatoes
4 eggs

Heat fat and cook dried beef in it for a few minutes. Add tomato and when hot, add cheese. Stir until cheese is melted. Break eggs into the mixture and stir until thickened. Serve on buttered toast.

Fried Cauliflower

1 egg
Bread crumbs
Salt
Butter
Cauliflower (hard head)
Pepper

Steam cauliflower until slightly tender. Cool. Beat the egg. Cut the cauliflower in slices, dip in egg, roll well in crumbs and fry in butter until brown. Season with pepper and salt.

Apple-Nut Salad

Apples
½ cup nut meats
1 stalk celery
½ cup seeded raisins
Mayonnaise

Remove core and enough of the pulp to leave a large cavity, without breaking through the skin. Fill the cavity with a mixture of celery, nut meats, raisins, and as much of the apple pulp as one wishes. Moisten with mayonnaise, and top with dressing and a "turtle" made of a raisin with five cloves placed in it to make a head and four feet. Serve on lettuce.

CREAM OF ONION SOUP
POTATO SALAD SARDINES
TRANSPARENT CUSTARD PIE

THERE are a number of ways of making onion soup, and while the French method is probably the most popular and also most suitable for a dinner menu, the creamed soup seemed more desirable for a luncheon. Of course we have milk in the Custard Pie for dessert, but the main course is not heavy and the meal will stand a little milk at both ends. There are now creamed soups on the market, and soups to which cream is added, which are very good. No one need—or should—go without soup at a meal because there is not time to make it. Having visited what is perhaps the largest canned soup factory in the world and seen the immaculate conditions under which it is made, the perfect specimens of meat and vegetables which go into its construction, as well as having consumed quantities of it, we have no hesitancy in recommending the use of commercially canned soup not as a substitute for the home-made variety, but as a valuable and convenient food. The cook who has imagination and food sense can concoct a more individual soup, one more to his liking, but those cooks who have neither will do well to stick to a soup that is made by rule. Croutons or hard toast offer contrast in texture.

Cream of Onion Soup

6 white onions
1 tbsp. butter
1 qt. water
1 pt. milk
1 tbsp. flour
½ tsp. sugar
½ tsp. salt
¼ tsp. white pepper
Pinch of mace
3 eggs
1 cup cream

Peel and slice the onions and put in soup kettle with one tablespoonful of butter. Let cook for ten minutes. Then add water, milk and all seasonings. Simmer for one hour, then press through a sieve. Return to fire and add one teaspoonful of flour in a little cold milk and bring again to boiling point. Cook ten minutes, then lower flame to a gentle simmer and stir in the beaten yolks of three eggs mixed with one cup of cream. Serve immediately with croutons.

Potato Salad

4 large potatoes boiled
1 cup chopped cucumber
½ cup chopped onion
½ cup chopped celery
French Dressing
Mayonnaise

Cut potatoes in cubes and mix with the chopped cucumber, onion and celery. Add green pepper or pimiento if desired. Put all together in a bowl and barely cover with well-seasoned French Dressing. (A clove of garlic in the dressing bottle adds flavor.) Add salt if necessary. Let stand to marinate and chill one hour or longer. When ready to serve mix with mayonnaise well seasoned and colored with paprika and put in salad bowl which is lined with lettuce leaves. Serve at once.

Transparent Custard Pie

½ cup butter
1 cup sugar
2 egg yolks
1 tsp. vanilla

Cook in double boiler until thick. Spread a layer of blackberry jam on a previously baked crust and pour in custard. Cover with meringue and brown.

LOBSTER AND MUSHROOMS IN CREOLE SAUCE
MOLDED SAUERKRAUT—VEGETABLE SALAD
WASHINGTON SHORT CAKE

THE lobster, who considers himself an aristocratic crustacean, may claw the air at being obliged to hobnob with so plebeian a vegetable as sauerkraut, but it will do him good. He needs taking down—and sometimes keeping down. Sauerkraut is always digestible—and cheap. Thus do we attempt to balance the budget as well as the meal. In fact, it wouldn't hurt the whole lobster family to get a little better acquainted with the vegetable kingdom. Take a shore dinner, now. Charging what they do for this luxury-class menu, you'd think they could throw in a little sauerkraut once in awhile, or something other than a nubbin of corn in season. But do they? As for the Washington Short Cake no claim is made for its parentage. George Washington, himself, would doubtless have preferred a wedge of mince pie. The city of Washington has not sponsored it, nor yet has the state. Not even Port Washington knows about it—from us. Washington is a free name—and we used it. It is a good name—and a good cake. However, it is not copyrighted and any one can rename it who likes.

Lobster and Mushrooms in Creole Sauce

4 tbsp. butter or cooking oil
3 tbsp. chopped green pepper
1 cup canned tomatoes
Salt, pepper
3 tbsp. chopped onion
3 tbsp. flour
1 cup brown stock
1½ cup lobster meat
½ cup sautéed mushrooms

Cook onion and green pepper in the fat for a few minutes without browning them. Add flour and blend smoothly. Add tomatoes and stock and cook until thickened, stirring constantly. Season to taste with salt and pepper, add lobster meat and mushrooms and serve with Creole Sauce. (See page 204.)

Molded Sauerkraut—Vegetable Salad

1 tbsp. gelatin
2 tbsp. cold water
2 cups sauerkraut juice
½ cup diced beets
½ cup diced carrots
¼ cup diced celery
3 tbsp. sugar

Soften the gelatin in cold water and dissolve in the hot sauerkraut juice. Add the sugar and let cool. Pour half of the mixture into a mold and let this harden, then add the other half, mixed with the vegetables. Chill. The attractiveness of this salad will be increased if the carrots and beets are cut with a fancy vegetable cutter. Serve on lettuce with Sour Cream Dressing. (Page 196.)

Washington Shortcake

½ recipe of sponge or plain butter cake
2 tbsp. gelatin
¼ cup cold water
2 cups mashed sweetened strawberries
1 tbsp. lemon juice
¾ cup boiling water
Whipped Cream

Bake the cake in a layer cake pan. Soften gelatin in cold water and dissolve in boiling water. Add strawberries and lemon juice and turn into a pan of the same size as the cake pan. When firm turn out on to the cake, cover with whipped cream and garnish with whole berries.

MINTED LIME COCKTAIL
JELLIED TONGUE
CORN-COB STICKS   VEGETABLE SALAD

THE Corn-Cob Sticks call for a corn-cob baking pan. This is of heavy aluminum and as it is inexpensive, might well be added to the list of kitchen equipment. The Corn-Cob Sticks are quite realistic and while the result would be about the same if the "Sticks" were made in muffin tins, the appearance of the "ears" as they come from the suggested mold, are very attractive. Tongue, either beef or calves', is a delicate meat and can be served in a variety of appetizing ways. The dish here suggested takes a little time to prepare but is a handsome one when served and quite good enough for company. If a dessert is wanted to finish off the meal with we suggest a Peanut Brittle Fluff. Put about a third of a pound of Peanut Brittle through the meat grinder. Beat a cup of heavy cream stiff and combine the two. Add a few drops of vanilla and drop a spoonful on individual servings of sponge or white cake.

Minted Lime Cocktail

1 cup white grapes
1 cup diced pear
1 cup diced grapefruit
½ cup lime juice
15 After Dinner Mints

Mince all ingredients and put in refrigerator for several hours, or over night. Serve in cocktail glasses and garnish with fresh mint leaves.

Jellied Tongue Aspic

1 tbsp. gelatin
¼ cup cold water
Salt, pepper
3 cups consommé, or
3 cups hot water and
2 bouillon cubes

Skin and trim a boiled beef tongue. Lay the whole tongue on a glass platter and garnish the top with slices of hard cooked egg, putting them through the center and not too close together; one egg will be enough. Crosswise on the tongue between the slices of egg alternate narrow strips of green pepper and pimiento. Around the tongue on the platter arrange a wreath of cold cooked vegetables cut with fancy cutters. Make an aspic according to the above ingredients and when about ready to set pour it over the tongue and vegetables. Let set and chill. Serve as soon as taken from the refrigerator and garnish with parsley, cut radishes and white pickled onions at rim of platter. Serve with Tartar Sauce or Henry VI Sauce. (See page 205.)

Corn-Cob Sticks

1 cup yellow corn meal
½ cup flour
½ tsp. salt
¾ tsp. baking powder
1 cup sour cream
½ tsp. soda
1 tbsp. sugar

Mix the corn meal with flour, salt, sugar, baking powder, which have been sifted together, into the sour cream in which the soda has been stirred. Pour this batter into a hot greased "corn cob" baking pan and bake in 375-400 oven.

CORN AND SALMON LOAF
PINEAPPLE SALAD
VERMONT CUSTARD PIE

If anybody ever offered us stock in a pineapple field—or even a pineapple canning factory, we should be tempted to grab at the chance. We simply cannot get along without our pineapple. And we have found out other things about pineapple: that the juice, for instance, standing beside our bed when a sore throat or a racking cough is making the night miserable, sipped frequently is soothing and healing. And *we* have found it helpful in mild attacks of indigestion. Doctors may not agree, and, so far as we know, the growers of that ubiquitous fruit make no such medicinal claims. And nobody pays us a cent for the tribute, either. It is all pure philanthropy on our part—passing along a bit of personal history that has brought us relief. At any rate we thought it did—and so the thing was as good as done. The "Vermont Custard" came to us under the name of "Coolidge Custard," but as we were unable to verify the late and greatly honored Mr. Coolidge's taste in custards, we thought rechristening it for his native state was fair enough.

Corn and Salmon Loaf

1 large can red salmon
2 eggs
Salt and pepper
1½ cups water
2 tbsp. butter
4 or 5 tbsp. catsup
2 cups rolled bread crumbs
2 strips bacon
3 tbsp. flour
1 cup milk
Parsley
2 cups canned corn
Lemon slices

Drain liquor from salmon and reserve. Remove bones, and mince with a fork. Add corn, eggs, bread crumbs, salt, pepper to taste, and mix well. Form into loaf. Use more crumbs if needed. Place in an open baking dish, cover with strips of bacon, add water and bake about 45 minutes in moderately hot oven. When done remove to platter and pour dressing over loaf.

Dressing

Blend flour, butter and one-half teaspoonful of salt and dash of pepper well together. Stir paste into milk and boil, stirring continuously until thick. Then beat in catsup. Pour over loaf and garnish with parsley and lemon slices.

Pineapple Salad

1 box lemon gelatin
1 can shredded pineapple
1 small onion, chopped
1 small tin pimiento, chopped
1 pt. boiling liquid

Strain pineapple and use juice with water to make one pint of boiling liquid. Pour this on lemon gelatin. Add pineapple, onion and pimiento and let cool and set. Serve on lettuce with mayonnaise or cooked salad dressing. (Page 196.)

Vermont Custard Pie

¾ cup sugar
1¼ tbsp. flour
2 beaten eggs
2½ cups milk

Mix sugar and flour, add a pinch of salt and the well beaten eggs, add milk, and pour into a previously baked pastry shell. When done remove from oven and sprinkle with nutmeg.

DEVILED SALMON

SWEET POTATO TEA CAKES

SALAD OF ALLIGATOR PEAR AND ORANGE

IN trying out this menu on our own family we used Lyonnaise potatoes instead of Sweet Potato Tea Cakes, but inasmuch as we are giving you the former in another menu we suggest the tea cakes here and you can do as you like. Lyonnaise Potatoes, however, deserve a little more attention than just the recipe given elsewhere, since they are often one of the Good Foods Spoiled by Poor Cookery. The greatest sin that is committed against them is to cut them—and the accompanying onion—in great hunks, fry them in any kind of fat and then serve them lukewarm. To chop them is likely to make them gaumy, and this they should not be. If, however, time is a compelling element, they may be chopped, but not too fine. The amount of onion depends upon liking, but Lyonnaise potatoes want to taste strongly of that lusty bulb. The onion should be chopped quite fine and slightly cooked in the fat before being combined with the potato. Part bacon fat and part butter is the best kind of fat to use, or fat from a roast of pork which is specially well flavored. The fat should be hot, the potatoes well browned and a little crisp.

Deviled Salmon

1 tbsp. butter
1 tbsp. minced onion
1 tbsp. minced green pepper
½ cup salmon liquid
2 tsp. dry mustard
Vinegar
1 tbsp. tomato catsup
Salt, pepper
2 cups flaked salmon

Melt butter in frying pan, add onion and green pepper, cook together for six or eight minutes. Add salmon liquid and mustard, mixed with vinegar to make a thin paste, cook slowly for five minutes. Add catsup, seasonings and salmon. Let simmer for about three minutes. Serve in patty shells.

Sweet Potato Tea Cakes

4 cups flour
2 tsp. salt
8 tsp. baking powder
1 tsp. nutmeg
¾ cup sugar
⅓ cup shortening
1½ cups mashed sweet potatoes
Milk

Mix and sift all dry ingredients. Rub in shortening and potato which has been pressed through a ricer or coarse wire sieve. Add milk to make a dough as soft as can be handled. Make into large flat cakes three or four inches in diameter and one inch thick. Place one-half inch apart on greased baking sheets and bake in moderately hot oven (375) for 25 minutes. Brush tops with a mixture of one teaspoonful of sugar and one fourth cup of milk as they begin to brown. Serve hot, or toasted when cold with butter and orange marmalade.

Salad of Alligator Pear and Orange

Cut entire sections carefully from fine seedless oranges, and divide an alligator pear into similar shaped slices. Arrange alternately three sections of orange and two of the pear, fitted together in a rounded segment, on a leaf or two of white lettuce, on individual salad plates, and sprinkle liberally with French Dressing, to which a few drops of Worcestershire and a bit of catsup is added. Use lime juice instead of lemon in the dressing, if liked.

OYSTER SOUP
CHICKEN RAPHAEL
ORANGE ICE BOX CAKE

MOST of the soups recommended in these luncheon menus are cream soups because they are nourishing and aid in formulating a complete meal with few dishes. Those suggested for dinner, such as consommé and bouillon have little food value, and even tomato soup without milk and many of the canned soups are stimulating without providing much nourishment—a quality desirable in a first course at dinner. The menu given here is rather too elaborate and too heavy for a family meal and is not so intended. But for a company luncheon it should prove satisfactory. A light fruit or vegetable salad, somewhat acid in flavor would go well with the chicken, such, for instance, as sliced tomatoes, endive or Romaine with French Dressing. Something tart should be found in almost every meal, even though it is no more than a salad dressing or a bit of fruit as dessert. Some colorful jelly on the table, or a dish of radishes and celery would lend spice to this menu as served. The Chicken Raphael is a famous dish served at the Cocoanut Grove, Los Angeles.

Oyster Soup

1 pt. oysters
1 pt. rich milk
3 tbsp. butter
1 tbsp. minced parsley
1 tbsp. minced celery
Seasonings

Drain oysters. To the liquid add parsley, celery, salt and pepper. Simmer for ten minutes and skim. Heat milk to boiling point and add butter. Cook oysters in hot liquor until edges curl and pour into a hot tureen. Add hot milk and season to taste. Serve with oyster crackers.

Chicken Raphael

2 ozs. diced fresh mushrooms
1 diced artichoke heart
1 pt. cream
1 tbsp. watercress chopped fine
2 ozs. butter
2 cups diced breast of chicken
Flour
1 small glass sherry
2 fresh eggs

Cook the mushrooms in butter. Add artichoke and chicken. Dust lightly with flour. Let simmer for a few moments so flour will blend. Add cream, previously heated. Season to taste. Let cook a moment longer. Add the chopped watercress and sherry. Simmer lightly a moment. Thicken with yolks of eggs lightly whipped with a little cream. Serve with fresh toast.

Orange Ice Box Cake

2 cups milk
2 tbsp. cornstarch
1 cup sugar
2 eggs
2 tbsp. cold water
¾ cup orange juice
1 tsp. grated orange rind
2 doz. lady fingers
1 tbsp. gelatin

Heat milk in double boiler. Add sugar and cornstarch. Cook ten minutes, stirring until thickened. Add beaten eggs, cook three minutes, stirring constantly. Add gelatin, soaked in cold water, orange juice and rind. Line spring form with lady fingers. Fill with alternate layers of orange mixture and lady fingers, having lady fingers on top. Set in ice box for several hours or overnight.

NUT CELERY LOAF
ARKANSAS SALAD
FRUIT CREAM PIE

THE salad given here is so named because while we were studying just what kind of salad would go best with a nut loaf, and carefully considering the contents of this, it occurred to us that to an Arkansan in the midst of a dust storm this salad, properly chilled and free from grit, might taste particularly good. And so, according to this sentiment, we named it. And with better reason at that, we believe, than some dishes we have encountered have been named. There was a story going around awhile ago to the effect that when the popular novel "The Postman Always Rings Twice," was finished the author could not find a suitable name for it. He racked his brain for days, and suddenly, while he was thus racking, the postman came—and rang twice. The harassed author clapped his hand to his brow and cried: "The very thing! The postman always rings twice!" And so he typed these words at the head of his book and sent it off, and a publisher read it because he wanted to see what the postman's ringing twice had to do with the book. He never found out, but he figured others would read it for the same reason, which they did. In the same way, it would seem, we often name a food dish.

Nut Celery Loaf

1 cup chopped nut meats
1 cup chopped celery
1 cup soft stale bread crumbs
½ tsp. salt
Dash red pepper
1 tsp. onion juice
2 tsp. melted butter
1 cup hot milk
Poultry Seasoning

Mix nut meats, celery and slightly moistened bread crumbs. Flavor with poultry seasoning, salt, red pepper and onion juice. Mix lightly, moistening with melted butter and hot milk, knead with hands and form into oval loaf. Place in buttered mould and bake in moderate oven, basting with mixture of melted butter, hot water and a few drops of Kitchen Bouquet. Serve with a Cream Sauce flavored with minced parsley. (Page 203.)

Arkansas Salad

1 pkg. lemon gelatin
1 crisp cucumber
1 tbsp. vinegar
¼ tsp. salt
3 slices canned pineapple diced
½ can pimientos
Juice from can of pineapple

Combine vinegar and pineapple juice with enough water to make one pint. Heat and add lemon gelatin. Let this stand to the setting point, then add finely diced cucumber, salt, chopped pimiento and pineapple. Pour in rinsed individual molds and chill. Serve on lettuce with mayonnaise, or cooked salad dressing (Page 196) with crisp wafers.

Fruit Cream Pie

2 cups whipped cream
1 cup berries
Sugar to taste

Lay berries (peaches or apricots) in baked pastry shell, sprinkle with sugar, cover with whipped cream dusted with confectioners' sugar, and serve.

ORANGEADE
BOILED SALMON—CUCUMBER SAUCE
INDIVIDUAL PEACH SHORTCAKES

IF salmon can be boiled without losing its color it makes a very attractive dish. By tying in cloth and plunging it into boiling water, it is more likely to keep both shape and color. There are various sauces suitable for salmon, such as Hollandaise, mayonnaise, caper, cucumber, tartar. Cold boiled or steamed salmon with cucumber sauce or tartar sauce is a most appetizing hot weather dish. Salmon requires longer and slower cooking than white fleshed fish and should be simmered, and not brought to a bubbling boil. To make this menu entirely suitable for a hot day dinner serve the salmon cold, and add a Chinese cabbage, endive or Romaine salad, with potato chips. Serve a sour cream dressing (Page 196) on Chinese cabbage for a change. Chinese cabbage, by the way, is a vegetable too seldom used. It is usually found in Italian markets and along with leeks, fennel, and others whose acquaintance we might well make.

Orangeade

One orange to each person to be served. Thin skinned, juicy oranges are best. Cut a slice squarely off the top, and with a sharp spoon dig out the inside; put this pulp through a sieve to strain it. To this juice add one-third as much maraschino cherry juice (or claret wine) as ginger ale. If this is not enough liquid to fill the orange cups, add more orange juice. Pour this into the orange cases, cut two holes in the tops and put them back on. Insert two straws in each cover and serve very cold on glass plates or set in glass sherbet cups.

Boiled Salmon—Cucumber Sauce

Buy a salmon steak three inches thick. Scrape and wash the skin. Wrap in a piece of cheese cloth. Put in a suitable pan for boiling and cover with water. Into the same kettle put a small onion sliced, a bay leaf, a blade of mace, a fourth of a cup of tarragon vinegar and a teaspoonful of salt. Simmer (do not let come to a boil), allowing ten to twelve minutes to the pound. Lift out carefully, unwrap without breaking, and lay on a platter. Garnish with sprigs of parsley, flowerlets of raw cauliflower, slices of cucumber and quarters of lemon. Serve hot with Sauce Tartare, or cold Cucumber Sauce. (See page 203 for sauce.)

Individual Peach Shortcakes

1 tbsp. sugar
1 tbsp. butter
4 tbsp. confectioners' sugar
Peaches

Make the regular biscuit dough, using four tablespoonsful of butter for shortening, and add the tablespoonful of sugar. Bake each biscuit in two layers with melted butter between. When the biscuits are done, separate them and on one-half lay a mixture of sliced peaches sprinkled with confectioners' sugar. Put a layer of peaches on top and serve with whipped cream.

SCALLOPS EN CASSEROLE
BOSTON FRIED CARROTS
CABBAGE PINEAPPLE SALAD
STRAWBERRY SHERBET

THE "scallop" is really the eye of one of the edible bivalves found off the eastern coast of the United States. That portion which we eat is the muscle by which the creature opens and closes its shell. This is torn from the shell and is one of the most delicately flavored of sea foods. It is sometimes cooked the same as oysters, but is commonest served fried in deep fat. We think, however, that the scalloped dish will be found good. In place of the cabbage and pineapple salad, a pickle or relish may be served, or sliced cucumbers in vinegar or in a sour cream dressing. Beets would make another suitable vegetable and would give color to the plate when served. With any dish of neutral coloring such as the scallops will be, some colorful garnish is needed.

Scallops en Casserole

Butter a baking dish and put in a layer of scallops; sprinkle with salt, pepper and flour. Cover with a layer of fresh mushrooms that have been sautéed in butter and cut in pieces; alternate scallops and mushrooms until dish is nearly filled, then pour over it a thin white sauce highly seasoned—just enough to moisten—and cover with mixed cracker crumbs and grated cheese. Bake in hot oven (450-500) fifteen minutes or until crumbs are browned and the scallops cooked through.

Boston Fried Carrots

3 cups finely cut carrots
3 tbsp. butter
½ tsp. salt

Melt the butter in a frying pan and add the cut carrots and salt. Cover closely and fry until tender and slightly brown—about fifteen minutes.

Cabbage Pineapple Salad

3 cups shredded cabbage
1 cup diced pineapple
¼ cup mayonnaise
½ cup celery cut fine
½ cup whipped cream
1 tbsp. horseradish

Mix the cabbage, celery and pineapple together; mix the mayonnaise, horseradish and whipped cream together; stir this through the cabbage mixture and season to taste. Add a dash of paprika.

Strawberry Sherbet

2 tbsp. granulated tapioca
3 cups boiling water
1½ cups sugar
4 tbsp. lemon juice
1 cup strawberry purée
1 egg white
Pinch of salt

Add tapioca to boiling water with salt and cook in double boiler until tapioca is clear. Add sugar, lemon juice and strawberry purée (crushed fresh strawberries put through sieve). Cool and add stiffly beaten egg white. Pack in mixture of three parts ice to one of salt and freeze. If frozen in refrigerator trays allow three to four hours depending on temperature. Stir several times first hour or two.

CLAM SOUP
SPAGHETTI WITH BACON SAUCE
APPLE-WATERCRESS SALAD

CANNED clams are usually obtainable when fresh ones are not. Chicken stock may be substituted for veal. This soup alone with a salad would make a suitable, nourishing and sufficiently hearty luncheon for any one who had not been doing a heavy morning's work, and where a substantial dinner would follow. Often in these menus we give a menu—particularly luncheon—that we feel is too heavy for the family where luncheon is merely a stop-over between a good breakfast and a better dinner, but in this way we allow for selection. In this menu for instance, the soup and salad would make a meal, or the spaghetti and salad. As it stands, and with a dessert to follow it would make a very good dinner. As we have said before—the menus are but suggestive and yet taken as given are suitable to the right purpose.

Clam Soup

1 dozen clams
1 qt. veal stock
½ cup sliced celery
¼ cup sliced onion
1½ cups canned tomatoes
4 tbsp. granulated tapioca
1 cup cream
Paprika, pepper, salt
Parsley

Scrub clams, cover with boiling water and cook until they open. Strain liquid and add to veal stock. Bring to a boil, add vegetables and tapioca and cook rapidly for fifteen minutes, then simmer for thirty minutes. Mince clams, discarding tough parts, and add. Season, bring to a boil and add one cup of cream. Serve sprinkled with parsley or cress, and serve toasted fingers or bread or crackers.

Spaghetti with Bacon Sauce

3 oz. pkg. spaghetti
1½ cups diced bacon
½ cup chopped green pepper
Salt
½ cup chopped onion
2 cups thin tomato sauce
1 tsp. chili powder
½ cup grated cheese

Cook spaghetti in salted boiling water for fifteen minutes and drain. Make the following sauce: Fry the one and one-half cups of diced bacon slightly and add chopped pepper and onion to it. Sauté until onion is light brown. Add to this the tomato sauce, chili powder and salt to taste and cook for ten minutes. Turn cooked spaghetti into a glass casserole, pour the bacon sauce over it, sprinkle with the grated cheese and set in slow oven until cheese is melted.

Apple-Watercress Salad

3 large red apples
1 cream cheese
Currant jelly
French Dressing
Watercress

Wash, polish and core apples. Do not peel. Cut crosswise in middle. Mix currant (or other syrup) jelly with cream cheese to form paste. Spread this on apple slices allowing one-half apple to each serving. Dip cress in French Dressing and lay on plate. Place apple on this.

BOILED TONGUE IN BROWN SAUCE

PEAR SALAD

CARROT PANCAKES

No specific study whatever is made in this book of bodily needs, or the various contributions made of different foods to these needs. And yet it is essential that any one who is planning daily meals for a family should know something of both. Different kinds of engines require different kinds of fuel. The human engine must have fuels that go under the names of carbohydrates, fats, proteins, minerals, water, vitamins, calcium. These fuels are found in foods, but no one food has them all. If sufficient variety is provided during the day, the various necessary chemicals for bodily nourishment will be taken care of. The main thing to be sure of is that no one type of food is being given preference to the loss of others. Too much starchy food should not be given at a meal, such as bread, potatoes, cream soups and sauces, cake, puddings. Neither should meat or vegetable predominate. A well balanced menu, or series of menus throughout a day, will take care of the requirements of the normal body.

Boiled Tongue in Brown Sauce

Parboil a beef's tongue or several calves' tongues until they are tender, with one bay leaf, a pinch of thyme, a red pepper, and a cut bud of garlic tied in a muslin bag. Skin the tongue while hot and slice. Melt a generous tablespoonful of cooking fat in a saucepan and brown in it two tablespoonfuls of flour. When well blended, add enough stock to cover the sliced tongue. Add sliced tongue to sauce, salt to taste, add the juice of one lemon, and boil gently for about six minutes. Serve with slices of hard cooked egg.

Pear Salad

Drain canned pears. Place two halves on a crisp, curled leaf of lettuce and in the cavity put a ball of cottage cheese rolled in crisp browned bread crumbs mixed with finely chopped nuts and grated cheese. Sprinkle two or three (not more) drops of onion juice and the same amount of lemon juice over each section and serve with French Dressing and crisp crackers.

Carrot Pancakes

1 cup grated carrots
1 tbsp. melted shortening
¼ tsp. salt
3 tbsp. sugar
½ lemon rind, grated
2 eggs
⅔ cup flour
½ tsp. baking powder

Grate carrots, add melted shortening, salt, sugar, grated lemon rind and well beaten egg yolks, then the flour sifted with baking powder. Mix well and fold in the stiffly beaten egg whites. Fry in butter or half butter and half bacon fat. Serve with jelly.

CHICKEN-PINEAPPLE CASSEROLE
SAVORY BAKED PEPPERS
CHERRY TORTE

WHATEVER we did before we had pineapple to cook with different meats, I cannot imagine. Not knowing what we missed, however, we managed to struggle along on plain fricasseed chicken and biscuits, or fried ham and eggs, with our fruit before or after. Now that we have it, however, and have learned what a delicious accompaniment it is to chicken, ham, pork, sausage and perhaps other meats, we find experimenting with it a pleasure. And not only pineapple but other fruits. Apricots, for instance, combine well with meats; so do raisins, pears, and plums. Try stewing large purple plums or ripe prunes until tender but not until the skin breaks, and using them somewhat sweetened, to garnish a roast of pork. Or a handful of ripe currants thrown into a beef stew. The creative cook—the one who has imagination and is not afraid to use it, is the one who originates the "unusual" in foods. These are the food artists and in most cases they are men.

Chicken-Pineapple Casserole

2 frying chickens
1 large can of sliced pineapple
½ cup butter
2 tbsp. lemon juice
2 tbsp. soy sauce
Flour
Salt, pepper

Cut the chicken into serving pieces, dip in flour seasoned with salt and pepper. Heat butter or cooking fat in frying pan and brown chicken on all sides in the fat. Remove to baking dish and cover with sauce made of pineapple juice, lemon juice and soy sauce. Cover and bake in slow oven (350 degrees) for thirty minutes or until chicken is tender. Dip drained and dried slices of pineapple in the seasoned flour and sauté in the frying pan after wiping it free of excess fat. Serve chicken on platter garnished with pineapple. Serve sauce in a boat.

Savory Baked Peppers

Thicken one can of vegetable soup with half bread crumbs, half boiled rice (or all bread crumbs) well seasoned. Remove seeds from green peppers and let stand in boiling salted water for five minutes; drain and stuff with soup and bread mixture. Sprinkle grated cheese over top. Bake in moderate oven until peppers are tender. As many peppers as servings. The stuffing should be just moist enough to handle.

Cherry Torte

6 eggs
2 cups confectioners' sugar
½ tsp. cinnamon
1 lemon rind
2 tsp. lemon juice
1 cup rye bread crumbs
2 cups unsweetened red cherries
¾ cup chopped almonds
1 cup whipping cream

Beat yolks of eggs, add sugar and beat until creamy. Add the bread crumbs, cinnamon, grated rind and juice of lemon; add cherries and half the almonds. Pour the mixture into a large buttered spring form. Sprinkle the top with sugar and remainder of almonds. Bake in slow oven at 325 for thirty minutes. Cool; turn from mold and cover with whipped cream; decorate with cherries or small sugar candies.

JELLIED CONSOMME
RAISIN PANCAKES
CANARY SALAD

JUST in case some one in your family is averse to raisins or feels that he already has an over-supply of iron in his system, blackberry jam might be substituted for raisins. The treatment would be the same—a good pancake batter (the one for banana pancakes on Page 13 is our favorite), and after a spread of butter on each cake, a layer of jam. Or, strawberry preserves. Or, again, shaved maple sugar. The possibilities are many, and although we should like to see our jellied consommé and canary salad used *some* time, we still feel that a luncheon for just the family (unless the men are hungry), and especially for the children, the pancakes, with a cup of coffee for the grown-ups and milk for the runner-ups, are about enough for anybody—so long as there are plenty of pancakes. And speaking of pancakes, we heartily recommend the electric griddle. In spite of the excellence of the buckwheat cakes that my mother used to bake on an old iron griddle over a wood fire, and the delectableness of which I can never hope to equal with all my devices—still, I bake my raisin pancakes on an electric griddle at the table.

Jellied Consommé

1 can consommé
1 pkg. cherry gelatin
1 cup pineapple juice
¼ cup honey
Juice of 1 lemon
Cream

Heat consommé almost to a boiling point and dissolve cherry gelatin in it while still on stove (be sure it is well dissolved). Remove from stove, add pineapple juice, honey and lemon. When cool put in refrigerator until firm. To serve: Break up jelly but *do not beat* and serve in glass bouillon cups or deep glass soup plates topped with a tablespoonful of *unsweetened* whipped cream, and a bit of finely chopped parsley sprinkled on the cream.

Raisin Pancakes

Use your favorite griddle-cake batter, and cook on a griddle in large cakes (size of dessert plates). Pile four or five on a hot plate as cooked, buttering each one, sprinkling with seedless raisins, and squeezing a little lime juice on each. Pour a little more melted butter over and around, and serve cut through the whole in pie-shaped sections very hot. Lemon juice may be used if preferred instead of lime.

Canary Salad

1 cup grated raw carrot
½ cup finely cut celery
Mayonnaise
½ cup chopped raw apple
½ cup finely cut orange
Lettuce

Mix vegetables and fruit together, combine with mayonnaise and serve on lettuce.

COD AU GRATIN

BANANA MUFFINS STEWED CUCUMBERS

CHERRY SLAW

THERE is, as the different menus calling for codfish as given in this book indicate, more than one way to use this humble member of the fish family. In fact, there are quite a number of ways that we have not yet mentioned. Fresh cod is not always to be found in every inland town, but salt cod stands on every grocery shelf from Whig Corners to the most exclusive store in Boston. (For that matter, it *ought* to be found in Boston—being born there, as you might say.) The cod, when I was a little girl and went to town with my father, did not repose on a shelf. He hung from the ceiling. Now he is cornered in a box or paraffin paper. The average cod weighs from six to ten pounds. The flesh is not fat. Cod-liver oil comes, as a perspicaceous person might judge, from the liver. Cucumber in its fresh natural state is so succulent an accompaniment to any fish that it may be preferred sliced cold with a French or sour cream dressing, but the adventurous cook who is not afraid to try anything once may like to experiment with a dish which is a favorite, we are told, with English cooks.

Cod au Gratin

Pick two cups of salt codfish into fine pieces. Cover with cold water and let stand three hours, changing the water once during that time. Drain and press out all the water. Make a cream sauce with two tablespoonfuls of butter, two of flour, one cup of milk. Add to this two tablespoonfuls of finely grated cheese and mix carefully with the fish. Put in a shallow, greased baking dish, sprinkle the top with cheese and brown in hot oven (450 degrees).

Stewed Cucumbers

Cut crisp fresh cucumbers lengthwise into quarters, sprinkle with mixture of salt, pepper, sugar, and roll in flour, and fry to light brown in butter. Barely cover with stock (in same frying pan) and simmer until tender. Thicken sauce with a little flour (mixed with milk), add a few drops of lemon juice, and serve hot.

Cherry Slaw

1 can large white cherries
2 cups cabbage, shredded
1 small bottle maraschinos
1 cup celery, cut fine
1 green pepper, shredded
Mayonnaise

Shred cabbage, celery and pepper very fine. Pit the cherries and cut both red and white in two. Mix all together with mayonnaise and chill. Serve on lettuce leaves.

Banana Muffins

1 cup banana pulp
1 cup brown sugar
4 tbsp. shortening
Pinch salt
2 cups flour
5 tsp. baking powder
1 cup milk
½ tsp. nutmeg

Sift flour, baking powder, salt, nutmeg and sugar together and mix in the shortening. Add milk to make smooth batter, add banana pulp and bake in well greased muffin tins for 25 minutes. Dust with confectioners' sugar.

CASSEROLE OF SWEETBREADS AND MUSHROOMS
TOMATO-CUCUMBER SALAD
CHERRY SHERBET ICE

In going over the menus in this book for perhaps the twentieth time (certainly no less) before letting them get out of our hands, it occurred to us that one might judge, from the frequency with which cherries are mentioned, that unless a considerable number of trees have been encouraged to take its place, the one that little George Washington cut down would be sorely missed. However, the crop seems to stand up pretty well even under the loss of this so famous one, and we suggest that a half dozen cans of both white and red cherries be kept on the supply shelf. They are a ubiquitous fruit, equally at home in pie, pudding, frozen dessert or salad. We have much to be thankful for in that little George did not destroy the *last* cherry tree. Both sweetbreads and mushrooms are—according to our estimation of foods—in the luxury class, at least most of the time. In certain seasons, however, mushrooms are plentiful and reasonable in price, and even if the menu is a little beyond the usual budget, it is intended for one of those times when you want something unusually good, and different.

Casserole of Sweetbreads and Mushrooms

1 pr. sweetbreads
1 cup mushrooms
3 tbsp. butter
1 pt. white sauce
1 pt. young peas
1 tbsp. vinegar
Salt, sugar and butter for peas

Soak the sweetbreads in cold water for one hour; cook for fifteen minutes in salted water to which a teaspoonful of vinegar has been added; remove from water, break into small pieces discarding membranes. Skin and slice mushrooms (measure after skinning) and stew for five minutes in the butter. Make a pint of white sauce, seasoning it highly and add sweetbreads and mushrooms to it. In the bottom of a well-buttered casserole place a pint of young green peas which have been cooked and seasoned with butter, pepper and salt, and one-fourth teaspoonful of sugar. Pour the sweetbreads and mushrooms over these, cover, and set in slow oven (325-350) for about half an hour.

Tomato-Cucumber Salad

Peel as many small, firm, ripe tomatoes as you will have servings. Cut a slice from the stem end and scoop out centers. Rinse out cavity with highly seasoned, salted French Dressing. Fill centers with a mixture of chopped cucumber and celery of equal quantity, a little onion, a few raisins, and mayonnaise. Set each tomato on a lettuce leaf and top with mayonnaise.

Cherry Sherbet Ice

1 can large white cherries
1 qt. water
1¼ lbs. sugar
4 large lemons

Place the can of cherries on the ice to chill. Drain cherries, remove pits and fill glasses about one-third full of the cherries and juice, filling up the glass with lemon ice:

Lemon Ice

Boil sugar and water. Grate rind of lemons and add to syrup. Boil five minutes. When cold add juice of lemons and freeze.

CHICKEN LITTLE
CORN PUDDING
WALNUT CREAM PIE

Of course it may as well have been "Little Red Hen" as "Chicken Little," but Chicken Little occurred to us first. If you stop to think about it, you can see how this matter of naming dishes, one after another, day in and day out, can get to be quite a problem. The proof, however, of the dish is in the eating and not in the name. We stopped, for a moment, to wonder why corn pudding seemed so logical an accessory to Chicken Little; why green corn goes so well with fried chicken, and corn muffins with roast chicken, and then suddenly it came to us—the chicken was *raised* on corn. Why separate them now? Corn pudding is better made with green corn scored and scraped from the cob, but the canned corn makes a fair substitute. If this is to be a company luncheon—and we think it good enough for any ordinary company—you may want to add a green salad which would seem to us a reasonable thing to do anyway. And of course nothing could be better, in season, than tomatoes. Out of tomato season we would recommend hearts of lettuce with roquefort dressing.

Chicken Little

1 year-old hen
3/4 pt. cream
1 tbsp. butter
1 cup mixed green and red pepper chopped
1 small glass sherry
Salt
Dash of cayenne
1/2 cup fresh mushrooms
Yolks of 2 eggs
1 pt. cream

Boil the fowl until meat is tender in just enough water to cover. (Save the stock for other purposes.) Cut meat from bones into dice. Simmer in a saucepan with three-fourths pint of cream, tablespoonful of butter, salt and cayenne for three minutes. Then add sherry, the cup of chopped peppers and the mushrooms. Simmer at boiling point for one minute then thicken with yolks of eggs mixed with pint of cream. Serve on small squares or triangles of toast and garnish with parsley.

Corn Pudding

2 cups grated or canned corn
4 egg yolks
2 tbsp. sugar
3 tbsp. flour
1 tsp. salt
1 1/2 cups milk
1 tbsp. butter

If canned corn is used, put it through a meat grinder using the finest knife. Add beaten egg yolks and the remaining ingredients. Pour into a well buttered baking dish and bake in a moderate oven until firm, about 45 minutes.

Walnut Cream Pie

3/4 cup sugar
2/3 cup flour
1/4 tsp. salt
1 cup chopped walnut or pecan meats
1/2 cup cold milk
2 cups hot milk
2 eggs
1/2 tsp. vanilla

Mix sugar, flour, salt and cold milk until smooth; add to hot milk, and cook until thick, stirring constantly (twenty minutes in double boiler). Add beaten egg yolks gradually and cook two minutes. Add nuts, vanilla, and pour into baked crust. Mix stiffly beaten egg whites with four tablespoonfuls of powdered sugar and spread over top. Set in slow oven to brown.

CREAM OF ASPARAGUS SOUP
TUNA FISH CASSEROLE
RED AND WHITE SALAD

WHILE the soup in this menu provides some vegetable, the meal would be improved by adding another. The salad, being of fruit, partakes of the nature of dessert, so some fresh green vegetable—lettuce, endive, Romaine or chicory with French Dressing would be an improvement. The limitations of space as well as a desire to rid our menus of any seeming arbitrariness leads us to mention only the outstanding features, and this introductory paragraph is designed to give us opportunity to make wider suggestions. So long as the general *plan* of the menu is followed, the judgment, tastes—and larder of the one who puts it into use, can be trusted to vary it according to need or wish.

Cream of Asparagus Soup

2 cans asparagus
Onion juice
3 tbsp. butter
3 tbsp. flour
2 cups milk
3 tbsp. grated cheese
¾ tsp. salt
¼ tsp. pepper
1 cup thin cream
1 hard cooked egg

Drain the asparagus. Cut off tips and reserve. To the rest of the stalks add the asparagus juice and a little onion juice and simmer until soft. Pass through a colander. Make a white sauce of the butter, flour, milk, cheese, salt and pepper. Add to asparagus pulp together with thin cream and tips. Reheat and serve garnished over the top with the hard cooked egg, which has been riced.

Tuna Fish Casserole

1 can tuna fish
1 cup celery diced
1 cup cooked peas
1 small can pimientos
1 cup cooked noodles or diced cold potato
White Sauce

Mix all ingredients together, add two cups of white sauce, and put in casserole. Make small baking powder biscuits and place on top of creamed mixture. Bake 15 minutes in hot oven.

Red and White Salad

1 box lemon gelatin
1 cup boiling water
½ pt. cream
1 pkg. cream cheese
1 small can crushed pineapple
½ can pimientos
½ doz. chopped red cherries

Dissolve gelatin in boiling water. Let cool and whip to consistency of whipped cream. Whip the cream, add cheese, pineapple, pimientos and cherries. Mix well, then add all to the whipped gelatin. Chill and mould. When ready to serve, unmold and serve on lettuce leaves. Garnish with a cherry on top and dressing at side. Serve with crackers.

CREAM OF SPINACH SOUP
POTATO NEST WITH EGGS
LEMON PUDDING

WE have remarked elsewhere on the advantages of using evaporated and condensed milk in certain cookery. Certainly we are no enemy of the friendly cow—in fact, how should we get either evaporated or condensed milk if it were not for the cow; to say nothing of *our* favorite beverage, buttermilk? Moreover, when it comes to drinking milk, or cream for our coffee, strawberries, pudding, or as a natural dressing for our peas and asparagus, we will take ours straight. But in cream soups, cream pies, in sauces, gravies, and in our baking, we prefer evaporated milk. Unless, that is, plenty of real cream and butter are used which, to most of us, is prohibitive. Evaporated milk *is* butter and cream. Except on the farm where milk is part of the produce, it is an economical as well as a convenient alternative, and should be stocked on the shelves along with other staples.

Cream of Spinach Soup

1 No. 1 can spinach
Juice from can diluted to 2½ cups
1 tbsp. butter
2 tbsp. flour
1 tsp. salt
1 tall can evaporated milk

Drain spinach and put through sieve. To spinach juice add water to make two and one-half cups. Melt butter (do not brown) and blend flour and salt with it. Add diluted spinach juice stirring continuously, and cook until slightly thickened. Add spinach and evaporated milk and stir smoothly until very hot but not boiling.

Potato Nest with Eggs

6 cups mashed potatoes
2 well beaten eggs
Bacon
6 eggs
Salt, pepper

Season potatoes well with salt, pepper and butter, and mix with two well-beaten eggs. Place in round casserole or baking dish and make six depressions about one inch deep with a tablespoon. Break an egg into each depression, and place a thin strip of bacon between each two eggs. Salt and pepper slightly and bake in moderate oven until eggs are set and bacon browned.

Lemon Pudding

6 eggs
½ cup sugar
2 lemons, rind and juice
4 tbsp. boiling water
2 oranges, juice

Separate the eggs. Beat the yolks, add sugar and mix. Stir into it the boiling water, fruit juices and rind. Cook over hot water until thick. Fold in the stiffly beaten whites of eggs. Cool. Serve in tall glasses topped with whipped cream.

LOUISIANA SHRIMP
ASPARAGUS ITALIAN
MARSHMALLOW PARFAIT

A SHRIMP, in spite of the suggested homeland of those designated in this menu, is pretty much a shrimp wherever he hails from, and, if you use the tinned shrimp as most of us do, even the shrimp would not remember where he came from. This recipe came from Louisiana, however, with the assurance that this is one way, at least, in which the Southern cooks use this most palatable bit of muscle. As for the Asparagus Italian—we do seem to be skipping pretty lightly around the world, and perhaps we should have called this Asparagus Alabam just to bear out our approval of neighborliness. As a matter of fact, this is a favored way of preparing asparagus out in Iowa and "Italian" was tacked on just because names were sort of running out. No attention need be paid to it. The Marshmallow Parfait is just a plain home-grown variety of sweet finish to a meal although it is one of those things that might easily have come to you as "Angels' Delight"—or worse!

Louisiana Shrimp

1½ tbsp. chopped onion
5 tbsp. butter
3 tbsp. flour
2½ cups shrimps
2½ cups cooked rice
1½ cups cream
1 cup evaporated mill
1 tsp. salt
1 tsp. celery salt
½ cup tomato ketchup

Cook the onion with butter for a few minutes. Add flour and stir until smooth. Add shrimps broken in pieces, rice, cream and evaporated milk. Bring to boiling point, stirring constantly. Add seasonings and ketchup. (This could be prepared early, but do not add the ketchup until reheated and ready to serve.)

Asparagus Italian

1 small onion
1 green pepper
2 tbsp. flour
1 small can tomatoes
½ cup water
Salt and pepper
½ cup cheese cut small
Asparagus
Toast

Chop and fry onion and pepper together in fat. Add flour and small can of tomatoes. Cook until thick and add water. Season with salt and pepper and add cheese cut in small pieces. Place heated asparagus on toast and pour sauce over all.

Marshmallow Parfait

½ lb. marshmallows
2½ cups cranberry sauce
½ pt. whipped cream
Pecan nut meats

Cut marshmallows in pieces and dissolve over hot water. Let cool and add whipped cream. Then add one-half cup of the cranberry sauce and mix lightly. Pour the remaining two cups of cranberry sauce in deep sherbet glasses; then the marshmallow mixture on top. Let stand in ice box until thoroughly chilled, and serve with a dab of whipped cream. Sprinkle a few finely chopped pecans over and top with a cube of cranberry sauce.

SWEETBREADS IN BATTER WITH TOMATO SAUCE
CORN MUFFINS
MARSHMALLOW FRUIT SALAD

SWEETBREADS are usually looked upon as a company dish, and while this menu is reasonably complete as it is, since the Marshmallow Fruit Salad takes the place of both salad and dessert, a soup would make it more complete. The tea biscuits might take any of the forms elsewhere suggested. With a vegetable added this menu could easily be translated into dinner. It should be rather a coarse, and preferably an acid vegetable such as sauerkraut, cabbage, chard, chicory or other greens. The ever popular marshmallow is met with in these pages almost as frequently, perhaps, as the cherry, pineapple, and some other of our favorites, but usually in association with some contrasting ingredients rather than, as is sometimes done, too closely affiliated with other cloying sweets. With acid or semi-acid fruits the marshmallow is an excellent foil, and its value as a garnish is great, but, unless purely as a confection, its charm is greater under some contrast.

Sweetbreads in Batter with Tomato Sauce

1 pair sweetbreads
1 tbsp. flour
1 tbsp. milk
1 egg
Pinch of salt

Soak sweetbreads in cold water for fifteen minutes and parboil for twenty minutes. Dip in batter made of the flour, milk, egg beaten light and salt. Fry in hot fat until a golden brown, and serve with tomato sauce. (Page 205.)

Corn Muffins

½ cup corn meal
1 cup flour
3 tsp. baking powder
1 tbsp. sugar
1 tbsp. melted butter
¾ cup milk
1 egg slightly beaten
½ tsp. salt

Mix and sift dry ingredients; add milk and egg. Thoroughly mix and add melted butter. Bake in a moderate oven, 375, 25-30 minutes.

Marshmallow Fruit Salad

18 marshmallows
4 tbsp. pineapple juice
1 tbsp. lemon juice
1 cup diced pineapple
1 cup canned peaches
¼ cup cream
¼ cup mayonnaise
1 cup grated cheese

Cut marshmallows into quarters. Combine pineapple and lemon juice, pour over marshmallows and let stand. Dice one cup sliced pineapple and one cup of canned peaches and drain. Drain juices from marshmallows and combine these with diced fruit. Now add one cup of grated American cheese. Make a dressing of one-fourth cup of cream whipped and one-fourth cup of mayonnaise, and mix three tablespoonfuls of this with fruit and cheese. Serve on lettuce leaves and garnish with remainder of cream-mayonnaise sprinkled with paprika.

STUFFED BACON SLICES

PORCUPINE SALAD

CHOCOLATE ICE CREAM WITH MARSHMALLOW MINT SAUCE

HERE is our old friend the shrimp again. This time entirely out of his element, capering about on a head of cabbage and the two of them masquerading under the name of a little animal that would doubtless turn up his nose at both. It does, however, make an interesting salad and goes particularly well with the bacon dish. It would go equally well as a dinner salad. The dessert suggested for this menu is good enough for *any* company meal, so if it seems best to reserve this for a more elaborate meal, a simple fruit dessert would do well here. For instance, small ripe cantaloupe cut in half, chilled, and the cavity filled with sliced ripe peaches, topped with whipped cream, and sprinkled with finely chopped candied ginger.

Stuffed Bacon Slices

Sliced Bacon
Olives
Bread stuffing

Make a bread stuffing as for poultry and add to it chopped stuffed olives (according to quantity and taste) and lay a tablespoonful or so on each good sized slice of bacon. Roll up, fasten with toothpick, and bake in 400-450 oven until bacon is done, slightly brown but not crisped.

Porcupine Salad

1 small hard head cabbage
12 small sweet cucumber pickles
1 can shrimps
Mayonnaise
Slaw

Trim the cabbage of coarse leaves. Cut a slice from top and remove center leaving a shell. Remove core from cabbage shreds, chop fine and let stand in Cole Slaw Dressing (see page 10) for two or three hours. Chill cabbage. When ready to serve, fill center of cabbage with cole slaw. Dip shrimps in French Dressing, stick a toothpick into each and then into the outside shell of cabbage, alternating with pickles. Top the cole slaw with chopped cucumber or grated carrot. Set the cabbage head on a salad plate and serve with Sour Cream Dressing No. 1. (Page 196.)

Chocolate Ice Cream with Marshmallow Mint Sauce

Chocolate ice cream
1 cup sugar
½ cup water
16 marshmallows
2 egg whites
2 drops oil of peppermint

Boil the sugar and water five minutes. Add the marshmallows cut in pieces and pour slowly on to the egg whites beaten stiff. Flavor with oil of peppermint Serve with either home-made or commercial chocolate ice cream.

CREOLE EGGS
ORANGE BISCUITS
LOG CABIN SALAD

THE orange biscuit in this menu calls up many possibilities. Blueberry muffins, for instance, would do as well, or date muffins, or cinnamon rolls which are quite easily made of rich biscuit dough rolled rather thin, spread with butter, cinnamon and sugar, rolled up like a jelly roll and cut in slices. The slices are laid flat side down on a greased tin and baked in a moderately hot oven. The log cabin salad might be a clever conceit to perpetrate on Lincoln's birthday—or, for that matter, it might be tried on St. Patrick's Day with a shamrock laid on top. Or, if shamrock is scarce, mint jelly can be cut in the shape of a shamrock leaf. Or—why not use it just to please the children and so coax them into eating more vegetables. As to the Creole Eggs, a vegetable oil can be used instead of olive oil if either the flavor or price of olive oil are objectionable.

Creole Eggs

1 tbsp. olive oil
1 tbsp. finely chopped onion
1 tbsp. chopped green pepper
1 tbsp. melted butter
3 tbsp. tomato pulp
2 tbsp. cooked rice
½ tsp. salt
Eggs

Put olive oil in frying pan and when hot add onion and fry soft. Add chopped pepper and tomato and simmer until thick. Add rice and salt. Put this in bottom of shallow glass baking dish and break over it as many eggs as will cover it without crowding, or as needed. Pour over the dish a tablespoonful of melted butter and bake at 350 degrees until eggs are set.

Orange Biscuits

2 cups flour
4 tsp. baking powder
½ tsp. salt
2 tbsp. sugar
3 tbsp. shortening
⅓ cup orange juice
About ½ cup water
Orange sections

Mix and sift dry ingredients and work in shortening. Add orange juice and water to make a dough that can be handled. Roll dough to one-half inch in thickness, and cut with a round cutter. Place a section of orange on each round, moisten the edges, fold the biscuit over, and press the edges together. Bake in a hot oven until well browned.

Log Cabin Salad

Pile leaves of endive log-cabin fashion on individual salad plates. Fill the center with a mixed vegetable salad—lima beans, raw shredded carrot, celery previously marinated in French Dressing. Serve mayonnaise separately.

POTATO PANCAKES APPLESAUCE
LETTUCE AND WATERCRESS SALAD
PRUNE SOUFFLÉ PIE

SPEAKING of applesauce, there is a subject worthy of some contemplation. Making good applesauce is not just the simple toss-it-over-your-shoulder process that some people seem to think. In the first place, not all apples make good sauce and how a marketer not brought up in the shadow of an orchard is going to tell which will and which will not is one of the consumer problems you hear about. An apple man coming to town with fruit from his own orchard can—and will tell you, but the huckster will tell you what he wants you to know, or at least what will sell his apples. Even if you knew the names of apples that make good sauce, such for instance, as Greenings and Northern Spies and Gravesteins and so on—unless you know the apple too, you are not much better off. The best thing to do is to become personally acquainted with the apple market. It would be an interesting study.

Potato Pancakes

12 large pancakes
2 cups boiling milk
2 eggs
3½ tbsp. flour
2 tbsp. baking powder
2 tbsp. butter
½ tsp. salt

Peel potatoes and throw into cold water. When all are peeled dry one potato at a time and grate. Drain off liquid and pour two cups of boiling milk over. Add melted butter, beaten eggs, and the flour, baking powder and salt which have been sifted together. Beat throroughly and fry on hot griddle. Serve with applesauce.

Lettuce and Watercress Salad

Wash and separate a head of lettuce, shake dry and chill. Shred outside leaves by cutting in fine strips with scissors. Lay on salad plate and arrange sprigs of watercress around the edge. In the center place a ball of cottage cheese that has been rolled in ground nut meats and sprinkled with paprika.

Prune Soufflé Pie

Whites of 2 eggs
6 tbsp. sugar
1 tsp. vanilla
1 cup prune purée
½ cup chopped walnut meats
Pinch salt

Cook enough prunes to make one cup of purée when pitted and put through purée sieve. Beat egg whites to stiff froth. Combine prune purée, nut meats and sugar and then fold in the whites of eggs. Add vanilla. Put into a previously baked pie shell and bake in a 350 oven for 15 minutes.

GRAPE AND GRAPEFRUIT COCKTAIL
CHICKEN SEVILLE
SHAUM TORTE

As most of our grandmothers did, and many of our country neighbors still do stock their shelves with all manner of preserved fruits, vegetables and meats against a less plentiful day, so now the thrifty and wise homemaking woman of town and city stocks her shelves with commercially preserved foods. As a general measure of good management, it does not pay the city dweller to buy foods for preserving. Not only is there the price of fuel as well as food to consider, but also freshness. Where one has access to a farmers' market, and certainly where one has a home garden or fruit it is just as good practice to can, preserve and pickle in season as it was fifty years ago. True, women have a multitude of interests other than housekeeping, but whether they have any that are more important than economical providing for family needs, must be a matter of individual judgment. At any rate, families must eat, and housewives must be responsible for providing food. And a hand-to-mouth existence of running to the store every time a can of soup is needed is both poor economy and poor management. All of which is called forth by the two cans of pressed chicken in the Chicken Seville. Of course fresh chicken can be used as well, but the tinned for such a purpose as this seems more convenient and more economical.

Grape and Grapefruit Cocktail

1 No. 2 can grapefruit
1 cup seeded white grapes
Lemon juice
Sugar
Fresh mint
Angelica

Drain grapefruit and mix with grapes. Sprinkle with two or three drops of lemon juice and sweeten to taste. Arrange in glasses, sprinkle with bits of angelica and put a small sprig of mint on top.

Chicken Seville

2 6-oz. cans pressed chicken
1 cup crumbs
½ tsp. salt
1 green pepper
2 tbsp. grated onion
1 chicken bouillon cube
¾ cup hot water
1 egg white
Stuffed olives

Shred chicken. Add crumbs, which should be fine and stale but not dry, salt, diced green pepper, and onion. Dissolve the bouillon cube in hot water and add. Add slightly beaten egg white. Place sliced stuffed olives on the bottom of individual greased baking dishes. Pack in the chicken mixture and bake in a moderately hot oven (375) until firm. Turn out and serve garnished with celery curls and triangles of buttered toast.

Shaum Torte

6 egg whites
2 cups sugar
1 tbsp. vinegar
1 tbsp. vanilla

Beat the egg whites to a stiff froth. Add sugar gradually, then vanilla and vinegar, beating all the while. Bake in two layers in a slow oven for one hour (300 degrees). When serving put whipped cream between the layers and on top. The appearance is improved by the addition of a few berries or three or four tablespoonfuls of jam.

TAPIOCA TOMATO BISQUE

GREEN PEPPERS STUFFED WITH BAKED BEANS

APRICOT SHORT CAKE

THE quick cooking tapioca is another modern discovery in the way of food products for which the homemaker may well give thanks. Not only as a common denominator for desserts quickly prepared, but as a thickener for soup and gravies that adds to flavor and nourishment but that requires no preparation. It is another of those food products that should be always on the shelf but never shelved. The beans with which the peppers are stuffed may also come off the shelf already cooked and seasoned. We believe that women who have taken on the responsibility of homemaking should learn to be good cooks. That they should be willing to spend time and thought and study on getting meals, and also willing to spend an hour getting a meal if it needs it, but we do not contend that they should cook things that are quite as good already cooked. In the recipe for "Tasty Beans"—the beans should be taken raw and cooked in the home oven. But for the beans to stuff these peppers, your favorite brand of canned beans is just as good—perhaps better on account of the seasoning.

Tapioca Tomato Bisque

1 pt. strained tomato
2 tbsp. quick-cooking tapioca
2 tbsp. melted butter
1½ pts. hot milk (part cream)
Salt, pepper, sugar
⅛ tsp. baking soda

To the tomatoes add butter, tapioca, salt, pepper, sugar (to taste) and boil fifteen minutes in a double boiler. Add soda. When ready to serve stir the hot soup into the milk (or evaporated milk diluted one-third) heated to the boiling point. Do not stir milk into the tomato as it may curdle.

Green Peppers Stuffed With Baked Beans

6 large green peppers
½ cup dry bread crumbs
1 medium can baked beans (with pork and tomato sauce)
2 tbsp. melted butter

Wash peppers, cut in halves and remove seeds. Place in boiling water, turn off the heat and allow peppers to remain in water about five minutes, to take sting out of peppers. Cool. Fill peppers with beans, cover with buttered crumbs and place in casserole. Pour a small amount of water around the peppers to prevent sticking and bake in a moderate oven (375) until peppers are tender, or for about thirty minutes.

Apricot Short Cake

½ cup sugar
4 tbsp. shortening
Yolk of 1 egg
4 tbsp. water
1 cup flour
2 tsp. baking powder

Cream the sugar, shortening and yolk of egg beaten to a froth; then add water and flour into which baking powder has been sifted. Beat until well mixed, pour into a greased layer cake tin. Bake twenty minutes in 350 oven. Split while warm (not hot) and fill with cooked dried apricots, mashed and sweetened. Now beat the white of the egg until stiff, then beat in half a glass of currant or raspberry jelly until it forms a stiff meringue. Pile this on the cake and garnish with pieces of apricot.

CREAM OF RICE SOUP
TOMATO ASPIC AND CHEESE SOUFFLÉ
PINEAPPLE CAKE

THE recipe for Pineapple Cake calls for a frying pan that can be put in the oven. Most frying pans have handles and handles are in the way in an oven. Any shallow biscuit pan will do for this recipe if not too large. A good heavy tin pan is good for this purpose, for baking biscuits or old-fashioned short cake. A 6x10 is a practical size or 6x12. Such a tin bakes better after it has been used awhile and becomes seasoned. Glass is excellent for casseroles, and one shallow oblong glass dish for cooking fish, baking apples, etc., should be kept on hand. Heavy aluminum, steel or iron are best for top of stove roasting. Enamel for boiling; iron muffin rings for pop-overs. Glass for pie baking and bread, although we like the old time tin bread pans too. Enamel ware is not recommended for baking, but is for refrigerator dishes, as is also glass.

Cream of Rice Soup

- 2 qts. chicken stock
- 1 cup rice
- 1 qt. top milk
- 1 small onion
- 1 stalk celery
- Salt and pepper
- 1 tbsp. butter

Wash rice and add to stock with chopped onion and celery. Simmer for two hours, put through a sieve, add milk (which has been heated to boiling point) and seasoning to taste. Add butter and serve hot in cream soup cups with sprinkling of paprika.

Tomato Aspic and Cheese Soufflé

- 1 can tomato soup
- 1 tbsp. vinegar
- 1 pkg. prepared lemon gelatin
- 1 cup boiling water
- Hard cooked eggs
- Stuffed olives
- ¾ lb. cream cheese
- 1 cup whipped cream
- ½ cup chopped blanched almonds
- ½ tbsp. gelatin
- 1 tbsp. cold water
- ¼ cup boiling water

To the soup add the vinegar and lemon gelatin, dissolved in boiling water. Decorate a ring mold with slices of hard cooked egg and stuffed olive slices. Pour in a little of the tomato aspic and allow to harden. Then add half the remaining aspic and place on ice to harden. Prepare the cheese soufflé by beating together the cream cheese, whipped cream, almonds and gelatin, softened in cold water and dissolved in boiling water. When the aspic is firm, arrange a layer of the cheese mixture over it and then pour in the rest of the aspic. Serve on lettuce with mayonnaise. Prepare the day before using.

Pineapple Cake

Melt in a handleless pan three tablespoonfuls of butter and let this run around pan. Sprinkle on this one-half cup of brown sugar. When this has melted into the butter, place in the pan as many slices of pineapple as the pan will accommodate. Let this stand while preparing:

Batter

- 1 cup granulated sugar
- 2 eggs beaten stiff
- 1 cup cold water
- 1 cup flour
- 1 tbsp. baking powder
- ½ tsp. salt
- 1 tsp. vanilla

Sift flour, sugar, salt and baking powder. Mix with water and eggs and beat thoroughly. Add vanilla and pour over pineapple in pan. Bake forty minutes in 350 degree oven. When done invert over large plate and serve with whipped cream.

LOBSTER AND GREEN PEA NEWBURG
SWEET POTATO BISCUITS
BOSTON PIE

BETWEEN the Lobster and Green Pea Newburg and the Sweet Potato Biscuits, a salad should be read, but because we wanted to give you these two recipes—with that of the Boston Pie—and the page being bound by iron rules, we shall have to leave it to you to include one of your own favorites or one taken from some other menu. It should be something a little sharp and crisp. The texture of our menu is a little soft, so something a bit crunchy like raw carrot or cabbage or cauliflower would be good with a hard wafer. Young white turnips peeled and sliced very thin with French Dressing, are rich in flavor. The Jerusalem artichoke (if you know where to find one) treated in the same manner, is a pleasant change from tomato and cucumber. The Boston Pie, we *think,* came from Michigan. But we like Boston and have spent many pleasant years there so it seemed only the decent thing to name a pie for it.

Lobster and Green Pea Newburg

1½ tbsp. butter
1½ tbsp. flour
1½ cups light cream
Salt, paprika
2 6-oz. cans lobster
1 No. 1 can peas (or fresh)
1 egg yolk
1 tbsp. lemon juice
2 tbsp. sherry

Make a white sauce of the butter, flour and cream. Season and add the lobster in large pieces. Add drained peas and slightly beaten egg yolk. Add lemon and flavoring, and serve with toasted bread croustades. If you do not care for the sherry, either the wine or the flavoring, a dash of nutmeg combines well with the lemon.

Sweet Potato Biscuits

1 tbsp. sugar
1 tbsp. butter
1 cup sweet potato mashed
1 cup buttermilk
2 cups flour
½ tsp. soda
1 tsp. salt

Add butter and sugar to hot mashed potato, then add buttermilk and beat well. Sift flour, salt and soda together twice and add to potato mixture. Roll out (pat out, with fingers), cut with biscuit cutter and bake in quick oven (450-457).

Boston Pie

¼ cup butter
¾ cup sugar
2 eggs
½ cup milk
1½ cups flour
2½ tsp. baking powder
½ tsp. vanilla

Blend butter and sugar and add the eggs well beaten. Sift flour, baking powder and a pinch of salt together twice and add to first mixture alternately with milk. Add flavoring last. Bake in two round layers. When done and slightly cooled, spread raspberry, strawberry or blackberry jam on one layer, place the other over it and dust the top with confectioners' sugar.

HAM TOAST SANDWICHES
BEET AND POTATO SALAD
RASPBERRY FLUFF

THE Ham Toast Sandwiches given in this menu are particularly good just as given, but if you don't happen to have any left-over ham in the house, and do have a little cold lamb, or chicken, or pork, or any other meat, try that. Whatever meat used should be highly seasoned, and if cold minced beef is used, add some chili sauce or a little Worcestershire. The beet and potato salad would be improved, according to our thinking, with either chopped or sliced onion, but we have thrust the onion into so many places where the Onion Haters would not have it, that we have grown a little sensitive on the subject. However, to the Onion Addicts, we recommend cutting up some scallions (with quite a good deal of the green top), or the addition of Spanish onion thinly sliced to whatever amount is wanted. And you will note that we repeatedly say "Rub the salad bowl with garlic." Always rub the salad bowl with garlic, except for fruit salads.

Ham Toast Sandwiches

Minced cooked ham
Bread, butter
1 egg
Mayonnaise
Prepared mustard
Milk

Mix mayonnaise and prepared mustard with minced ham according to amount required. Spread slices of bread with butter, then spread one slice with minced ham and lay the other over. Press together and trim off crusts. Cut in two. Dip in beaten egg diluted with milk as for French Toast, and fry on both sides in butter until brown. Lay on a platter and garnish with parsley. Serve tart jelly and sweet pickles separately.

Beet and Potato Salad

1½ cups cold boiled potatoes
1½ cups cold boiled beets
2 hard cooked eggs
2 tsp. dry mustard
Vinegar
4 tbsp. melted butter
Salt, pepper
Parsley

Dice both potatoes and beets before measuring. Make the following dressing: Yolks of two hard-cooked eggs mashed to a paste with dry mustard, melted butter, salt and pepper to taste and vinegar to a consistency of heavy cream. Mix the potato and beet with this dressing and put in a salad bowl that has been rubbed with garlic. Chop the egg whites, toss lightly with coarsely chopped parsley and sprinkle over the top.

Raspberry Fluff

½ pt. cream.
Ripe raspberries

Whip the cream, sweeten to taste, mix lightly with as many raspberries as it will attractively include, and serve in compote glasses. Garnish with a few fresh berries. Any other berries, or peaches or apricots can be used.

ESCALLOPED OYSTERS AND SHRIMP
FRESH VEGETABLE SALAD
APRICOT TRIFLE

ESCALLOPED dishes are so popular and so economical—in use of cooking equipment as well as in food combinations that it pays to have several casseroles on hand suitable for different purposes and different sizes. We personally favor glass casseroles because with these you can watch the progress of the cooking. They are less likely to break than some, at least, of the pottery dishes we have tried, and can be used as serving dishes as well which aluminum or other metal dishes cannot. At least they look better on the table than most of such do. And they clean easily. If food has been burned on, or is badly stuck on (which should not happen if the dish was well greased) just put it to soak for a little while in a strong solution of baking soda and water. We suggest small hot biscuits to accompany this meal.

Escalloped Oysters and Shrimp

1½ pts. oysters
2 cans shrimps
2 cups cracker crumbs
1¼ cups melted butter
½ tsp. salt
¼ tsp. paprika
2 dashes cayenne
1 dash white pepper
1 tsp. celery salt
Oyster liquor
Thin cream

Strain oysters of juice. Remove intestinal vein from shrimp and break in three pieces. Toss the cracker crumbs in melted butter and divide into three parts. Butter a glass serving dish, put in one part of the buttered crumbs, then one half the oysters. Sprinkle with part of the seasonings which have been mixed together, and pour over this layer four tablespoonfuls each of the oyster liquor and the thin cream; add a layer of the shrimp with another dusting of the seasonings; then another part of the buttered crumbs, the rest of the oysters, seasonings, four tablespoonfuls each of cream and oyster liquor; then the rest of the shrimps and seasonings, and finally the rest of the buttered crumbs to top with. Bake in a quick oven (400-450) for thirty minutes.

Fresh Vegetable Salad

Lettuce
Tomatoes
Cucumbers
Green beans (cooked)
Sweet onion
Celery

Cut small firm tomatoes into eighths. Slice cucumbers; cut beans into inch pieces; dice celery; slice onion very thin. Put all together and pour French Dressing over. Toss together until thoroughly blended. Arrange lettuce around sides of a salad bowl that has been rubbed with garlic, and put the mixed salad in it. Serve mayonnaise with it.

Apricot Trifle

1 qt. can apricots
1 cup apricot syrup
½ cup sugar
3 egg whites

Drain apricots and boil one cup of the liquid and the sugar together to a syrup. Mash the drained apricots, put through a sieve, and add this pulp to the hot syrup. Beat the egg whites very stiff, then fold in the apricot mixture. Chill. Pile in mounds on serving plates and serve with whipped cream.

SHRIMP SALAD
PANNED POTATOES
JELLIED PEARS

ONE might think, perhaps, that the shrimp was a poor relation of ours and we were trying to introduce him into good society. Still, and at that, you haven't met up with the shrimp as often as you will with hamburg steak in one form or another. But the shrimp is worth knowing. He is a modest fellow—mild almost to a fault as compared (in flavor) with the mackerel, for instance. But he is a luscious morsel and takes to mayonnaise like mustard to ham. And he, too, has a fellow feeling for the ubiquitous pineapple. *There's* a pusher for you, into everything. If you think you have run up against the shrimp here and there, *what* do you think of the pineapple! And if this menu seems a little light to you, try adding one of those hot breads mentioned elsewhere, or a fried mush. Not necessarily corn meal, but try Cream of Wheat, oatmeal (or rolled oats) or hominy. It will be more than is needed, with the potatoes, but it will be good.

Shrimp Salad

1½ cups cooked shrimp
1½ cups diced pineapple
1 cup chopped celery
¼ tsp. paprika
12 large stuffed olives
½ tsp. salt
Onion juice
Mayonnaise

Remove black thread from shrimps and cut in pieces. Marinate in French dressing. Chill. Cut sliced pineapple in pieces and chill. Combine pineapple, shrimp, celery, salt and paprika and mix with mayonnaise. Serve on lettuce leaves and garnish with sliced olives.

Panned Potatoes

4 medium raw potatoes
3 tbsp. butter
½ tsp. salt
Dash of pepper
1 tbsp. cream

Chop potatoes fine and put in shallow glass baking dish. Add the butter cut in pieces, salt, pepper, cream, and cover with bread crumbs. Bake in moderate oven forty-five minutes.

Jellied Pears

1 can pears
3 tsp. sugar
1 cup water
2½ tsp. gelatin
¼ cup cold water
Inch stick cinnamon
Juice from pears

Combine juice from pears with sugar, water and cinnamon and boil three minutes. Soak gelatin in cold water and dissolve in syrup. Arrange pears in a mold and strain the juice over them. Let set until firm and cold, and serve with whipped cream.

CREAM OF LIMA BEAN SOUP

EGGS A LA MALAGA—HOT ROLLS

CURRY APPLES

THIS is another menu that, with a raw vegetable salad added, would make a very creditable dinner. On the other hand, the Lima Bean Soup and apples, or some preferred salad, would do for a family luncheon. The egg dish is a hearty one and very delicious. The recipe for "curry apples" calls for an individual flat baking dish. These may be found in pottery and in glass. We have found a yellow pottery with white lining to stand up better than some other kinds, and the glass still more durable. Whatever dish is chosen it should be one that can be sent to the table as it comes from the oven in order not to disturb the egg.

Cream of Lima Bean Soup

1 qt. young green limas
1 pt. milk
1 pt. veal stock
1 tbsp. butter
2 tbsp. flour
2 egg yolks
Salt, pepper

Boil lima beans slowly in water to cover for thirty minutes. Drain and press through colander. Heat milk in double boiler. Heat stock and add bean purée to it. Rub butter and flour together and add to boiling milk, stirring until it thickens. Add this to stock and beans. Bring to the boiling point and add beaten yolks of eggs. Serve hot with croutons.

Eggs a la Malaga

(A Spanish Recipe)

Tomato sauce or chili sauce
Eggs
Peas
Shrimp, oysters or cold ham
Asparagus
Cheese

Into a buttered individual flat baking dish pour about two tablespoonfuls of hot tomato sauce or chili sauce; break into this a raw egg, and arrange scattered on top, carefully so as not to break egg, one or two raw shrimps, oysters, or pieces of cold ham; asparagus cut in inch pieces and a few peas, and cover with a coating of grated cheese. Put in hot oven and allow to bake until the egg is firm. Serve hot with sweet rolls or muffins.

Curry Apples

6 apples
1 tbsp. curry
2 ozs. grated cheese
1 cup fine bread crumbs
Milk

Peel medium-sized apples, cut in two crosswise and make a cavity in the middle of each half. Mix together the cheese, curry powder and bread crumbs to form a paste with a little milk. Fill each cavity with this mixture and bake in moderate oven till the fruit is cooked. Serve hot on squares of fried bread (French Toast).

MACARONI LOAF
FROZEN TOMATO SALAD
DELICIOUS PIE

If the Tomato Salad is frozen in the refrigerator allow from three to four hours, according to the temperature of the refrigerator. If a simpler salad is preferred, use one of the same nature since the macaroni loaf is starchy and should have an accompaniment of some sharp nature such as tomato, cole slaw, cucumber in French Dressing or vinegar. If a soup is wanted, let it be a consommé, thin vegetable, or anything but cream. A fruit cocktail would be better. The frozen tomato salad might be done in individual molds or in a ring mold, served on lettuce with mayonnaise in the center.

Macaroni Loaf

½ cup elbow macaroni
1 cup scalded milk
1 cup soft bread crumbs
1 tbsp. butter
1 tbsp. chopped onion
1 tbsp. chopped green pepper
1 tbsp. minced parsley
3 eggs
1 tsp. salt
½ cup American cheese grated
Butter

Cook macaroni until tender and rinse in cold water. Sauté onion, pepper and parsley in butter until soft. Beat yolks and whites of eggs separately. Mix sautéed vegetables, egg yolks and salt with macaroni. Stir in whites of eggs. Put a layer of macaroni in well oiled or buttered baking dish; cover with a layer of vegetables, add a layer of cheese mixed with bread crumbs, and alternate layers, with cheese and bread crumbs on top. Pour milk over and dot generously with butter. Turn out onto platter. Serve with mushroom sauce (Page 206) and with small sausages around the edge. Garnish with parsley and radishes.

Frozen Tomato Salad

1 can tomatoes
1 onion (small)
1 tsp. sugar
½ tsp. salt
1 peppercorn
1 tsp. pepper
Bit of bay leaf
2 tsp. granulated gelatin
2 tbsp. cold water
1 tbsp. mild cider vinegar

Cook tomatoes with onion, sugar, salt, pepper, and bay leaf. When thoroughly cooked, strain the mixture over the gelatin which has been soaked five minutes in the water. Stir until the gelatin is dissolved, add the vinegar and freeze. Serve with mayonnaise.

Delicious Pie

1 cup sugar
2 eggs
1 tbsp. vinegar
½ cup pecans ground
½ cup raisins ground
1 tsp. nutmeg and allspice mixed
1 tbsp. flour
½ cup butter

Cream butter and sugar; add egg yolks and flour and beat well; add vinegar and spices, nuts and raisins. Fold in stiffly beaten whites of eggs and bake slowly in uncooked crust. Top with whipped cream and sprinkle cocoanut over.

CHIPPED BEEF AND MUSHROOMS
BOILED POTATOES SQUASH SOUFFLÉ
JELLIED PINEAPPLE SALAD

CHIPPED beef in cream gravy is one of the standbys of the economically minded family, but it needs a little change once in awhile just to vary its nature. Evaporated milk is excellent for making cream gravies and cream sauces, as well as for many other uses. If plain milk is used it should be top milk or part cream and butter added as well. People who live in a dairying country have no reason for using evaporated or condensed milk, especially farmers. But for those who live in cities where milk and especially cream is expensive, evaporated and condensed milk are both an economy and a convenience. In cream soup, white sauce, creamed potatoes and gravies, evaporated milk is an improvement over raw milk and takes the place to some extent of butter and cream.

Chipped Beef and Mushrooms

1 cup chipped beef
2 cups fresh mushrooms
3 tbsp. butter
1½ cups thick cream sauce
Pepper, salt, paprika

Peel mushrooms and slice across. Season with salt and pepper. Put in a frying pan and sauté in the butter. Shred the dried beef and rinse in cold water. Add to the cream sauce with the mushrooms and their juice. Heat all together thoroughly, blending smooth. Place on rounds of toast and sprinkle with paprika.

Squash Soufflé

3 lbs. summer or Italian squash
2 eggs
2 tbsp. olive oil
2 tbsp. bread crumbs
Grated cheese
Butter
Salt

Wash squash but do not pare. Cut in pieces and steam until tender. Place in baking dish, add the eggs, olive oil, bread crumbs. Mix all together. Sprinkle top thickly with grated cheese (Parmesan is best) and dot with butter. Bake in moderate oven (350-375) until brown.

Jellied Pineapple Salad

2 tbsp. gelatin
¼ cup cold water
1 No. 2 can sliced pineapple
2 tbsp. lemon juice
½ cup mayonnaise

Dissolve gelatin in the cold water. Heat juice from drained pineapple and enough water to make a pint of liquid and add this to the gelatin. Add lemon juice and cool. When about to stiffen, add the mayonnaise and the diced pineapple. Put in individual molds and let set and chill. Serve on lettuce topped with Honey Salad Dressing (page 197).

CREAMED COD BAKED POTATOES
BROCCOLI WITH HOLLANDAISE SAUCE
PINEAPPLE—CUCUMBER SALAD
RICE FLIMSY

"CODFISH gravy" as it is so often made, skimped in butter and without an egg, is a not too palatable dish, but creamed cod, or even the old-fashioned "gravy" is not only an economical food but a delicious one. Plenty of butter, however, is a necessity, and a beaten egg added to the gravy just before it is taken from the stove, makes it an altogether different matter from that which we too often meet. The "Creamed Cod" of this menu is even more delicate. Potatoes either baked or boiled belong with codfish even as either onions or mushrooms have an affinity for beefsteak.

Creamed Cod

1 large slice fresh cod
¼ cup consommé
1 tsp. minced parsley
¼ pint cream
1 tbsp. flour
¼ tsp. powdered sugar
1 tsp. lemon juice
1 chopped green onion
1 tbsp. butter

Boil the cod and while hot break it into flakes. Put the butter into a saucepan and stir in the tablespoonful of flour; add the cup of consommé or stock gradually stirring until it thickens. Add the chopped green onion or scallion. Simmer for ten minutes, add sugar, parsley and lemon juice. Put the fish into this sauce and heat but do not let it boil. Serve in a deep dish and sprinkle with paprika.

Broccoli with Hollandaise Sauce

Choose thick-stemmed broccoli with large firm heads. Trim off the lower end of stalks and coarse leaves. Cook in boiling water until tender, adding salt when nearly done, about half an hour. Drain and serve with Hollandaise Sauce (page 206).

Pineapple-Cucumber Salad

1 cucumber
1½ cups pineapple juice
2 tbsp. lemon juice
⅓ cup sugar
2 tbsp. gelatin
½ cup cold water
1 cup crushed pineapple
1 tbsp. chopped green pepper

Peel and chop cucumber; season with salt and pepper; pour onto this the hot pineapple juice, lemon juice, sugar and dissolved gelatin. Add the crushed pineapple and chopped green pepper. Place in a wet mold to chill. Serve with mayonnaise in which an equal amount of sour cream has been beaten, with necessary seasonings added.

Rice Flimsy

¾ cup cooked rice
¾ cup peaches cut fine
¾ cup powdered sugar
¾ cup whipped cream
Maraschino cherry

The rice should have been slightly salted in the cooking. Mix all ingredients together, folding the whipped cream in last. Put in individual serving glasses to slightly chill and top with maraschino cherry.

NOODLE RING
ASPARAGUS AND CHEESE IN PATTY SHELLS
COFFEE CREAM

THE price of potatoes fluctuates with the season and the whims of Providence, becoming at times and at certain seasons almost prohibitive to the moderate purse. Products of the wheat fields—macaroni, spaghetti and noodles are also more or less at the mercy of the elements but not to so great an extent. The price seldom varies and so not only as a change in starchy food content but as an economical measure, we should introduce one or the other of these into our menus more frequently than some of us at least do. Nothing will ever quite take the place of the potato but there are times when we have to look upon it as something of a luxury and substitute other things for it. Rice is another substitute that is usually inexpensive in price and one which goes a long way. If potatoes only had a way of swelling up the way rice does—but unfortunately they shrink in the peeling, especially in the hands of the careless cook.

Noodle Ring

1 small pkg. egg noodles
3 eggs
1 cup milk
Pinch salt
Pepper

Boil noodles until soft in water to which salt has been added. Mix the well beaten eggs and milk with the drained noodles and pack in a ring mold in a moderate oven until firm. Remove from mold and fill the center with left-over meat chopped, cooked and minced spinach, or creamed tuna fish. Garnish with parsley or other green.

Asparagus and Cheese in Patty Shells

1 tbsp. butter
2 tbsp. flour
1 cup milk
1 can asparagus tips
1 cup blanched almonds
1½ cups American cheese

Melt butter and add flour. Add milk gradually and cook until thickened, stirring constantly. Add liquid from canned asparagus and bring to the boiling point. Add asparagus tips cut in small pieces, chopped almonds and grated cheese. Serve in previously baked patty shells.

Coffee Cream

40 marshmallows
1 cup very strong coffee
½ pt. cream
½ cup pecans chopped

Cut the marshmallows in pieces in a deep bowl; pour the hot coffee over them and stir until smooth. When cool stir in the cream whipped, and the nut meats. Chill.

DINNER MENUS

DINNERS

THE dinner menus which follow are, in general, meant for family consumption, or at least to give the perplexed housewife suggestions for making her own menus. Many of them, however, are quite suitable for company meals where simplicity is the rule. The accessories to the main dish which is usually meat of some sort, are, we believe, always in keeping but are meant to be merely suggestive of what will make a tasty and proper *kind* of accompaniment. If we say broccoli with roast lamb it simply means that some green vegetable of that type would be suitable. Of course we always think of peas with roast lamb, onions or mushrooms with beefsteak, boiled onion with fowl and so on, which is quite all right because they do go well together and we do not repeat such meals so often that we get tired of the accompanying dishes. On the other hand, unless we keep our minds reasonably alert we are likely to miss some of the many kinds of vegetables and fruits that are such a valuable addition to the diet. It is our intention, therefore, merely to stimulate the memory or the interest to further investigation of food products and to make suggestions that may or may not be carried out as given.

Getting meals is far more interesting if you have interesting things to work with. Of course there are countless devices in the way of cooking equipment that are more of a nuisance than a help. But there are also many that do save time and energy and that are worth having. A visit to the housekeeping departments of large stores is always stimulating. We have referred to various such articles throughout these pages, as the plank for meats, fish and vegetables, the casserole, and others especially useful in making salads and mentioned in the pages immediately preceding the section devoted to that subject. Amongst others that are new and that I have recently been testing are: a nut meat grinder—small mill in colored enamel fitting closely over a glass jar; a food grater similar in construction but larger, suitable for grinding bread or cracker crumbs, cheese or other dry foods. These are both very attractive, practical and inexpensive. A grapefruit corer which bites the core from half a grapefruit gives a much neater appearance than a knife will do and saves time over any other method we have tried. An ice crusher takes cubes or chunks of ice and reduces them to fine pieces suitable for beverages or cooling cocktails or melon. Egg beaters of various types—nothing especially new but even with the electric beaters and mixers, a valuable addition to the cooking equipment. These can be had at any price and in any quality, but it pays to get the better quality, one with eight blades and of stainless steel having given us the greatest satisfaction. The blades are flattened to reach near the bottom of the bowl. Can openers also are of many kinds, but we like one that fastens to table or shelf, or to the wall, although a more simple kind should also have its place in the drawer for picnics. There is a new food grater and potato ricer that is very convenient, and some kind of grater or sieve is essential. There is also a bean slicer and stringer which saves time and gives a uniform size to the cut pieces. As for a pea sheller, its greatest advantage in our opinion is in protecting the nails. In shelling peas by hand it is almost impossible to keep from getting green stain under the thumb nail. The pea sheller is not so much of a time saver as a nail saver. To these small conveniences we would add paper towels and a wall container to hold them. These are handy for wiping the hands and also for draining fried foods. Not only are they more convenient to use in many ways than a cloth but they help to give a cleaner appearance to the kitchen since they can be destroyed immediately upon using.

Plenty of refrigerator dishes, too, are more than a convenience; they are a necessity for preservation of food. In both glass and enamel they are made to fit one on top of another and so conserve space. Plenty of sharp knives with a sharpener to keep them so, sturdy scissors of stainless steel, long handled forks and spoons, steel skewers and spatulas are other necessities. Of stainless steel they will be easier to keep looking well than those of cheaper materials.

With frying pans in different sizes, kettles, sauce pans, double boilers, roasters, baking pans and complete equipment for washing dishes and keeping sinks and stoves and cooking dishes clean, that highly important part of homemaking which must be carried on in the kitchen is easily and pleasantly accomplished.

TOMATO JUICE COCKTAIL
POT ROAST OF BEEF   HORSERADISH SAUCE
BROWNED POTATOES   HARVARD BEETS
SPECIAL PRUNE WHIP

MOST tomato juice that comes canned for cocktail use can be bettered by a little judicious dressing, no matter what the canner may say. A little lemon juice, more salt, a dash of sugar, perhaps, a few drops of onion juice, and a little celery salt will tone it up, and make it different. Nothing gives a hostess more pleasure than to have her special concoctions praised for their individuality. Tomato juice should be highly seasoned and served very cold. A lukewarm tomato juice is not an appetizer, it is an irritant—to the disposition. If a soup is preferred with this menu let it be a thin consommé.

Pot Roast of Beef

4 lb. cut of round
Piece of suet
2 onions sliced
Salt, pepper

Melt the suet in a heavy kettle. Nothing is better than an iron kettle for such roasts. When hot, put the meat in (wiped but not washed) and sear on all sides. Then add 1 cup of hot water and the onion and cook slowly for three hours or until tender. One half hour before it is done, add the seasonings. As the water boils away add a very little more, just enough to keep the meat from sticking. The meat should *roast* in its own juices. Turn the meat from time to time so that all sides will be brown. When the meat is done, remove to a hot platter, add one cup of hot water to the liquid in the kettle and thicken with flour. Add a tablespoonful of Worcestershire Sauce and serve the gravy separately. The potatoes are boiled until nearly done, then browned with the meat.

Horseradish Sauce

3 tbsp. fresh horseradish
1 cup cream
1 tbsp. tarragon vinegar
½ tsp. salt
1 tsp. paprika
½ tsp. pepper

Whip the cream to a stiff froth; add the horseradish, vinegar and seasonings. Serve with roast hot or cold.

Harvard Beets

3 cups cooked beets diced
¼ cup vinegar
¼ cup cold water
½ tbsp. cornstarch
½ tsp. salt
2 tbsp. butter
2 tbsp. sugar

Dice cooked and skinned beets: heat water and vinegar together, add salt, sugar and pepper; blend cornstarch with water and add. Cook in double boiler until it thickens, stirring constantly. Add butter and when melted add the diced beets and heat through. Serve warm.

Special Prune Whip

3 cups large cooked prunes
½ cup crushed pineapple
1 cup combined juices
1 tbsp. gelatin
½ pt. whipping cream
2 cups cut marshmallows

Pit the prunes and cut in small pieces; soften gelatin in one fourth cup of cold fruit juice. Heat the one cup of combined juices and add dissolved gelatin. When this mixture begins to thicken, add the cream whipped and the marshmallows. Reserve a little of the whipped cream to garnish the servings. Chill before using.

POTATO-ONION SOUP
MEAT PIE WITH BISCUITS
TOMATO SALAD WITH RICE BALLS
LEMON PIE

THIS menu follows the Pot Roast of Beef dinner to suggest a use for left-over meat. With a good refrigerator, a day or two may elapse before serving this menu, allowing for another meat before having beef again. Any other left-over meat may be used as well as beef. Of course, plain cold roast beef is delicious in itself, so we suggest that if the roast was a good sized one, one meal be made from cold slices and the pie from tag ends. No potatoes are needed as a separate course in this dinner because there are potatoes in the soup and rice in the salad. We suggest lemon pie as a suitable dessert.

Potato-Onion Soup

4 onions
½ cup flour
1 tbsp. butter
1 pint water
3 potatoes cooked, mashed
1 qt. milk
Salt, pepper, paprika

Peel onions and fry in hot butter until soft; stir the flour into the butter and onion until browned; add the water slowly; have milk heated in double boiler and stir hot mashed potatoes into it. Add this to the onion and flour and water mixture and season. Serve in cream soup cups, sprinkle with paprika and add a small triangle of toast.

Meat Pie With Biscuits

Cut left-over meat into small pieces and put in bottom of greased casserole. To any left-over gravy, add enough stock, consommé or hot water with dissolved bouillon cube, to make 1 pint. Thicken this with flour, season with salt, pepper, 1 tablespoon of Worcestershire Sauce, 1 tablespoonful Chili Sauce. Pour over meat to cover. On top of this place small baking powder biscuits and bake 20 minutes at 450 degrees.

Tomato Salad with Rice Balls

2 green peppers
6 green scallions
8 large stuffed olives
1 hard cooked egg
1 tbsp. Worcestershire Sauce
4 small firm tomatoes
1 tbsp. prepared mustard
1 cup cooked rice
1 tsp. paprika
Few grains cayenne
½ tsp. salt
Head of lettuce
French Dressing

Chop onions, olives, green pepper and egg together; add Worcestershire Sauce and prepared mustard; then add warm rice and mix together with seasonings. Form into small balls and cool; add a grated garlic clove to some French Dressing (or use vinegar in which a garlic clove has been soaked to make the dressing) and pour over a small head of washed and chilled lettuce. Put lettuce on plates, arrange a thick slice of tomato on each and on this place a rice ball. Pour French Dressing over tomato and rice.

CABBAGE STUFFED WITH SAUSAGE
SWEET POTATO WITH APPLE
GRAPE JUICE SHERBET

THE stuffed cabbage will be found a very substantial meal, and with boiled rice instead of the sweet potato dish, is easily prepared. No salad is needed with the tomato bouillon and the cabbage for vitamins and the light dessert is recommended. In making the white sauce for the meat and cabbage dish, we suggest that a generous quantity be allowed for it is exceptionally good, and especially if rice or potatoes are substituted for the sweet potatoes, it will be too quickly gone. This sweet potato dish would be good with ham. The jellied tomato bouillon is made by adding dissolved gelatin, one tablespoon to a pint, to hot strained tomato juice and beef bouillon half and half, and highly seasoned.

Cabbage Stuffed with Sausage

1 large head cabbage
1 lb. pork sausage
¼ loaf bread
Cream Sauce

Mix the sausage (highly seasoned) with the bread (using fresh bread). Add no other seasonings providing the sausage is well seasoned. Cut the top squarely off a head of cabbage as in cutting a pumpkin for Jack-o'-Lantern. Cut out the insides of the cabbage leaving a shell of leaves (enough for the required number of servings) and fill the cavity with the bread and meat mixture. Put the top back on and tie the whole in cheese-cloth to keep it intact. Steam for 1 hour. Serve with a generous quantity of cream sauce poured over, and further quantity in gravy boat. See page 203 for Cream Sauce.

Sweet Potato with Apple

3 good sized sweet potatoes
4 large tart apples
¾ cup brown sugar
6 slices bacon
Butter

Peel the potatoes and cut lengthwise in medium thin slices. Boil in salted water until tender but not until they break. Drain. Place a layer of potatoes in a well buttered baking dish, then a layer of raw, unpeeled but cored apple cut in thin crosswise slices. Over these lay the thin slices of bacon which have been partly cooked in a frying pan. Alternate layers with bacon on top. Pour the bacon fat over, dot with a little butter, sprinkle with salt and bake in a moderate oven for 45 minutes.

Grape Juice Sherbet

2 cups grape juice
½ cup sugar
1 egg white
1 tsp. gelatin
¼ tsp. cold water
Juice 1 lemon

Soak gelatin in cold water. Heat the grape juice and add gelatin, lemon and sugar to it. Pour into refrigerator trays and let set one half hour. Remove to a bowl and whip stiff; fold in the egg white, return to tray and freeze for 4 hours. Stir every half hour for first two hours, then let freeze.

ROAST LEG OF LAMB
GREEN PEAS   STUFFED PEPPERS
MINT SALAD

JELLIED consommé would be an ideal first course for this dinner if used in the summer. In that case fresh fruit might well be used as either a first or last course. Lamb, like veal, requires slow and thorough cooking. Rare lamb is indigestible as well as unappetizing although underdone mutton is liked by some. Thirty minutes to the pound should be allowed for lamb. A little longer will do no harm. There is not much danger of over-cooking if the meat is frequently basted. The clove of garlic inserted in the meat at the joint gives an unusual flavor, but should be removed before serving.

Roast Leg of Lamb

Leg of lamb
Clove of garlic
½ cup hot water
1 tsp. ginger
1 tbsp. butter
3 tbsp. flour
1½ cups warm water
½ cup sour cream
Salt and pepper

Wipe the meat with damp cloth. Make a mixture of the salt, pepper, and ginger and rub the meat with this. Insert the garlic clove in the meat at the joint. Place the leg in a roasting pan with the half cup of hot water in which the butter has been melted. Roast until tender allowing thirty minutes to the pound, and baste frequently. When the meat is tender remove the leg to a hot platter. Pour off all the fat in the roaster but about three tablespoonfuls and into this blend three tablespoonfuls of flour stirring until smooth. Add gradually the warm water and sour cream, and continue to stir until the gravy is thick and well cooked. Season to taste and thin with hot water if desired. Serve in gravy boat.

Stuffed Green Peppers

6 green peppers
6 slices bacon
1 onion
1 can tomato soup
1 can pimientos
1 tsp. Kitchen Bouquet
Salt, pepper
Boiled Rice

Cut tops from peppers and remove seeds. Parboil for 5 minutes in salted water. Cut the bacon in small pieces and fry until crisp. Remove bacon from pan and in it sauté the onion until soft. Add to this the boiled rice (about 2 cups full) the can of soup, the chopped pimientos, salt, pepper and Kitchen Bouquet. Stuff peppers with this and bake in hot oven (400) 15 to 20 minutes. Serve one on each plate with the meat. Pour gravy over the pepper.

Mint Salad

2 cups crushed pineapple
1 pkg. mint gelatin
4 sweet pickles
Lettuce

Heat pineapple and juice. Dissolve gelatin in ¼ cup cold water and add to hot pineapple. Let stand until partly thickened, then add pickles chopped very fine. Turn into individual molds. When ready to serve turn out onto lettuce or cress and garnish with white, red or green cherry. Serve mayonnaise separately.

GRAPEFRUIT AND CHERRY COCKTAIL
VEAL LOAF
CANDIED PARSNIPS   SPINACH SOUFFLÉ
ADELAIDE'S RICE PUDDING

EITHER fresh or canned cherries may be used in the cocktail. If canned we recommend the large sweet cherries. Fresh ox-hearts would be delicious and all that is required to make the cocktail is to mix either fresh or canned pineapple with the pitted cherries and add a few drops of lemon juice. If potatoes are desired they may either be added to the menu or substituted for the parsnips. If potatoes are served we recommend a lighter dessert, perhaps a custard or sherbet. Not fruit, since we have fruit in first course.

Veal Loaf

4 cups ground veal
2 tbsp. ground onion
2 tbsp. chopped pepper
¼ cup fine cracker crumbs
2 eggs
1 tbsp. minced parsley
1 tbsp. chopped celery
1 tsp. salt
¼ tsp. pepper
1 tbsp. fat or butter
Milk

Mix together the ground meat, chopped onion, celery and green pepper. Moisten cracker crumbs with milk or stock, add beaten eggs, and all seasonings. Use just milk or stock enough to moisten the loaf and not make it wet. Turn into a greased baking tin and bake in a moderate oven for two hours.

Candied Parsnips

Cut parsnips in lengths and boil until tender. Lay in a baking dish and sprinkle lightly with brown sugar and just a dash of cinnamon. Add salt. Put one marshmallow on each piece and set in oven until marshmallow is toasted.

Spinach Soufflé

2 cups cooked spinach
1 tbsp. butter
¼ cup flour
¼ cup butter
1 cup milk
¼ cup grated cheese
3 eggs
Salt, pepper

Heat the two cups of spinach with the tablespoonful of butter and cut the spinach crossways first one way then the other. Melt the ¼ cup of butter and blend the flour into it, stirring until smooth. Then add the milk and cheese and season. To this add the spinach and the egg well beaten. Fold in the beaten whites last and put in buttered baking dish to reheat for ten minutes.

Adelaide's Rice Pudding

4 tbsp. rice
2 qts. milk
8 tbsp. sugar
1 tsp. salt
2 tbsp. butter
1 cup raisins
Nutmeg and cinnamon to taste

Soak the rice in 1 quart of milk for 2 hours. Add remainder of ingredients and put in buttered pudding dish. Bake in moderate oven for 2 hours.

CRANBERRY—APPLE COCKTAIL
BAKED WHITEFISH RICED POTATOES
SLICED CUCUMBERS
FRUIT PUFFS

THIS is a simply prepared dinner and only the dessert needs preparation beforehand. Plain sliced cucumbers seem a more desirable relish with baked fish than a cucumber salad—although in our opinion a sour cream dressing is more delicious than just vinegar. If cucumbers are not available almost any kind of tart relish will do. If another vegetable is desired, a dish of greens of whatever is seasonable is suggested; or a vegetable soup may take the place of the fruit cocktail.

Cranberry—Apple Cocktail

- 6 bright red apples
- 1 cup crushed pineapple
- 1 cup cooked unsweetened cranberries
- ½ cup cider
- 1 tbsp. sugar
- 2 cloves
- Pinch salt

Polish apples and cut a slice from the stem end of each. Remove core but do not peel. Scoop out pulp with a potato-ball cutter, being careful not to break the skin. Mix together 1 cup of apple balls, the crushed pineapple and cranberries. Boil the cider, sugar and cloves together. Cool and remove cloves and pour liquid over the fruit mixture. Fill the apple shells with this, put back tops, stick a clove in each as a stem, and serve very cold on glass plates on each of which is a grape leaf or an autumn leaf or a leaf of green lettuce.

Baked Whitefish

- 4 lbs. fish
- 1 pt. bread crumbs
- 4 tbsp. melted butter
- 1 lemon
- 4 slices thin salt pork
- 1 tbsp. grated onion
- ½ tsp. white pepper
- ½ tsp. salt
- 1 cup oysters
- White sauce
- Minced parsley

Clean and bone the fish and sprinkle with salt. Make a stuffing, of one cup of the bread crumbs, one half the oysters (chopped), the melted butter, minced parsley, grated onion, juice and grated rind of the lemon, salt and pepper. Fill the body of fish with this and sew up the opening. Put the salt pork in the bottom of a baking dish and lay the fish on it. Bake in a hot oven (450) for 15 minutes. When the fish begins to brown, add hot water to the pan and baste with this liquid. Reduce heat to 400 and bake slowly for 40 minutes basting every ten minutes. At the end of this time remove the pork, cover the fish with a medium white sauce to which the remainder of the oysters (chopped) have been added, sprinkle with the rest of the bread crumbs and bake until crumbs are brown. Remove to a hot platter, sprinkle with minced parsley, garnish platter with slices of lemon.

Fruit Puffs

- ⅓ cup butter
- ¾ cup sugar
- 2 cups flour
- 3 tsp. baking powder
- ½ cup milk
- 1 cup fruit
- 2 egg whites

Cream butter and sugar. Mix and sift dry ingredients and add to first mixture alternately with milk. Fold in egg whites stiffly beaten and add fruit—cherries, berries, peaches. If canned fruit is used it should be drained. Put in individual greased glass molds and steam 40 minutes. Serve with or without cream. Serves 6.

COLD SALMON LOAF—CUCUMBER SAUCE
BRAISED LIMA BEANS
CHERRY FLOAT

THIS is a good hot weather menu, and might be ushered in with jellied chicken soup, or cold fruit juice. Salmon, like hamburger, being one of the economical foods, is likely to become monotonous unless touched up sometimes with other ingredients that will take away a little of the fish taste and add more zestful flavors. With the beans, no bread is needed, but if the family is bread-minded we would suggest small hot biscuits or rolls crisped in the oven.

Cold Salmon Loaf

1 can salmon
2 small onions
1 green pepper
1 tbsp. chopped parsley
1½ cups sweetened spiced vinegar
2 tbsp. lemon juice
1 tbsp. gelatin
¼ cup celery chopped fine

Drain and trim the canned salmon. Mix with it the minced onion, celery, pepper, parsley; dissolve the gelatin in some of the cold vinegar. Heat vinegar and lemon juice and add gelatin. The sweetened vinegar from a can of pickles is excellent for such purposes. Pour liquid over fish mixture, place in a mold and set away to chill.

Cucumber Sauce

1 medium cucumber
1½ cup mayonnaise
½ cup sour cream
1 tbsp. horseradish
Salt, pepper
Paprika

Chop cucumber, not too fine; beat the sour cream into the mayonnaise and add horseradish and cucumber. Season to taste. Serve in mayonnaise dish.

Braised Lima Beans

1½ cups Lima beans
½ cup chopped onion
½ cup chopped carrot
½ cup chopped celery
1 cup boiling water
1 cup consommé
1 chopped pepper
1 tbsp. butter
Salt and pepper

Soak the beans overnight. In the morning parboil for ten minutes. Mix with other vegetables; put in buttered casserole and sprinkle with salt and pepper. Pour the heated consommé over and bake in moderate oven for an hour and a half.

Cherry Float

¼ cup butter
½ cup sugar
¼ cup milk
1½ tsp. baking powder
1 cup flour

Soften the butter, add sugar and milk stirring carefully, alternating with dry ingredients sifted together. Beat smooth, then pour into a buttered deep pudding dish. Mix the following and put over the dough:

1½ cups drained sour red cherries
½ cup cherry juice
½ cup sugar
¼ tsp. salt
¼ tsp. cinnamon

Bake in oven at 350 for 45 minutes. Should be nicely browned. Serve with whipped cream or cherry sauce.

SPANISH STEW

FLEMISH CABBAGE   BOILED POTATOES

MOCK SHERBET

THIS is a rather heavy meal and if any first course is desired it should be a very light one, perhaps a thin soup. Plain riced or boiled potatoes are best with this menu since there is a delicious gravy to eat on them. However, with the noodles in the stew no potatoes at all are necessary, nor is any kind of bread. The Flemish cabbage takes the place of a salad, and the sherbet tops off the meal with a pleasant taste and is not too heavy.

Spanish Stew

1 lb. lean fresh pork
1 tbsp. butter
1 cup chopped celery
1 No. 2 can small peas
1 large green pepper
2 cups boiling water
1 pkg. broad noodles
¼ tsp. black pepper
Salt, Curry and Chili powder to taste

Cut the meat in small pieces and sauté in the butter. Add chopped onion and pepper and cook slightly, then add the celery. Season with salt and pepper and add 2 cups of boiling water. Simmer gently for half an hour. Meanwhile boil a package of broad noodles in slightly salted water. When tender, rinse and drain in colander. Add these to the meat mixture with more hot water if necessary. Lastly add the can of peas with liquor. Simmer all together until well blended. Add Chili and Curry powder to taste and salt. Serve a relish or pickles with the stew.

Flemish Cabbage

1 medium head red cabbage
2 medium onions
2 tart apples
2 tbsp. sugar
3 tbsp. butter
¼ cup vinegar
Salt and pepper
1 green pepper, chopped
Meat broth

Melt 2 tablespoonfuls of butter in a deep pan and slice the onions in it. On top of these put the finely shredded cabbage. Season with salt and pepper and add a little vinegar. Cover with meat broth or 1 cup of hot water in which a bouillon cube has been dissolved. Let come to a boil and then add the apples cored but not peeled, sliced crossways. Cover and cook for one hour. When nearly done add two tablespoonfuls of sugar and the rest of the butter.

Mock Sherbet

½ cup quick-cooking tapioca
¼ tsp. salt
1 cup sugar
2 cups boiling water
2 lemons
2 egg whites

Cook tapioca, salt, sugar and water in double boiler until clear. Add juice and rind of lemons (grated) and cool. When it begins to set, add the beaten egg whites and beat until light and foamy. Chill. Serve very cold in individual sherbet glasses garnished with cherries, mints or small candies in color.

HAM BAKED IN PINEAPPLE
RICE AND ONION CASSEROLE
CUCUMBER AND CARROT SALAD
BUTTERSCOTCH CREAM

BAKING smoked ham in fruit juices is a variant for cooking this particularly delicious meat developed in recent years. Our grandmothers would as soon have thought of cooking chicken in hard cider as baking ham with pineapple (if they had had the pineapple) or apricots, raisins or peaches. And yet not only are all of these combinations good, but the meat is improved by the addition of grape juice, cider, ginger ale or almost any kind of fruit juice. These should, of course, be used in moderation.

Ham Baked in Pineapple

Have a center slice of ham cut about an inch and a half thick. Brown it on both sides—preferably in its own fat, or in butter. Then place it in a baking dish, sprinkle lightly with a mixture of brown sugar and dry mustard, and pour around it the juice from a large sized can of sliced pineapple. Bake covered in a moderate oven until the ham is tender (about an hour) basting frequently to keep moist. Sauté the slices of pineapple in the hot fat after browning the ham, and use them to garnish the platter on which the ham is served.

Onion and Rice in Casserole

2 cups cooked rice
4 tbsp. butter
8 medium onions
½ cup cheese grated
1 cup milk
2 tbsp. flour
1 tsp. salt
½ cup pimientos

Pare and parboil the onions until almost tender. Make a cream sauce by melting the butter in a frying pan, adding flour and stirring to the simmering point but not to brown. Add cold milk, stirring constantly. Add salt and cheese and stir until well blended. Finally stir in the chopped pimientos. Put a layer of onions in the bottom of a well buttered baking dish, then a layer of rice, cover with the white sauce and alternate. Bake 20 minutes in a 350 oven.

Cucumber and Carrot Salad

Grate or grind raw carrots (according to number of servings) and mix with tart mayonnaise and cream—one-fourth cream to three-fourths mayonnaise. Season with salt and pepper if necessary. Chop cucumbers coarsely and mix with the same salad dressing. Serve a small mound of the carrot mixture on a lettuce leaf, surrounded by the cucumber mixture. Sprinkle with paprika.

Butterscotch Cream

4 eggs
1 pint diluted evaporated milk
½ lb. butterscotch candy
1 cup cream
Grain of salt

Beat egg yolks, add milk gradually beating all the time. Cook in double boiler, stirring constantly until the mixture coats the spoon. Remove from fire and add the crushed butterscotch candy. Cool and add the cream and beaten whites of eggs, and freeze in refrigerator trays or in freezer. If frozen in trays, stir the mixture twice during the first hour, then freeze for three hours longer.

VEAL CUTLET IN MILK
SWEET POTATO SOUFFLÉ
TOMATO ASPIC
BROWN SUGAR PUDDING

VEAL is a meat that is lacking in fat and so some fat, preferably butter, should be added in the cooking. Cutlets are not satisfactory either broiled or pan broiled, which means frying. They are best browned and then cooked in some kind of moisture. Veal also must be *well* cooked, and cooked slowly. Mashed potatoes or rice may be substituted for the sweet potatoes. A green vegetable may also be added to advantage and green beans, peas, asparagus or spinach are recommended. A jelly—preferably tart, such as currant, plum or cranberry are also suitable accompaniments, although in this menu the tomato aspic is sufficient to make a well balanced meal. A sherbet would be sufficient dessert.

Veal Cutlet in Milk

1½ lbs. veal steak
1 egg yolk
1 tsp. water
Toasted bread crumbs
Salt and pepper
1 pint hot milk
2 tbsp. melted butter

Cut thick slice of veal into serving pieces. Beat the egg yolk to stiff froth and add water. Into this dip the veal, then roll it into the toasted bread crumbs which have been seasoned with salt and pepper. Brown the veal on both sides in hot melted butter in a frying pan. Remove to baking dish, pour over it the hot milk, cover and cook in a slow oven (350) until tender. Remove cover for last fifteen minutes. Serves six.

Sweet Potato Soufflé

2 lbs. sweet potatoes
¼ tsp. salt
2 tbsp. butter
½ cup brown sugar
¼ cup seedless raisins
Dash of pepper

Boil sweet potatoes until soft. Peel and mash while hot. Add salt, pepper, butter and brown sugar and beat thoroughly. Lastly add the seedless raisins. Pile in greased baking dish and bake in moderate oven until browned.

Tomato Aspic

3 cups stewed tomatoes
1 onion
1 stalk celery
1 tsp. sugar
¼ cup cold water
1 tsp. lemon juice
1 clove
1 tsp. allspice
Salt
1 envelope gelatin
1 large green pepper
Lettuce

Cook tomato, onion, celery and all spices together. Strain. Dissolve the gelatin in cold water and add to the hot liquid. Pour in individual molds. Chill. When ready to serve, unmold and set each mold on a ring of green peppers placed on a lettuce leaf. Top with mayonnaise.

Brown Sugar Pudding

1 cup brown sugar
1½ cups boiling water
¼ cup cornstarch
½ cup chopped nuts

Cook brown sugar and water together five minutes. Thicken with cornstarch dissolved in small amount of cold water. Cook until it clears. Add nuts. Chill and serve with whipped cream.

BREADED PORK CHOPS—ONION SAUCE
CORONET OF CAULIFLOWER
GLAZED SWEET POTATOES
APPLE CRISP

PORK, to be digestible, must be thoroughly cooked. Moreover, the process of long slow cooking develops flavor. Pork chops may be pan fried (fried in the spider) but they are better baked. They should, in any case, be kept from getting dry, at the same time allowing them to cook through and to brown at the last. Loin chops are always best, although shoulder chops if not from too old a hog are very good and usually cheaper. Other recipes for cooking pork chops will be found elsewhere in this book.

Breaded Pork Chops—Onion Sauce

Have loin chops cut about one and a half inches thick. Wipe with a damp cloth (do not wash) and sprinkle with salt, pepper and a dusting of sage. Dip them in beaten egg (diluted with a very little water) then in bread crumbs and lay them in a baking dish. Cover and bake for one and a half hours at a temperature of 350 to 375, or until tender, basting occasionally with hot water in which butter or fat from the meat has been melted. Uncover for the last 15 or 20 minutes with the heat turned up to 500 and let brown. Serve with:

Onion Sauce

Slice ten or twelve medium sized onions and cook in salted water until soft. Drain and put through a coarse sieve. There should be 1 cup of strained onion. Make a white sauce of two tablespoonfuls of butter melted in a frying pan, to which two tablespoonfuls of flour are blended. Then add one cup of cold milk slowly and stir constantly; season with salt and pepper and a dash of cayenne. Serve in a gravy boat to be poured over chops.

Coronet of Cauliflower

Cook a large head of fine cauliflower in salted water until tender (about 20 minutes.) Remove from water and arrange slices of small cooked and buttered carrots amongst the outer edge of flowerlets. Just before serving sprinkle with grated cheese.

Glazed Sweet Potatoes

6 medium sweet potatoes
1 cup sugar
¼ cup water
2 tbsp. butter
Salt and pepper
Paprika

Cook potatoes until tender; peel and slice lengthwise. Melt butter in frying pan, add sugar and let brown very slightly. Add water and let come to a boil; put slices of potato in this, baste with the sauce until glazed.

Apple Crisp

6 apples
1 tsp. cinnamon
¼ cup butter
½ cup water
¾ cup flour
1 tsp. baking powder
1 cup sugar
Pinch salt

Cut the peeled apples in thick slices. Sprinkle with cinnamon and sugar mixed. Make a batter of flour into which salt, baking powder, and sugar have been sifted, water, and melted butter, and pour over the apples. Bake in moderate oven for 30 minutes or until apples are tender.

SPINACH SOUP

STUFFED ONIONS PLANKED

FROZEN FRUIT SALAD

In general, the soup course at dinner is merely a stimulation to appetite—something warm and zestful to start the digestive juices. This, of course, when a full and nourishing meal follows. At times, however, a rather light dinner is planned, or one quite suitable for children in which case the soup may form part of the nourishment. A cream soup, too, is one way to give the children a little more milk. In the soup suggested there is the added value of spinach. Of course a cream soup is better for lunch than dinner, and in this instance a tomato juice or sauerkraut cocktail may be substituted for the soup.

Spinach Soup

1 cup cooked chopped spinach
2 tbsp. flour
2½ cups cream sauce
1 tsp. sugar
Salt, pepper

Make a medium cream sauce (see page 00) and add the chopped cooked spinach and season. Serve hot.

Stuffed Onions Planked

6 large onions
1 lb. ground beef
¼ lb. salt pork ground
3 tbsp. melted butter
Mashed potatoes
Peas—carrots
6 large mushrooms

Mix ground beef and pork together and season with salt and pepper. Peel and parboil onions in salted water until slightly tender. Drain and cool. With a sharp knife cut a slice squarely off the top of each onion and with a fork scoop out the center leaving a shell that will hold together. Chop these centers fine and add one-half the quantity to the meat, together with the melted butter. Mix thoroughly. Fill the onions with this mixture, lay a large mushroom on top of each, set in a greased baking tin with a tablespoonful of hot water, and bake in a hot oven until tender and slightly browned. Heat a well oiled plank and on it place the onions, around them arrange first a ring of green peas, then, with a pastry tube a wreath of mashed potatoes (seasoned) and lastly a row of overlapping slices of carrot. Set the plank back in the oven to lightly brown the potato.

Frozen Fruit Salad

1 cup crushed pineapple
⅓ cup mayonnaise
½ cup cherries chopped
2 bananas
1 cup heavy cream
1 cup sugar
2 tbsp. lemon juice
1 cup fruit juice
1 tbsp. gelatin

Beat cream, add mayonnaise and sugar, mix well together; add pineapple, chopped cherries and bananas mashed. To one cup of combined fruit juices, heated, add the gelatin dissolved in cold fruit juice and stir all together. Put into a refrigerator tray and freeze 3 to 4 hours, stirring every half hour for first hour and a half.

BAKED HAM—CAULIFLOWER GARNISH

LIMA BEANS CANDIED SWEET POTATOES

TURNED SALAD

APRICOT ICE

PLANNING a week's menus ahead, as women have sometimes asked us to do, is not always satisfactory. There are likely to be left-overs that you have not planned on, or there is a special sale on something, or you get invited out, and the schedule is upset. It is not a bad idea, however, to make a rough plan so that you have something to work toward. If you have roast beef on Sunday, you know pretty well that at least three other meals are taken care of, and that will make it easy to fill in alternating days with something entirely different. Almost any plan, however, is better than none. The woman who doesn't know what she is going to have for dinner at night until after lunch at noon is a poor manager and an unhappy one.

Baked Ham

Cover ham with cold water and bring slowly to simmering point. Cook until nearly tender, twenty minutes to the pound. Remove skin from shank, score into squares, stick a clove into each square. Cover with a paste of brown sugar, prepared mustard, salt, pepper, moistened with maple syrup. Pour one small bottle of ginger ale in the roaster and bake until tender. Garnish with cauliflower flowerlets boiled for twenty minutes, and spiced crab apples.

Lima Beans

Boil lima beans until tender in salted water. Drain, put into skillet with hot bacon fat and fry until brown. Stir, but do not break.

Turned Salad

Put into large salad bowl, crisp lettuce leaves, sliced cucumbers, green pepper rings, avocado sliced lengthwise, sliced radishes and thin slices of Bermuda onions. These should be very cold. Serve at table as separate course. When ready to serve, pour French Dressing over, then with salad fork and spoon, turn and turn until every ingredient is coated. Serve on cold plates.

Apricot Ice

1 cup sugar
2 cups water
½ cup white corn syrup
4 tbsp. lemon juice
1 No. 2 can apricots

Cook sugar, corn syrup and one cup of water to soft ball stage. Remove from fire, add lemon juice, 1 cup of water; add apricot juice and mashed fruit. Cool. Put in refrigerator trays and freeze. Makes two quarts. Allow three hours or more for freezing, according to temperature of refrigerator.

CHICKEN-NOODLES IN CASSEROLE
CARROT IN PEPPER RINGS
STRAWBERRY SHORTCAKE

A SPECIAL plea is made for the strawberry short cake. Here in particular is a place to be lavish with butter, and open-handed with berries. Strawberries have a short season, even though we begin with the earliest that are reasonable in price, and they are perhaps the most popular of berries. We should in all fairness give them every advantage. Make your biscuit dough rich—(and *make* it biscuit dough, not cake dough) and spread the butter on while the biscuits are hot—so hot that the butter will hide itself within the flaky folds almost before the berries are laid on. Spread the tops too, after the two halves are put together, and before the dressing of berries is added. Let the juice run down in a limpid pool of lusciousness—and serve a spoon with it!

Chicken-Noodles in Casserole

1 small fowl
2 pkgs. noodles
Salt, pepper
1 onion
½ cup celery
½ cup cream

A year old hen does very well for this dish. Disjoint and cook the fowl in water to cover, until the meat comes readily from the bones. Cool, and then cut the meat in small pieces. The sliced onion and diced celery are cooked with the fowl. Cook noodles in separate kettle, drain and chop not too fine, or break in small pieces before cooking. Butter a casserole and lay a portion of the noodles in the bottom. Sprinkle with salt and pepper, dot with butter; over this put a layer of chicken meat and repeat this until all noodles and all meat are used. Thicken the broth in which chicken was cooked to a very thin sauce, and add a half cup of cream. Season well and pour over the chicken and noodle dish. Set in a moderate oven to cook through.

Carrot in Pepper Rings Salad

½ pkg. lemon gelatin
1 cup boiling water
2 tbsp. vinegar
4-5 small new carrots
3 sweet green peppers
3 slender sweet pickles
Salt

Dissolve gelatin in boiling water and add vinegar. Let stand until it begins to set. Grate carrots or chop fine, and season with salt. Add to gelatin and mix well. Remove seeds from peppers and scald. In center of each pepper place a pickle upright and pack with carrot. Let set and chill. Cut in slices about ¾ inch thick. Serve on lettuce with mayonnaise.

Strawberry Shortcake

2 cups flour
4 tsp. baking powder
4 tbsp. shortening
½ tsp. salt
¾ cup milk

Sift flour, baking powder and salt together. Cut in shortening. Add just enough milk to handle in soft dough. Roll on floured board and cut as biscuits. Bake at 400-450 for fifteen minutes. When done split, butter both halves generously. Spread one half with crushed strawberries, lay other half on top, brush with butter, cover with berries, one whole one on top.

SAUSAGE BALLS—TOMATO SAUCE
BAKED CABBAGE
BLACKBERRY PUDDING

IT doesn't pay to get too serious over "balanced meals" and "food values." About all you have to remember is that plenty of green vegetables and a suitable amount of milk are about the best health protectors there are and the remainder of the essential food will take care of itself. We are almost certain to have some kind of meat once a day anyway, and we are more likely to eat too much sweet than not enough. So be sure of two or three different kinds of vegetables for the main meal, and an appetizing vegetable or fruit salad is about as good as anything we can think of for the everyday lunch unless there are workers who require a heavier meal.

Sausage Balls with Tomato Sauce

1½ lbs. pork sausage highly seasoned
1 cup rice
4 hard cooked eggs

Press sausage firmly around each egg (shelled). Roll in corn meal and fry in deep fat until brown. Cut in half and lay on a bed of cooked rice. Cover with

2 cups tomato soup
1 tbsp. flour
½ tsp. sugar
1 tsp. celery salt
½ tsp. salt
1 tbsp. Worcestershire Sauce
Paprika
5 drops Tobasco Sauce

Tomato Sauce

Blend flour into tomato soup. Add sugar, salt and celery salt and cook in double boiler until thick; then add Worcestershire, Tabasco and paprika.

Baked Cabbage

1 head new cabbage
2 eggs
2 tbsp. butter
½ cup cream
Bread crumbs
Grated cheese

Boil new cabbage for twenty minutes; drain and cool. Chop, and add two beaten eggs, two tablespoonfuls butter, one-half cup cream, pepper, salt. Put in baking dish and cover with bread crumbs, sprinkle with grated cheese and bake until brown.

Blackberry Pudding

1 cup sour milk
½ cup sugar
1 tsp. soda
1 egg
Flour
1 cup berries

Beat egg and add sugar. Mix soda with sour milk, add berries and flour to make batter of consistency of waffle batter. Bake twenty minutes in moderate (350) oven. Test with cake tester to be sure it is done. Serve with

Blackberry Sauce

1 cup water
1 cup berries
1 tbsp. butter
½ cup sugar
1 tbsp. arrowroot or cornstarch

Mash berries through purée sieve. Add sugar, arrowroot, water and cook in double boiler ten minutes. Add butter and stir. Serve hot.

VEAL POT ROAST WITH DUMPLINGS
SPANISH PEPPERS—SOUTHERN STRING BEANS

If you are a beginner at cooking, try the simplest dishes first. Roasts are not difficult, and once you have mastered the art of making fluffy dumplings you will find many places where they will take the place of both bread and potatoes. The fewer dishes you undertake at a time the less tired you will be when the meal is done, and the less worn your nerves. With the fewer dishes, however, the greater is the necessity for careful balancing. So long as you make sure to have plenty of vegetables—at least one raw, you are not likely to go astray. As a dessert for this menu we suggest peach short cake.

Veal Pot Roast with Dumplings

4 lbs. veal
2 tbsp. butter
1 cup hot water
6 potatoes
Salt, pepper
Flour

Cut veal into serving pieces. Put butter in iron or steel kettle or Dutch oven and heat. Brown meat in this, turning to brown all sides. Sprinkle with flour. Pour in one cup hot water, cover closely and cook slowly for two hours. Twenty minutes before the meat is done put in the potatoes, peeled and quartered, and dumplings.

Dumplings

1 cup flour
1 tsp. baking powder
Salt
Milk to make stiff batter

Sift flour, baking powder and salt, and stir to thick batter with milk. Drop from spoon into kettle, cover and cook twenty minutes. Make a gravy with juice left in kettle, adding one pint of hot water, two bouillon cubes and seasoning.

Spanish Peppers

6 green peppers
3 cups corn
1 onion
1 cup tomatoes
Salt, pepper
Paprika
½ cup cracker crumbs

Seed peppers and scald five minutes in boiling water. Chop the corn if from can, or use fresh grated corn and mix with chopped onion, tomatoes, cracker crumbs and seasonings. Fill peppers with this. Sprinkle with cracker crumbs, dot with butter and bake in glass baking dish, the bottom of which is just covered with water.

Southern String Beans

1 tbsp. butter or pork fat
1 qt. string beans
Seasonings

Put fat into heavy skillet and heat. Put in beans (washed, trimmed and cut) with just enough water to keep from burning and cook until tender, about twenty minutes. Stir frequently.

HAM LOAF—HORSERADISH SAUCE
GREENS—MASHED TURNIPS
LEMON SNOW PUDDING

SEVERAL different recipes for horseradish sauce will be found in these pages. There are any number of combinations which will render this piquant relish suitable for different kinds of meats and salads. You may have your own favorite and care for none of them. But at least a bottle of fresh horseradish is one of the things that should be kept on the shelf, but it should not be kept too long, for it loses its zest in time. The best way to get horseradish is to buy it from some one who digs it from his garden (or dig it from your own garden) and learn what *fresh* horseradish can be like when it takes a good hold of the tongue.

Ham Loaf—Horseradish Sauce

1½ lbs. ham
¾ lb. fresh pork
3 eggs
1 No. 1 can tomato soup
2 cups bread crumbs
1 onion

Have the ham and pork ground together; add the beaten eggs, tomato soup, bread crumbs, and chopped onion. Make into a loaf two or two and a half inches thick and bake in slow oven (350°) for one hour. Serve hot or cold

Horseradish Sauce

2 tbsp. butter
2 tbsp. flour
2 cups meat stock
4 tbsp. horseradish

Melt butter and blend flour with it and cook slowly until slightly brown, stirring constantly. Add well-seasoned stock gradually, stirring, and cook until thick. Add horseradish and serve hot with hot meat or cold with cold meat.

Greens

Swiss chard, escarole (American endive), dandelions, beets, or whatever "greens" can be had. Greens should be washed in several waters and then cooked in as little water as possible. A small piece of salt pork or a few slices of bacon will lend flavor. Otherwise they should be drained, chopped coarsely, and dressed with butter, pepper and salt.

Lemon Snow Pudding

1 cup milk
1 cup sugar
1 tbsp. butter
2 eggs
1 tbsp. cornstarch
2 lemons (grated rind of one)
Pinch of salt

Heat milk, add sugar and cornstarch blended with some of the cold milk, butter, salt and yolks of eggs. Beat. Cook in double boiler until thickened. Transfer to serving dish; beat egg whites to stiff froth, add two tablespoonfuls of sugar, and spread over pudding. Set in slow oven to brown.

CHILLED WATERMELON BALLS

CREOLE MEAT BALLS SUCCOTASH

PEAR AND CHEESE SALAD

IF melons are not available, either another fruit or a soup may be substituted. If a melon of any kind is used, chill it by placing in the refrigerator for several hours, or by serving it in a plate of chopped ice, never by putting ice in the melon. The salad seems almost superfluous and it all depends on whether a simple family meal is being served or one more elaborate. Cottage cheese is easily digested, and even though we have a fruit to begin with the melon and pear are both so light in value that the cheese will upset no dietary rules beyond repair.

Creole Meat Balls

1 lb. chopped beef
1 slice of stale bread
4 onions
1 egg
2 green peppers
½ tsp. pepper sauce
1 tbsp. mustard
1 tbsp. vinegar
1 tbsp. orange juice
1 large garlic clove
1 tbsp. paprika
1 tbsp. tomato soup
Salt, pepper
6 potatoes
Boiling water
Bacon fat

Mix beef, bread crumbled, minced onion, beaten egg, chopped pepper, pepper sauce, prepared mustard, vinegar, orange juice, salt and pepper together and form into balls or patties. Fry one large minced onion in bacon fat. Add garlic (minced) and paprika to this. Lay the balls in a roasting pan for top of stove cooking. In with the meat balls lay raw, pared and sliced potatoes. Add a very little water and the tomato soup and cover closely. Simmer for two hours, adding a little boiling water as necessary to keep from sticking. When potatoes are tender, take up meat balls on hot platter, alternating with potatoes and garnish with cress, parsley, small green onions, radishes, or small pickles. Add a bouillon cube and cup of hot water to the liquid in the pan, thicken, season highly and serve in a boat.

Succotash

1 pt. young lima beans
1 pt. corn scraped from cob
1 tbsp. butter
½ pt. top milk or evaporated milk
⅛ tsp. soda
Salt, pepper

Shell the beans and cover with boiling water, add teaspoonful of salt and boil twenty-five minutes; then add ⅛ teaspoonful of soda, boil one minute longer, drain and rinse in hot water. Score the corn and scrape it from the cob, add it to the beans, then add the milk, butter, salt, pepper. Stir over the fire continuously for five minutes and serve. If dried beans are used in winter they should be soaked overnight.

Pear and Cheese Salad

Stuff the cavity of halved canned or fresh pears with cottage cheese, sprinkle with paprika, serve on lettuce with mayonnaise or cooked salad dressing.

PORK TENDERLOINS—APPLE SAUCE

BAKED TOMATOES RICED POTATOES

PECAN PIE

IF we neglect to mention spaghetti and macaroni as often as we might, don't *you* forget them. Our idea in this book is to remind you of things you might forget, or tell you of something you didn't know, and we are sure to neglect a good many of the stand-bys. So, sometimes when we say potatoes, or leave out a starchy food entirely, you say to yourself "macaroni!" or "spaghetti!" Our personal preference is for potatoes with pork, but with veal or lamb or fowl—noodles, macaroni or spaghetti is excellent. We have, however, mentioned these good starchy foods so often in our luncheon dishes, that we shall leave them mostly to your own judgment with the dinners.

Pork Tenderloins

Dip each tenderloin in beaten egg, then in cracker crumbs, salt and pepper. Brown on both sides in hot spider, using part butter and part other fat. Place in a roasting pan; pour milk over them until almost covered. Set in oven at 400 and roast, covered, for three hours. Just before serving turn up heat, take off cover and brown. Make a gravy by thickening sauce left in pan with flour and water paste. Season.

Baked Tomatoes

6 large tomatoes
½ cup rice
2 tbsp. minced onion
2 tbsp. minced green pepper
2 tbsp. cracker crumbs
1 tbsp. bacon fat or oil
1 tbsp. minced parsley
½ cup stock
Salt, pepper, paprika
½ cup grated cheese

Cook rice in boiling, salted water. Drain. Heat the fat and sauté onion, pepper and parsley. Add the rice and stock and cook until stock is absorbed. Season to taste. Cut a slice from each tomato and spoon out insides, leaving thick shell. Fill with the rice mixture; combine bread crumbs and cheese and sprinkle over the top. Set in baking pan and bake until tomatoes are tender (about thirty minutes), and cheese brown. Moderate oven, 350.

Pecan Pie

2 cups brown sugar
1 cup raisins (chopped)
1 cup pecan meats
4 eggs
1 tbsp. butter
½ tsp. allspice
1 tsp. vanilla
3 tsp. vinegar

Mix sugar and butter; add yolks of eggs, spices, nut meats, raisins and vinegar. Beat whites of eggs and add to mixture last. Pour into a pie plate lined with short crust and bake 20 to 30 minutes in 350 oven. Serve with a spoonful of whipped cream on each piece. Makes one large or two small pies.

CHICKEN SPINACH SOUP
BAKED HALIBUT
CARROTS IN PEANUT BUTTER CREAM
COFFEE BAVARIAN CREAM

IF fresh fish happens to be unobtainable when you want to try this menu, try frozen fish. The frozen food industry is a new one—developed almost entirely within the last ten or fifteen years, and has already proven itself a most valuable asset to the home market. Not only can fresh fish be had at any time of the year and in almost any locality, but also frozen fowl, vegetables and fruits. Frozen peas, for instance, are infinitely superior to canned peas, and can hardly—if at all—be distinguished from fresh peas. Taken fresh from the field or sea or yard, these products are frozen almost instantaneously while at their very best. If you have not already investigated frozen foods, it will be to your advantage to do so. We suggest adding sliced cucumbers and tomatoes in French Dressing to the menu.

Chicken Spinach Soup

2 qts. spinach
2 cups chicken stock
1 tbsp. butter
1 tbsp. flour
2 cups milk
Salt, pepper

Wash the spinach and cook in three cups of boiling water. Drain, chop and press through a vegetable sieve. Add the water in which the spinach was cooked and the stock, and heat to boiling point. Rub butter and flour together; add the milk slowly and cook until smooth. Add the spinach to this, heat, but do not boil. Serve at once.

Baked Halibut

1 slice of halibut (or swordfish)
Salt, pepper
Bread crumbs
Juice of 1 lemon
1 small onion diced
Flour
Bacon

The slice of fish should be about two inches thick. Sprinkle with salt and pepper and diced onion. Squeeze the juice of a lemon over the top side. Put in baking dish, sprinkle with bread crumbs, lay strips of bacon over, and bake one hour at 400.

Carrots in Peanut Butter Cream

3 cups milk
2 tbsp. flour
2 tbsp. peanut butter
2 cups cooked sliced carrots
1 tsp. salt

Heat the milk in double boiler; thicken with flour moistened with a little cold milk; cook ten minutes. Soften the peanut butter with some of this sauce and add to the mixture with salt; add the carrots. Put in vegetable dish and garnish with strips of pimiento.

Coffee Bavarian Cream

1 envelope gelatin
¼ cup cold water
½ cup strong coffee
½ cup sugar
1 tbsp. lemon juice
2 cups cream whipped
¼ tsp. salt
1 tsp. vanilla

Soften gelatin in cold water and dissolve in hot coffee. Cool, and when it begins to thicken beat, fold in whipped cream and flavoring. Turn into mold that has been rinsed with cold water and chill.

GRILLED HAM WITH
RAISIN SAUCE
WHITE TURNIPS STUFFED WITH RICE
AVOCADO-GRAPEFRUIT SALAD

STUFFING vegetables is something of a new wrinkle in food preparation, but it is a good one. In that way you get two dishes in one. Almost any vegetable that has much body to it can be stuffed. With stuffed onions we are already quite familiar—there are at least two recipes in this book. But stuffing turnips will be new, we hope, to some of you. And when you have tried that, try an egg plant some day, or a carrot that has a husky butt. The rice that usually forms the base for such stuffing takes the place of potatoes and bread (it should be potatoes *or* bread, for never are both needed), and the trimmings that go into the rice help to add up the vitamin column. Stuffed cucumbers are not half bad either and we recommend experimenting with them some day.

Grilled Ham with Raisin Sauce

Spread a slice of smoked ham about 1½ inches thick with prepared mustard and grill. Serve with:

Raisin Sauce

¾ cup raisins
1 cup water
4 or 5 cloves
¾ cup sugar
1 tsp. cornstarch
1 tbsp. butter
1 tbsp. vinegar
Dash of pepper
½ tsp. Worcestershire Sauce

Cover raisins and cloves with cold water and simmer until raisins are tender. Combine dry ingredients, add to mixture, and stir until thickened. Add remaining ingredients and serve hot.

White Turnips Stuffed with Rice

Trim and wash as many nicely shaped white turnips as required for servings. Cook in plenty of boiling water until tender. Drain, cut a slice from the top and scoop out insides, leaving a thin shell but thick enough not to break in handling. Salt and pepper the insides and brush with melted butter. Make a stuffing of boiled rice, chopped green pepper and onion, moisten with tomato soup, season to taste and fill turnip shell. Put a piece of butter on each, cover with bread crumbs or grated cheese, and bake fifteen minutes in 400-450 oven. Tomatoes, onions, eggplant or peppers may be used instead of turnips. The stuffing can be diversified by using different soups for moistening. The cup may be topped with a large mushroom, a slice of cucumber or tomato. Use the insides as another vegetable, or in soup stock. This dish allows for many variations.

Avocado-Grapefruit Salad

1 medium avocado
1 pink grapefruit
¼ cup crushed pineapple
¼ cup chopped cucumber
¼ cup chopped onion
½ cup mayonnaise

Peel avocado and grapefruit. Cut avocado in half, remove the stone, then cut in lengthwise slices. Divide the grapefruit into sections. On each salad plate lay a bed of cress, white chicory hearts, very young dandelions or lettuce. Place avocado and pink grapefruit on this in alternate layers. Mix pineapple, cucumber, onion and mayonnaise together and season well. Put a tablespoonful of this dressing in center of salad. All ingredients should be chilled.

SMOTHERED STEAK
SQUASH AU GRATIN   BOILED POTATOES
COLE SLAW—MUSTARD SAUCE
FRUIT

How to economize in money and still feed a family on the required foods suitable for nutriment, and also cater to personal taste, is no light job that can be tossed off between other duties. This particular item in the list of responsibilities that make up household management is perhaps the most nerve-racking of all; at least it demands a good deal of thought and study. Meat and eggs are expensive—at least in many localities and excepting that time of year when eggs are at the lowest price. And yet nutritionists agree that we need a certain amount of these in our diet. The main problem, then, is to select, especially in meats, the most nutritious for the least money and then devise appetizing ways of cooking them.

Smothered Steak

3 lbs. round steak
Flour
2 cups tomatoes, strained
1 large onion
Salt, pepper

The steak should be at least one inch thick. With a sharp knife cut criss-cross gashes on both sides and into these sprinkle salt and pepper. Rub over with a garlic clove, and dredge lightly with flour. Melt two tablespoonfuls of fat in a roasting pan and lay the steak in the hot fat over a flame to sear on both sides. Now cover with the sliced onion, the tomato and cook in slow oven two and a half to three hours according to size of steak. Remove to hot platter and pour gravy over.

Squash au Gratin

4 small green squash
½ cup milk
⅓ cup bread crumbs
2 eggs
⅓ cup grated cheese
2 tbsp. butter
1 tsp. sugar
Salt, pepper

Cut squash in half crossways, clean out seeds and steam until tender. Scrape out some pulp, leaving a thick shell. Mash the pulp and mix with milk, beaten eggs, butter and seasoning. Pack this stuffing into the shells and sprinkle tops with bread crumbs and cheese. Set in moderate oven (350) to brown crumbs and melt cheese. One-half squash to each serving.

Cole Slaw—Mustard Sauce

1 small hard head of cabbage
3 tbsp. melted butter
1 egg
1½ tsp. sugar
⅛ tsp. white pepper
¼ tsp. dry mustard
½ cup vinegar

Cut cabbage in quarters; shred very fine with sharp knife, discarding core; let stand in ice water one-half to one hour.

Mustard Sauce

Cream the butter and beat the egg. Combine these and add sugar and seasonings Into this pour the hot vinegar gradually. Cook in a double boiler until slightly thickened, stirring constantly. Let cool. Drain the cabbage by shaking in cheesecloth. Mix with the dressing and serve cold.

MARYLAND CHICKEN BAKED IN CASSEROLE
GLAZED ONIONS RAW CAULIFLOWER SALAD
RASPBERRY SHERBET

THERE are no "formal dinners" in this book. Indeed, no sensible modern hostess ever tries to serve a formal dinner in these days. Only hotels and clubs attempt such functions and stupid affairs they are. Most of the menus given here are for home folks, for the perplexed homemaker who says to herself day in, day out, "*What* shall I have to eat?" A few there are, however, which, we think, are good enough for company or holidays. This is one. Raw cauliflower salad may be new to you, but if you will take our word for it and try it you will not be sorry. It should be very young and tender cauliflower, and white. The flowerlets should be broken off, all green leaves removed and sliced very thin. And don't forget to soak the cauliflower first for half an hour or so in cold salted water. If there are any insects secreted about it, this will drive them out. We suggest boiled rice with the chicken instead of potatoes. Bread is not needed, but small hot biscuits would please the children.

Maryland Chicken Baked

1 three lb. chicken
1 egg
1 tsp. salt
2 cups fine bread crumbs
2 tbsp. butter
1 tbsp. chopped parsley

Cut chicken into serving pieces, discarding back, neck and giblets. Split breast, disjoint legs. Beat egg and salt together. Dip each piece of chicken in this and then roll in bread crumbs. Place in well buttered two-quart glass baking dish, dot with the butter, cover and bake one to one and one-half hours according to size of chicken. Temperature 400. Serve in same dish or on hot platter, and garnish.

Glazed Onions

2 cups small white onions
½ cup butter
3 tbsp. sugar

Peel onions and cook in salted water until almost tender. Drain and set kettle back on stove, shake dry. Melt butter in frying pan and add sugar, letting it melt, but do not burn. Add onions and cook over simmering flame until quite tender, stirring occasionally until glazed. Use these for garnishing the chicken.

Raw Cauliflower Salad

2 cups thinly sliced cauliflower
½ cup finely cut celery
½ cup Italian onion
French Dressing

Mix the cauliflower, celery and onion shredded together and chill. Pour French Dressing over and serve on lettuce leaf with thin slices of radish and green pepper for garnish.

Raspberry Sherbet

1½ cups canned raspberries
1 lemon (juice)
1½ cups cream
1½ cups sugar
1½ cups milk

Put raspberries through fine sieve to take out seeds. Heat to boiling point and dissolve sugar in them. Cool and add milk and cream, lemon juice last. Pour in refrigerator tray and freeze from three to five hours, depending on temperature. Stir with spoon every half hour for first two hours, until it begins to harden.

CANTALOUPE ADE

FRESH PORK SHOULDER WITH SAUERKRAUT

BOILED POTATOES

APPLE-PECAN SALAD

SAUERKRAUT is nothing more or less than pickled cabbage. But it is not only pickled, it is also fermented. Farmers say it has "worked." If you suddenly lift the cover off the barrel of sauerkraut when it is finally ready for eating you may justly think it has worked overtime. And so it has, night and day, ever since it was brought fresh from the field, shaved into the barrel, and bruised down with salt to cover it to stew in its own juice. It is the fermentation that preserves it: Lactic acid fermentation. Sauerkraut is one of the most valuable foods that comes to our table—and it comes too seldom. It cleanses the digestive tract; prevents intestinal poisoning. It contains Vitamins A, B, C, and E (and so uses almost as many letters as the New Deal.) It is rich in mineral salts, calcium and phosphorus. It is more nutritious raw than cooked. The moral is—forget the smell and cultivate the taste.

Cantaloupe Ade

With vegetable cutter cut small balls from ripe cantaloupe and chill. When ready to serve put in sherbet glasses and pour over each a small glass of ginger ale. Put a strawberry, cherry, or some colorful fruit on top.

Fresh Pork Shoulder with Kraut

1 qt. sauerkraut
2 lbs. pork shoulder steak
2 tbsp. flour
2 tbsp. vinegar
Bacon fat
2 tbsp. brown sugar
2 small onions
Sliced potatoes
1 tsp. caraway seed

Put two tablespoonfuls of bacon fat in a heavy kettle to heat. When very hot add one half the kraut. On this place the shoulder steak and the onion sliced, season with salt and pepper and sprinkle with half the flour. Cover with the rest of the kraut, sprinkle over with the brown sugar and vinegar. Now cover this with the potatoes sliced. Cover with boiling water and cook slowly for about two hours.

Apple-Pecan Salad

2 tart apples
2 cups chopped pecan meats
Salt
Mayonnaise
Lettuce

Peel, quarter and slice apples. Throw into cold water so they will not discolor. Chop pecan or walnut meats. Drain apple and season with salt; mix with nut meats and then with mayonnaise highly seasoned with paprika. Serve on lettuce leaves.

TOMATO SOUP
BOILED BEEF—HORSERADISH SAUCE
ORANGE ICE

NOTHING is said about potatoes in this menu, but it is such a homely meal that any husky boy or man would feel himself cheated if he did not have them. A gravy made from boiled beef is not as good as that made from a pot roast or roast beef. It may *taste* as good, but because the meat has not roasted it will be rather colorless in appearance. So it might be well to save the stock from the meat for other purposes and have mashed potatoes today. But remember that mashed potatoes require a good deal of pampering in the way of butter and cream, and that they should be fluffy and not soggy. Good mealy potatoes, well drained, then mashed and made rich with cream and butter, seasoned with salt and pepper, and with a little well at the top half filled with butter for the server to dispense, do not need gravy. If, however, boiled potatoes are preferred, then thicken a little of the stock and give it color with kitchen bouquet. Another vegetable or a salad should be added.

Tomato Soup

1 qt. (or can) tomatoes
1 pt. water
4 cloves
1 small onion
2 tsp. sugar
1/8 tsp. soda
1 tsp. salt
2 tbsp. butter
2 tbsp. flour

Cook tomatoes, water, cloves, onion, sugar and salt together for twenty minutes; strain, reheat and add the soda; blend flour and butter and add to the other mixture.

Boiled Beef

4 to 5 lbs. rump beef
1 onion
Salt, pepper
Suet

Put a small piece of suet in heavy roasting kettle and try out. Wipe the beef with a heavy damp cloth and put into the hot fat with a sliced onion. Brown on all sides. Cover with boiling water, cover and cook slowly, adding water as necessary to partly cover. Season with salt and pepper when partly tender (4-5 hours). Cook until done. Remove from kettle and serve hot or cold with horseradish sauce (see page 57).

Orange Ice

2 cups water
1 cup sugar
1½ cups strained orange juice
1 tbsp. lemon juice
1 egg white
Grated rind of one half orange

Boil sugar and water together for five minutes. Cool and add orange juice and grated rind and lemon juice. Pack in ice and salt and freeze to a mush. Add stiffly beaten white of egg and finish freezing. If packed in refrigerator tray, stir every half hour for two hours and allow three to four hours for freezing.

HAM AND EGGS—FRIED MUSH
ASPARAGUS RING—MASHED POTATOES
CUCUMBER AND CRESS SALAD
BLUEBERRY PIE

HERE is a good old farmer menu—ham and eggs and fried mush. But no housewife need blush if this happens to be the day when her husband takes a notion to bring the sales manager home to dinner, or even one of his old classmates. The man doesn't live who wouldn't welcome this dish—so long as it is well prepared. And here is where the test of a good cook is made. Not in some fancy canapé she happened to see a food demonstrator make, but in the perfect cooking of a slice of ham, and the frying in its succulent fat a nice fresh egg. The small Daisy or Scotch hams are delicately flavored and not so expensive as the inner cuts of a large ham. In frying these smaller slices care must be taken not to overdo them. Ham should by no means be rare, neither should it be fried hard and dry. The egg white should be "set" and firm, the yolk a little runny.

Ham and Eggs

Ham should be sliced about one-half an inch thick. Trim off fat and try it out in a frying pan. Fry the ham in this about fifteen minutes, turning it once. Take out and lay on a hot platter. Break eggs one at a time into hot fat, and do not crowd. Spoon the hot fat over them until the white is set and yolks coated. Do not turn them over. Take out carefully with a wide spatula and place around the ham. Garnish with parsley.

Fried Mush

Cut slices of cold corn meal mush or cold boiled hominy half an inch in thickness. Fry on both sides in hot ham or bacon fat. Serve on plate with ham and eggs.

Asparagus Ring

2 cans of asparagus tips
3 tbsp. butter
3 tbsp. flour
1 cup evaporated milk diluted one-third
3 eggs
Salt, pepper

Heat the butter and blend into it the flour, add the cold milk very slowly; season with salt and pepper. Beat the egg yolks to a froth and stir into the sauce. Cool, and fold in the beaten whites; then stir in the asparagus, cut into one-inch pieces. Place in a buttered ring mold, set in a pan of boiling water and bake in a moderate oven one-half hour, or until set. Unmold onto a large round plate and fill center with mashed potatoes. Serve with White Sauce.

Blueberry Pie

1 qt. blueberries
½ cup sugar
1 tbsp. lemon juice
Yolk of 1 egg
2 tbsp. sour cream
¼ tsp. cinnamon

Line a plate with plain pastry. Put in the washed berries, sprinkle over the sugar, lemon juice and cinnamon. Beat the yolk of egg and add cream to it. Pour this over the berries, cover with top crust and bake in hot oven (500) until bottom crust is done (15 minutes), then lower heat and bake for 25 minutes longer.

CROWN ROAST OF PORK
APPLESAUCE
SAVORY BEET SALAD
CHERRY ICE

CERTAIN meats taste better in some kinds of weather than in others. In hot weather, for instance, ham and bacon have an appetizing appeal while fresh pork seems to belong to cold weather. It is a heavy meat, and usually with considerable fat, and requires slow and long cooking. So around the crown roast of pork we have tried to build a menu that is suitable to late fall or winter. Of course the Cherry Ice might be even more delectable on a July day, but on the other hand, after a lusty meal of roast pork we cannot afford, for the sake of peaceful sleep, to have anything heavy. A fruit salad might be substituted for the Ice, if preferred.

Crown Roast of Pork

5 lbs. pork loin
Sliced bacon
Salt, pepper
Flour to dredge
1 can sliced pineapple
Potatoes
1 head cauliflower
Sage

Have the butcher prepare the crown roast. Season with a mixture of salt, pepper and sage and dredge with flour. Wrap the end of each rib with bacon, fasten with a toothpick. Put in a 500 oven to sear meat (15 to 20 minutes), then lower heat to 375 and roast, allowing twenty minutes to the pound. About thirty minutes before meat is done put into the roaster as many potatoes, peeled and of uniform size, as will be required for serving. Drain the pineapple rings, and sauté in some of the pork fat taken from the roaster (or bacon fat). Boil a head of very white, firm cauliflower. When ready to serve, remove the roast to a large platter. Arrange the potatoes around it, drain the cauliflower, season it with salt, pepper, paprika and butter, and set it whole, in the center of the roast. Garnish the platter with parsley and radish roses.

Savory Beet Salad

½ tbsp. gelatin
1 tbsp. cold water
¾ cup boiling water
½ tsp. salt
½ cup celery, cut fine
1 tbsp. sugar
½ tbsp. prepared mustard
2 tbsp. vinegar
2 tbsp. minced onion
2 cups cooked beets, diced

Soften gelatin in cold water and dissolve in boiling water. Add salt, sugar, mustard, vinegar and onion. When this mixture begins to stiffen, stir in beets and celery. Turn into individual molds. Serve on lettuce, cress or chicory, garnished with strips of hard cooked egg whites.

Cherry Ice

2 cups water
1 cup sugar
1 qt. sour cherries
1 lemon
1 tbsp. gelatin
2 egg whites

Boil sugar and water together for fifteen minutes. Pit the cherries and chop all but ½ cup. Soak the gelatin in juice of lemon. Add the chopped cherries and gelatin to the hot syrup and let cool. Rub through a fruit sieve and pour into freezing trays. At the end of 45 minutes, remove from trays, beat well and fold in the stiffly beaten egg whites and the whole cherries. Return to trays and freeze for three to four hours.

SHEPHERD'S PIE
SCALLOPED CORN AND TOMATOES
COMBINATION FRUIT SALAD

WITH a combination fruit salad, no dessert seems necessary, especially after a meat pie. This rule for a fruit salad is by no means arbitrary. Any combination of fruit may be made. This particular one can be put together quickly and at any time of year. Plain French Dressing as given on page 195 is our preference for a fruit salad, but others may like better the boiled dressing, the fruit salad dressing, or mayonnaise with cream in it. Cooked cabbage might be substituted for the scalloped corn and tomatoes, or squash could be baked in the oven at the same time with the meat pie.

Shepherd's Pie

Cold cooked meat
Mashed potatoes (hot)
Salt, pepper
1 tbsp. milk
Meat stock or gravy
1 egg
Onion, chopped
1 tbsp. Chili Sauce
1 tbsp. butter

Cut cold meat in small pieces; put gravy or thickened meat stock in the bottom of a greased casserole. Put in cold meat, cover with gravy or stock and add the onion which has been sautéd to tender, and the Chili Sauce. No more liquid should be added than just barely to cover meat. Add the well-beaten egg to the potato well seasoned and cover the meat layer with this. Brush the top with one tablespoonful of milk in which one tablespoonful of butter has been melted. Bake in moderate oven for twenty minutes.

Scalloped Corn and Tomatoes

½ doz. ears of corn *or*
1 can of sweet corn
6 ripe tomatoes
2 cups bread crumbs
¼ cup butter
Salt, pepper

Scrape corn from cobs; scald and peel tomatoes. Put a layer of corn in bottom of well-buttered casserole. Cover with layer of sliced tomatoes and add a layer of bread crumbs. Cut bits of butter over and season with salt and pepper. Alternate layers until all are used. Dot with butter, and bake one-half hour in a moderate oven.

Combination Fruit Salad

2 bananas
3 oranges
1 red apple
½ cup walnut meats

Cut bananas in two lengthwise and then into quarters. Divide oranges into sections. Core the apple but do not peel. Divide apple into quarters and then dice. Mix all together with

Fruit Juice Salad Dressing

2 eggs
½ cup sugar
½ cup pineapple juice
¼ cup water
Juice of 1 lemon

Beat eggs; add sugar and liquids. Cook in double boiler until thick. Stir while cooking. Chill and mix with fruit. Sprinkle salad with nut meats.

CORNED BEEF AND CABBAGE
PRUNE SOUFFLÉ

Two accusations that are often made against books of recipes and advice to the cook, are not going to be held against this book, if we can help it. One made by men is that the food is too delicate—tea-room variety, nothing for a husky man to lay hold of. And the other is even more heinous—that which we have called The Ruination of Good Food by Poor Cookery. Stodging up perfectly good food with ridiculous things that do not belong with it. Making what men call "messes." Take this menu, for instance: Corned Beef and Cabbage. Nothing fancy or delicate about that, is there? And the only reason we include it—it being such a very plebeian dish, is that we want to encourage its consumption. We have no cabbages to market, nor any beef to sell, but we have deep interest in seeing folks get good solid food, well cooked.

Corned Beef and Cabbage

4 lbs. corned beef
1 head cabbage
Potatoes
Turnips
Carrots

Put the corned beef on to cook in cold water to more than cover, and allow 3½ hours to boil very slowly. Skim off scum as it rises. The size of cabbage and quantity of other vegetables depends upon the number to be served. Turnips should be sliced across, carrots lengthwise; potatoes, if large, cut in two. Yellow turnips should be given at least fifteen minutes more time than other vegetables to cook; potatoes and carrots require about thirty minutes, and cabbage a little less, according to nutritionists. We cook ours longer.

In the opinion of the writer a pound of salt pork and a couple of parsnips add a desirable flavor to this dinner, but that is a matter of personal taste.

A corned beef and cabbage, or "boiled dinner," is another time and dish saving meal. Everything is cooked in one kettle, and everything may be served on one platter if you have one large enough. Vinegar and horseradish are usual accompaniments. Mustard or mixed pickles go well with this dinner.

Prune Soufflé

1 cup prune pulp
½ cup prune juice
½ cup chopped nut meats
½ cup bread crumbs
2 eggs
Grated rind of 1 lemon
1 tbsp. lemon juice
¼ tsp. salt

Cook prunes very tender in water to cover; remove stones and force prunes through a sieve. Mix all ingredients together except eggs. Beat yolks until light and creamy and add to mixture. Beat whites stiffly and fold in. Put in well buttered baking dish and set in pan of water. Bake in moderate oven until set, 25-30 minutes.

CORNED BEEF HASH

STEWED CELERY

FROZEN RASPBERRIES

CORNED BEEF HASH naturally follows a dinner of corned beef and cabbage. It need not follow on the very next day but it follows. This is another favorite among men—if well made. The trouble with most corned beef (or other) hash is that it is either chopped too fine so it is mushy, or so coarse that it is in hunks; it is either so dry it tastes gritty, or so much liquid is used that it runs down the throat before you know it is there. Or else there is too much potato for the amount of meat. Judging by these comments one might surmise that the making of good corned beef hash requires a certain amount of skill. The suspicion is correct. It requires skill—and some watchfulness. But when well made it is one of those dishes which the hungry Oliver would have given his starved little soul to partake of in plenty.

Corned Beef Hash

Take two-thirds as much cold boiled potato as corned beef. Chop the beef quite fine, and cut the potato into small dice. *Do not chop them together*. Mix, and season with salt, pepper, and add a chopped green pepper. Moisten with left-over gravy, cream, or tomato soup. Do not *wet* the mixture. It should be just moist enough to hold together.

Melt either pork, bacon fat or butter in a good sized frying pan and bring to a light, smoking heat. Put the hash in and spread over the bottom. Lower the heat and let cook 15-20 minutes or until cooked through and light browned on the bottom. Do not stir. When done fold one half over the other and with two spatulas (so it will not break) transfer to platter. Garnish with small pickled onions, gherkins, slices of beet and parsley.

Stewed Celery

1 qt. cut celery
1 tbsp. butter
1 tbsp. flour
Salt, pepper

Cut outside coarse celery stalks in inch slices. Wash and drain. Put in saucepan and cover with boiling water, add one-half teaspoon of salt and simmer for thirty minutes or until tender. Allow only enough water to cover and not let burn. When the celery is done, drain, and save the water. Blend together the flour and butter and stir into it one cup of the water in which celery was cooked. Cook to the boiling point. Add the celery, season to taste, and heat slowly for five minutes. If creamed celery is preferred, do not add the water, but make a thin white sauce and heat the celery in it.

Frozen Raspberries

1 No. 3 can red raspberries
Juice of 1 lemon
⅔ cup sugar
2 cups water

Mash the berries and remix with the juice. Add the lemon juice, sugar and water and bring to the boiling point to melt the sugar. Cool, freeze, using three parts of ice to one of salt.

MEAT CAKES WITH CHILI SAUCE
OYSTER PLANT EN CASSEROLE
GINGER-PEAR DESSERT

YOU will see that you are meeting your old friend Hamburg Steak quite frequently in these pages. Sometimes he masquerades as a Mexican, sometimes he wears a Spanish dress. But he is such a plain, homely fellow, though honest and wholesome withal in his native form, that the more we can smuggle him in under this guise and that the better. He is bound to be made a familiar of ours anyway, because he is so in accord with our pocketbooks at their lowest hour, and so why not fix him up and let him appear at his best. And if this is your first acquaintance with oyster plant (or salsify) we hope it will not be your last. Try it this time anyway.

Meat Cakes Mexican Style

2 cups cold cooked meat
½ cup cold rice or mashed potatoes
1 egg
1 tsp. chili powder
Salt, pepper

Chop meat and mix all ingredients together, and form into small flat cakes. Brown in skillet in hot fat, both sides. Place on hot platter, and pour over them

Chili Sauce

1 cup tomato soup
2 tbsp. flour
3 tbsp. butter
1 tbsp. minced onion
1 tsp. salt
1 tsp. chili powder
¼ tsp. essence of garlic
Dash of paprika

Blend flour and butter; add other ingredients and cook five minutes over direct heat or fifteen minutes in double boiler, stirring until thick.

Oyster Plant en Casserole

Wash, scrape and boil two bunches (depending on size) of oyster plant until tender. Drain and rub through colander. Season with salt, pepper, butter; add one egg beaten into one cup of milk. Put into buttered casserole, sprinkle fine cracker crumbs over and bake fifteen minutes at 375.

Ginger-Pear Dessert

1 can pears
1 lb. ginger cookies
Juice from pears
1 tbsp. gelatin
1 tsp. lemon juice
Whipped cream

Drain pears and lay in bottom of glass sauce dish. Dissolve gelatin in cold water and add to one pint of fruit juice and lemon juice (other fruit juice added to make up quantity) and pour over pears. Put in refrigerator to set and chill. At serving time crush the cookies with rolling pin and sprinkle thickly over pears. Top with whipped cream, more rolled cookies, and serve on glass plate.

PLANKED HAM

FRIED GREEN TOMATOES SAVOY CABBAGE

PEACH PUDDING

A PLANK for cooking purposes is not an expensive piece of equipment and allows for a number of dressy dishes. It also takes the place of several different serving dishes, and is easy to clean. You will find several recipes for planked food in this book: planked steak, planked fish, planked stuffed vegetables; so we suggest that if you do not already possess a plank with its metal holder, you take up a collection and make the house a present of one. Every house ought to have a birthday present, and then of course it cannot be neglected on Christmas. Houses are amongst the most appreciative recipients of gifts you ever saw.

Planked Ham

1 large slice ham (1 inch thick)
6 potatoes
2 large tomatoes

Salt, pepper
Paprika
Butter
Fat

Peel, slice (one inch thickness) and steam potatoes for ten minutes—keep hot. Heat the plank very hot and rub with oil or cooking fat. Lay the ham on it and broil slowly for fifteen minutes. Turn the slice of meat over. Place the slices of potato around the meat on the plank, lapping one slice slightly over another. Cut the tomatoes in half-inch slices and arrange them over the uncooked surface of the ham. Sprinkle them with salt, sugar, pepper and paprika, seasoning the potatoes with all but sugar. Dot each tomato slice with butter. Return plank to lowest broiler flame and cook slowly 30 minutes, or until the ham is done, the potatoes golden brown and the tomatoes tender. Garnish the plank with thin strips of green pepper and rose radishes.

Fried Green Tomatoes

Wipe firm green tomatoes and slice about one-half inch thick. Dip in egg, then flour and fry brown in hot fat—butter, vegetable oil, or bacon.

Savoy Cabbage

Trim off any broken leaves. Soak in cold salted water for twenty minutes. Put in boiling water and boil for thirty minutes. Drain, chop coarsely and season with salt, pepper and butter.

Peach Pudding

Butter a deep baking dish and dust sides and bottom with sugar. Cut thin slices of stale bread and brush with butter. Alternate slices of bread and sliced peaches sprinkled with sugar; the top layer should be of bread. Do not fill dish too full, but allow for the following custard to be poured over:

Custard

Juice from can of peaches
½ cup sugar
3 eggs
2 cups milk
Grated nutmeg

Set baking dish in a pan of water and bake slowly one hour. Serve warm (not hot).

BRAISED SHOULDER CHOPS WITH VEGETABLES
STUFFED BEET SALAD
FROZEN CHERRY CUSTARD

We suggest a cream of pea soup as an introduction to this menu, either home-made or canned. Whether it pays to make soup when you can buy good soups at so very low a price or not is all a matter of taste, time and preference. There are those who maintain that no commercial soup can compete with the home-made. Others, whose opinion is equally to be respected, say that in nine cases out of ten the commercial soups are better than most women can make—so there you are. When time is a factor, the commercial soups are certainly valuable. If they are not quite "tasty" enough, a little seasoning, a little butter, will improve them. It is a good plan, at any rate, to keep a supply on hand. It is an equally good plan to try your own hand at soup making once in awhile.

Braised Shoulder Chops with Vegetables

4 shoulder chops
Salt, pepper
1 cup carrots
½ cup turnips
½ cup celery
½ cup onion
1 cup stock or water

Chop vegetables coarsely. Brown chops on both sides in hot fat. Season with salt and pepper. Mix vegetables, add stock and spread over the chops. Cover closely and bake in moderate oven (375-400) until meat is tender—about 3 hours.

Stuffed Beet Salad

Cook small, new beets (or use canned), rub off skin; cut out center and stuff with olives which have been chopped and mixed with cottage or cream cheese. Serve on shredded cabbage or lettuce and top with mayonnaise.

Frozen Cherry Custard

¾ cup sugar
1 tbsp. flour
2 cups milk
1 cup canned cherries
1 tbsp. lemon juice
2 tsp. vanilla
1 cup cream
Pinch of salt
1 egg

Mix sugar, flour and salt. Add milk which has been scalded, and cook in double boiler for fifteen minutes. Add egg slightly beaten and cook until thickened. Cool, add cherries with their syrup, lemon juice, vanilla and cream whipped stiff. Pack in three parts ice to one of salt and freeze.

SWISS STEAK

FRIED EGGPLANT DUTCH LETTUCE

COFFEE TAPIOCA CUSTARD

THE compact lettuce heads are not so good for Dutch Lettuce as the loose leaved garden variety that people who have gardens are always glad to give away. Wilted lettuce is one of the many dishes that you have to experiment with until you learn how to make it exactly the way you and your family like it. Some like it quite sweet, others want it very tart. Try it the way we suggest and then, if that doesn't suit, make little ventures with more sugar—or less, with or without onion—until it is the way you like it best. The main thing is not to *cook* the lettuce. If to facilitate the wilting you want to put the lettuce into the saucepan with the fat and vinegar, turn it over and over until it has all come in contact with the heat and seasonings, and then take it out. If left in too long it becomes discolored and soft. Just *wilt* the lettuce and season it to a sweet-sour.

Swiss Steak

2 lbs. flank or round of beef
Flour
1 tsp. salt, dash pepper
Clove or garlic
Fat for frying
2 cups strained tomatoes
1 small can peas with juice

Pound into the flank as much flour as it will hold (using a meat tenderer or a wooden potato masher), first on one side and then on the other. Sprinkle with salt and pepper and rub with a clove of garlic. Brown on both sides in hot pork or bacon fat, add two cups of strained tomatoes, and the peas with juice. Season to taste. Simmer in Dutch oven or heavy kettle on top of stove, or cook in roaster in moderate oven for three and a half hours. It should be very tender when done and with a rich red sauce. Place the meat on a hot platter and pour sauce over.

Fried Eggplant

Peel an eggplant and cut cross-wise in thin slices. Beat an egg and add to it a tablespoonful of hot water. Dip each slice of eggplant into this and then into finely rolled cracker crumbs which have been seasoned with salt and pepper; fry in hot fat in a frying pan. Fry no more at a time than will cover bottom of pan comfortably and add hot fat as needed. Butter, or half butter will improve the flavor. Drain on paper toweling and keep hot until served.

Dutch Lettuce

2 heads garden lettuce
¼ lb. bacon
1 tsp. sugar
1 egg
2 tbsp. vinegar
¼ cup sour cream
Salt
Pepper

Wash two heads of garden lettuce and separate the leaves. Cut the bacon into pieces and fry out to a light brown. Add two tablespoonfuls of vinegar to bacon and fat; beat the egg lightly and to it add the sour cream. Stir this into the bacon fat and continue to stir until it thickens. Pour over the lettuce, cover closely and let stand until the lettuce is wilted. Serve hot with the juice.

Coffee Tapioca Custard

4 cups hot coffee
½ cup sugar
½ cup quick cooking tapioca

Place all ingredients in a double boiler and cook until clear. Pour in custard cups to chill. Serve with sweetened whipped cream.

VEAL AND HAM PIE

SWEET POTATO APPLE DISH RED CABBAGE STEWED

RED RASPBERRY SHERBET

Red cabbage is not quite so handsome a dish as some others, but there is a peculiarly delicious flavor to this kind. By pouring several baths of hot water over it you can reduce the color somewhat, but it will be a purplish red no matter what you do. Red cabbage, however, cannot be had at all times of year, and so green cabbage may be substituted. And if you are not partial to sweet potatoes, good plain white potatoes will do, or rice. If the time of year when this menu is used does not favor a sherbet, try a custard. The main thing is to have a light dessert after the heavy meal.

Veal and Ham Pie

Fill a deep baking dish (well greased) with alternate layers of lean cooked ham and veal cut in serving pieces. Sprinkle each layer with salt, pepper, minced parsley, chopped onion and green pepper. In the middle put a layer of sliced hard boiled eggs, highly seasoned and with a few drops of Worcestershire Sauce on each. Pour over the whole veal broth which has been boiled down and highly seasoned with salt, pepper, onion or a slight flavor of garlic. Cover with rich pastry and bake until browned. Serve cold or hot, in slices.

Sweet Potato Apple Dish

Steam sweet potatoes until nearly done; peel, cut in round slices about one-half inch thick. Slice tart apples in the same way, and put alternate layers of potato and apple in buttered glass casserole with potatoes on top. Sprinkle cinnamon and sugar, mixed, over each layer, a little salt and dots of butter. Bake until potatoes and apples are tender and a rich syrup has formed—about thirty minutes.

Red Cabbage Stewed

1 medium red cabbage
1 small onion
2 tbsp. fat
¼ cup vinegar
1 cup water
1 tbsp. brown sugar
Salt, pepper
Dash of nutmeg

Slice the onion and brown it in the fat. Add the cabbage, shredded, the vinegar, water and seasonings. Cook in covered stew pan until tender—about thirty minutes.

Red Raspberry Sherbet

1 qt. raspberries
1¼ cups sugar
1 egg white
1 cup water
2 tbsp. lemon juice

Boil sugar and water until it makes a thin syrup. Mash berries and add to syrup. Cool and add strained lemon juice. Freeze to a mush. Add beaten egg whites. Freeze and then let stand two hours before using. Canned berries require less sugar.

BRISKET POT ROAST—BOILED RICE
FRUIT ASPIC
CUBAN CREAM PIE

THERE are "born cooks" but there are also good cooks who have acquired the art. Not all women like to cook, but any intelligent woman who puts her mind to it can learn to cook. "Born cooks" are not so likely to work by rule—they do not have to. They are also likely to have more imagination and food sense, and to develop original dishes. But the woman who has to learn the art by rule can serve just as satisfactory dishes as the other. It does pay, however, for the young homemaker to take some good cooking lessons before doing too much expensive experimenting. Seeing the thing done is even more helpful than a good recipe book, but with a good book and conscientious effort any one can cook.

Brisket Pot Roast

4 lbs. brisket
1 cup tomatoes
1 onion, sliced
Salt, pepper
Dash paprika
3 small carrots, diced

Wipe meat with damp cloth and cut into serving pieces. Brown in very hot fat in heavy kettle; add vegetables, seasoning and tomatoes. Cover closely and cook very slowly for four hours. Add small amount of water to keep from burning if necessary. Serve with boiled rice.

Fruit Aspic

1 cup chopped pineapple
1 cup cherries
1 small can peaches
Juice of 1 lemon
1 tbsp. gelatin

Drain all fruit. Dissolve gelatin in ¼ cup cold fruit juice. Heat 1 pt. of fruit juice, and add dissolved gelatin. (Add water to make the pint if necessary.) Pour over drained fruit and mix. Set away to cool and chill. Serve on lettuce with mayonnaise.

Cuban Cream Pie

2 egg yolks
1 pt. milk
½ cup sugar
1 tbsp. flour
1¼ tbsp. cornstarch
1 tbsp. orange juice
⅛ tsp. salt

Beat egg yolks stiff. Sift all dry ingredients and mix with egg yolks. Add just enough milk so it can be stirred. Heat pint of milk in double boiler; pour egg and flour mixture into the milk and cook until it thickens, stirring constantly. Add orange juice when cool. Put into baked pastry shell. Make the following:

Meringue

2 tbsp. powdered sugar
½ tsp. orange juice
2 egg whites

Cover pie with this and brown in slow oven.

WATERMELON COCKTAIL
PLANKED WHITEFISH
CUCUMBER ASPIC
APPLE PIE AND CHEESE

HERE is another occasion for using the plank which we once presented to the house. A planked fish is a handsome dish, and makes serving a simple matter. Whitefish is one of the commonest of fresh water fish and can almost always be found in market, either fresh or frozen. The flesh is a little more fatty than some other fish and highly flavored. The eggs of the whitefish, salted and colored black are sold as caviar. Cold whitefish, dressed with minced celery, pepper, and onion and seasoned with lemon, capers, paprika and salt, served on lettuce and garnished with hard cooked egg, makes an excellent salad. Whitefish grow to a considerable size, sometimes weighing as much as thirty pounds.

Watermelon Cocktail

Cut small balls from watermelon pulp with a vegetable cutter. Fill sherbet glasses and over each pour 1 teaspoonful of lemon juice, 1 teaspoonful of confectioners' sugar, add two or three green cherries and a very little of the juice. Serve cold.

Planked Whitefish

2 or 3 lbs. fish
Melted butter
Salt and pepper
String beans
Mashed potatoes
Cauliflower
Carrots

Split the fish down the back, press open and remove backbone. Wipe inside and out with heavy damp cloth. Season with salt, pepper and melted butter. Place in a greased pan, skin side down and put under broiler or in hot oven to cook evenly for ten minutes. Fold the fish together, place on a hot, greased plank and bake in hot oven for 25 to 30 minutes. When done arrange around it on the plank, a row of cooked cauliflower flowerlets, a row of sliced carrots (boiled), a row of string beans, and at the outside a row of mashed potatoes put on with pastry tube. The vegetables should be previously seasoned with salt, pepper, butter. Set the plank in hot oven (500) to brown potatoes and heat through.

Cucumber Aspic

2 cups chopped cucumber
1 cup chopped celery
1 cup chopped green pepper
1 cup sugar
1 cup cold water
1 tbsp. lemon juice
½ cup chopped onion
1½ tsp. salt
¼ tsp. white pepper
1½ tsp. paprika
2 tbsp. gelatin
2½ cups chicken consommé

Soak gelatin in the cold water. Heat consommé to boiling point and dissolve gelatin in it. Peel and chop cucumbers. Chop all other vegetables very fine. Add all vegetables and seasonings to consommé. Turn into a rinsed ring mold and chill for several hours. Serve with mayonnaise.

CHICKEN POT-PIE WITH DUMPLINGS

BEETS WITH MINT

GRAPENUT-PEAR MERINGUE

THIS menu seems to us a good family dinner. Not that company wouldn't appreciate chicken potpie with dumplings, but we always seem to feel that for guests we must have either fried or roast chicken, while, as a matter of fact, they may themselves prefer the plainer meal. We might try it sometime as an experiment. If a soup is wanted with the dinner it should be a light one, not a cream soup. A cocktail or an appetizer would be better. For a family dinner perhaps the first course may be eliminated. And perhaps a salad will be desired. If so, endive, lettuce or chicory would be best.

Chicken Pot-pie with Dumplings

Clean and disjoint year old fowl. Put in kettle with water to cover and cook until tender—about an hour and a half; with it cook one onion, sliced, and a small bunch of parsley. When almost tender enough to take up drop the dumplings in from a spoon, and cook twenty minutes, covered.

Dumplings

2 cups flour
3 tsps. baking powder
1 egg
1 tbsp. butter
½ tsp. salt
½ cup evaporated milk
¼ cup water

Mix the flour and baking powder and salt together. Beat the egg, and add it to the milk and water combined with beaten egg. Stir this into the flour and drop from spoon into the kettle with chicken. Thicken the sauce that is left after taking up chicken and dumplings and pour over both meat and dumplings.

Beets with Mint

½ cup butter
3 cloves
2 tbsp. vinegar
1 tsp. sugar
1½ cups small cooked or canned beets
6 mint leaves cut in bits

Melt butter, add cloves, vinegar and sugar. Add small whole or sliced beets and simmer ten minutes or longer. Sprinkle with mint leaves shredded with scissors. Serve hot.

Grapenut-Pear Meringue

1 No. 2 can pears
¾ cup sugar
1 tbsp. lemon juice
2 cups pear juice
½ glass currant jelly
2 egg whites
½ cup sugar
Grapenuts
1 tbsp. gelatin

Soften gelatin in cold water, and dissolve in heated pear juice. Add lemon juice. Cool. Lay drained pears in serving dish (glass oven dish). Fill the cavity of each with cube of jelly. Pour over these the pear juice, cooled, but not set. Sprinkle with grapenuts. Beat whites of eggs, sprinkle sugar in, and cover the pear dish with this. Set in quick oven to brown, then set to stiffen.

HALIBUT VERSAILLES

AVOCADO AND CUCUMBER SALAD

AMBER APPLE PIE

WE have no axes to grind when it comes to baking dishes but we have preferences. Reasonable heavy dishes are better than light ones because they do not burn food quickly and they hold heat longer. For pies and casserole dishes we like glass, not only because you can watch the progress of your cookery, but because food can be served in the dish it was cooked in. This has a double advantage—better appearance than where the contents must be disturbed, and a saving in dishwashing. We have had some very attractive pottery wear but in general it has not stood up as well as glass. Of course that implies an oven glass, one that is made specially for baking purposes. A homemaking club might find a comparative study or survey of cooking utensils helpful.

Halibut Versailles

Butter well an oval casserole and pour in enough milk (or diluted evaporated milk) to just cover the bottom. Lay in a thick halibut steak, and sprinkle with salt and pepper. Over this lay alternate rows of thickly sliced tomatoes and medium or small mushrooms. Dot generously with butter and bake in moderate oven, allowing twenty minutes to the pound. Serve on hot platter, garnished with mashed potato, buttered beets and parsley.

Avocado and Cucumber Salad

1 large or 2 small avocados
1 Italian onion
2 slim medium sized cucumbers
1 green pepper
Lettuce—French Dressing

Peel avocado and cut in two lengthwise. Remove stone. Remove seeds and fiber from green pepper. Peel onion; cut onion and cucumbers into thin round slices. Cut pepper into thin lengthwise strips, and avocado into narrow lengths. Put a layer of lettuce hearts in salad bowl, and put vegetables and avocado in alternately. French Dressing.

Amber Apple Pie

6 medium apples
3 tbsp. sugar
¼ lemon rind, grated
1 tbsp. butter
2 egg yolks
2 egg whites
2 tbsp. sugar
¼ tsp. vanilla
Juice of ½ lemon

Peel and slice apples; stew in saucepan with butter, fruit sugar, grated rind and juice of lemon. When cooked press through a sieve and add egg yolks. Line a pie pan with rich pastry and pour in apple mixture. Bake in slow oven until firm. Beat whites of eggs until stiff and dry, then mix with 2 tablespoonfuls of sugar and three drops of lemon juice. Spread over pie and return to 300 oven until lightly browned. Sprinkle chopped maraschino cherries over top.

CRABMEAT COCKTAIL
VEAL POT-PIE WITH DUMPLINGS
LETTUCE SALAD WITH THOUSAND ISLAND DRESSING
RHUBARB BETTY

THIS is another good spring menu. If used on a cool day a thin soup or a tomato soup may be substituted for the cocktail. Vegetables are in the pot-pie, and so is all the starch needed. The salad is rich in vitamins and appetizing as well. Any other simple dessert will do as well as the Rhubarb Betty so long as it is not heavy, but spring is the time of year when rhubarb is at its best and since it is short lived it seems wise to take advantage of it. You will find dumplings accompanying several dinners, particularly stews—but, what would a stew be without a dumpling? And as a matter of economy in fuel, time and dishes—nothing could be better. The recipes for dumplings are not always the same, and yet, when you have found one perfect dumpling recipe it can be used for every purpose. See p. 195 for recipe for Thousand Island Dressing.

Crabmeat Cocktail

1 can crabmeat
2 tsp. Worcestershire sauce
2 tsp. vinegar
¾ cup catsup
2 drops tabasco sauce
Stuffed olives

Remove bones from crabmeat and place in chilled glasses. Cover with the sauce made by mixing other ingredients. Tarragon vinegar preferred.

Veal Pot-pie with Dumplings

2 lbs. veal neck
¼ lb. cubed raw ham
2 onions
5 small potatoes
1 cup diced carrots
½ tsp. pepper
1 bay leaf
¼ tsp. peppercorns
2 tbsp. flour
1 tsp. salt

Cut meat into serving pieces, cover with cold water and cook slowly one hour. Add vegetables and cook until nearly tender. Make a biscuit dough adding an extra tablespoonful of shortening and enough milk so the dough will drop from spoon. Drop in spoonfuls into the stew, cover and cook slowly for twenty minutes taking care that it does not burn. Take out dumplings and arrange on hot platter. Spoon out meat and vegetables and add to the dish. Add one cup of stock or hot water and a bouillon cube with one tablespoonful of butter to the juice in kettle and thicken with flour. Pour gravy over the whole.

Rhubarb Betty

1 qt. unsweetened cooked rhubarb
1 qt. fine bread crumbs
4 tbsp. melted butter
Cinnamon

Combine bread crumbs and butter and heat in oven, stirring to light brown. Place layer of rhubarb in buttered baking dish, then layer of bread crumbs and alternate until dish is full, crumbs on top. Bake uncovered for fifteen minutes in 400—450 oven, or until crumbs are slighty browned. Serve with whipped cream sweetened, and sprinkle with cinnamon.

CREAM OF CORN SOUP
HAMBURGER BALLS WITH PEPPERS
CABBAGE DUCHESSE
GRANDMOTHER'S DEEP APPLE PIE

HAMBURGER is the most economical meat one can buy and the chief trouble with it is that the family trying to economize is likely to use it too often in a monotonous fashion. Just plain hamburger fried two or three times a week—or even once—is extremely trying to the sensitive taste that longs for variety. Since, however, most of us do have to economize on meats, we have tried to devise a few unusual ways in which to serve one that is of good flavor, hearty, and nutritious but does need a little dressing up. If you meet your old friend hamburger several times throughout this book, try to look upon him as a friend who means well, and not one who simply tries to annoy by frequent appearance.

Cream of Corn Soup

1 No. 2 can of corn
½ cup celery
1 slice onion
2 cups water
2 cups thin white sauce
1 egg
1 cup cream
Salt, pepper

Simmer the corn, onion and water for twenty minutes. Rub through a sieve. Add this to the thin white sauce and season highly. Just before serving add the slightly beaten egg mixed with the cream, and heat in double boiler. Serve in bouillon cups with a spoonful of whipped cream on top, sprinkled with paprika.

Hamburger Balls with Peppers

1 lb. hamburger
1 sweet pepper ground
2 onions
6 strips of bacon
1 cup bread crumbs
1 can tomato soup
1 egg
1 tbsp. flour

Mix meat, bread crumbs and beaten egg together; add onion, pepper and seasonings and form into six balls. Wrap each ball in a strip of bacon and fry in a shallow pan. When done, remove from pan, add tomato juice to the pan, thicken with flour, heat and serve in separate dish.

Cabbage Duchesse

1 medium cabbage
3 tbsp. butter
4 tbsp. vinegar
1 tbsp. sugar
¼ tsp. salt
⅛ tsp. paprika
1 green pepper chopped
2 tbsp. pimiento chopped

Remove coarse leaves and shred cabbage into slices about one-fourth inch thick. Put into boiling water to which has been added salt and a pinch of soda. Boil fifteen minutes. Drain and pour over it a sauce made by melting the butter and adding to it the vinegar, sugar, salt, paprika and peppers.

Grandmother's Deep Apple Pie

1 cup cold water
1 tbsp. flour
1 egg
3 tbsp. sugar
¼ tbsp. salt
2 tbsp. butter
½ tsp. cinnamon
½ cup cream
Apples peeled and cored

Line a deep pie dish with rich pastry. Onto this lay thickly sliced quick-cooking apples to cover the bottom in a double layer. Over this pour the following custard: To the tablespoonful of flour add a cupful of water slowly, blending smoothly. Add the beaten egg, sugar and salt. Cook until smooth, take from stove and add the cream. Pour this over the apples, dot with bits of butter, sprinkle over with cinnamon, cover with top crust which has been slashed slightly in center to allow for escaping steam, and bake at 500 for fifteen minutes. Lower heat and bake at 400 for another twenty minutes.

CREAMED FINNAN HADDIE

BOILED POTATOES SPINACH

TOMATO CUPS

SELF-FROSTING LEMON PIE

In planning your meals, remember that the eye must be fed before the mouth. The first appeal as you sit down to the table is to the eye. If the eye is teased, the tongue begins to twitch. If with this dish of creamed finnan haddie we had mashed potatoes, white turnips, and, say, some other neutral colored vegetable, there would be little temptation to the palate no matter how well the food was prepared. The spinach and the tomato cups lend color and variety. If you do not care for spinach, substitute carrots instead. And it would be a good plan to add some beets as well.

Creamed Finnan Haddie

2 cups cream sauce
Parsley
2 lb. finnan haddie

Cover finnan haddie with cold water and heat slowly. Let simmer until tender; remove bones and break fish into flakes. Put into hot cream sauce and sprinkle with chopped parsley.

Spinach

1 pk. spinach
2 tbsp. butter
Hard-boiled egg
Salt, pepper
Vinegar

Wash spinach through several waters, trim off long roots and bruised leaves. Put in a kettle with no water except what clings; cover closely and let cook ten minutes. Drain, put in wooden bowl and chop fine. Add butter, seasonings, a few drops of vinegar or lemon juice. Arrange in vegetable dish and garnish with sliced egg. Serve hot.

Tomato Cups

6 firm tomatoes
½ bunch celery
French Dressing
1 cup mayonnaise
3 tbsp. horseradish
Lettuce

Cut thin slice squarely from top of tomato and scoop out pulp to leave thick shell. Pour teaspoonful of French Dressing (specially salted) in tomato and let stand while preparing sauce. Mince celery very fine and mix with horseradish; add this to mayonnaise. Turn tomatoes over to drain, then fill with sauce, and chill. Serve on lettuce, sprinkled with paprika, garnished with sprig of parsley.

Self-Frosting Lemon Pie

Juice of 1 lemon
1 cup sugar
3 tbsp. flour
Yolks of 2 eggs
¾ cup sweet milk
1 tbsp. butter, melted

Beat egg yolks, add sugar and melted butter; add flour and milk alternately; add stiffly beaten whites of eggs and lemon juice last. Bake in under crust for forty minutes at 325-350, or until pie is golden brown.

SAVORY HAMBURG LOAF
SQUASH PUFF BAKED POTATOES
APPLE SALAD
SPANISH CREAM PIE

THOSE of us who got our growth before ever vitamins were discovered seem to be struggling along toward a reasonably hale finish, but of course we shall never know how many of those who fell by the wayside might have survived if they had known about vitamins. It is like taking medicine. It may not seem to do much good but you will never know what might have happened to you if you hadn't taken it. The knowledge and understanding of vitamins (if anybody does understand them) has done this for us anyway: it has taught us that we should eat more vegetables, more fruit and more milk. No matter whereabouts in the alphabet these things come, they will help to keep us healthy if we use them freely.

Savory Hamburg Loaf

1 lb. hamburg
¼ lb. salt pork, ground
2 small onions chopped
1 green pepper, chopped
1 egg beaten
1 cup bread crumbs
2 tbsp. butter, melted
2 tsp. salt
1 can tomato soup
1 can hot water
Bacon

Mix all together except tomato. Put strips of bacon over top, cover with tomato soup and hot water and bake in moderate oven forty minutes.

Squash Puff

Cut a hard winter squash into pieces and remove seeds. Steam tender, scrape from shell and mash. Season with salt, pepper, generous amount of butter and cream to a consistency where it can be beaten. Beat until light, put in greased baking dish, dot with butter, sprinkle with black pepper, and heat through in moderate oven.

Apple Salad

4 tart apples
1 bunch celery
1 cup nut meats
Dressing

Pare, quarter and dice apples; cut celery in small pieces; mix, and add chopped nut meats, walnut, pecan or hazel. Serve with

Boiled Salad Dressing

½ cup sugar
⅔ cup vinegar
1½ tbsp. butter
½ tsp. white pepper
1 tsp. salt
2 eggs well beaten

Mix and cook in double boiler until thick. Chill and add to salad.

Spanish Cream Pie

1 cup sugar
½ cup cream
½ cup milk
2 tbsp. butter
2½ tbsp. flour
1 tsp. vanilla

Mix all ingredients and cook in double boiler. Fill crust and bake in moderate oven (350) for thirty minutes. Cool and cover with whipped cream.

VEAL BIRDS   CASSEROLE OF POTATOES
SALAD OF GREEN PEAS
BUTTERSCOTCH BANANAS

THIS is another good menu for warm weather because veal is not a heavy meat, and while string beans can be had throughout most of the season, they, as well as beets, are cheaper and fresher if used close to the day of gathering. Since cooked bananas are not a favorite with everybody we suggest a light pudding, ice, custard, or just crackers and cheese as a substitute for the last course, with a bit of fruit to top off with. If a first course is desired, a cocktail—cranberry, sauerkraut, tomato, or grape juice is recommended. Nothing heavy.

Veal Birds

- 2½ lbs. veal steak
- Cracker crumbs
- Celery salt
- 1 egg
- Salt and pepper
- Onion juice
- Melted butter

Have the steak cut one-half inch thick; cut this into four-inch squares. Chop the trimmings very fine and add one-fourth as much bread crumbs. Add the other ingredients and bind together with melted butter to make a paste. Spread a tablespoonful of this mixture on each piece of meat. Roll up and tie with string, or skewer. Dredge with a mixture of flour, salt and pepper and cook in fat in a frying pan until well browned all around. (25 minutes.) Drain on paper toweling.

Casserole of Potatoes

Peel as many potatoes as will be required and lay in cold water for an hour. Cut lengthwise into quarters; pack into a buttered baking dish and season with salt and pepper. Pour over these just enough milk (in which has been dissolved ⅛ teaspoonful of soda) to barely cover and add a tablespoonful of butter to each cup of milk. Cut the butter into small pieces and roll in flour. Over the top sprinkle chopped parsley and onion. Cover closely and set in a dripping pan of water. Bake in 400 oven for forty-five minutes, or until potatoes are tender.

Salad of Green Peas

- 1 tbsp. gelatin
- 1 cup cold water
- ¾ cup sugar
- 1 pt. hot water
- ½ cup lemon juice
- 1 No. 1 can peas (small)
- 4 pickles
- ¾ cup English walnuts
- 1 tbsp. chopped pimiento

Soak gelatin in cold water for five minutes, add to it the sugar, hot water and lemon juice. When beginning to harden, add peas, pickles, chopped fine, the walnuts and chopped pimiento. Put into molds and leave until firm. Serve on lettuce leaf with mayonnaise dressing.

Butterscotch Bananas

- 1 cup brown sugar
- 2 tbsp. light cream
- ½ cup whipping cream
- 2 tbsp. butter
- 1 tsp. vanilla
- Bananas

Cook together brown sugar, cream and butter, stirring until sugar is dissolved; let bubble for about five minutes. Cool, add vanilla. Pour over sliced bananas in individual dishes and serve with whipped cream.

MICHIGAN SAUSAGE AND APPLE

BAKED POTATOES KOHL RABI

PEACH PAULINE

THIS is a simple menu—as are all that are in this book; one that any average homemaker can put together without spending too much time or money, and with very little trouble. Another vegetable can be substituted for the spinach, according to season or inclination. Cabbage would be good, new cabbage boiled for twenty minutes and dressed with butter and seasonings; or baked Hubbard Squash if used later in the season; or the squash and spinach might be used together without the potatoes. No salad is needed with the apple in the meat dish and at least one other vegetable besides the potato.

Michigan Sausage and Apple

Fry either link sausages or sausage meat according to quantity needed; take thick slices of unpeeled tart apples and thinner slices of onion. Dip the slices of apple in a mixture of flour and sugar and fry in sausage fat taken from the sausage as it fries. Fry onion without dipping but until slightly brown. Turn apple and onion rings once. Keep these slices as unbroken as possible. Arrange the sausage in center of a hot platter and surround with alternate rings of apple and onion, seasoned with salt and pepper.

Kohl Rabi

This is a delicious member of the vegetable kingdom too little known. It is sort of a cross between a turnip and a cabbage, looking something like the former but tasting more like the latter. But this bulb grows on a stem something like Brussels Sprouts, and not in the ground. There are several ways of cooking it. You first cut the leaves from the bulb and then peel the skin from it as you do a turnip. Cut in quarters or slices and boil until tender in an uncovered kettle with a generous amount of water. Drain and shake over the fire to dry. Put in a serving dish and dress with melted butter, salt and pepper. Or, cook a sliced onion in four tablespoonfuls of butter until tender and then add two teaspoons of curry powder. Pour this over the cooked and drained kohl rabi (two bunches) and reheat.

Peach Pauline

1 can sliced peaches
½ cup sugar
2 tbsp. butter
2 cups bread crumbs
Lemon juice

Put a layer of peaches in the bottom of a buttered baking dish, sprinkle with a few drops of lemon juice and part of the sugar. Add a layer of bread crumbs and repeat until all ingredients are used, with crumbs on top. Pour over enough of the juice to moisten the dish but not enough to be sloppy. Bake at 400 for fifteen minutes or until hot through and crumbs brown. Serve with whipped cream.

JELLIED TOMATO BOUILLON
TENDERLOIN FILLETS
BRUSSELS SPROUTS
PEPPERMINT ICE CREAM

For a company dinner this is easily prepared because the dessert—which requires most time in preparation, should be made early in the morning. New potatoes would be delicious with this dinner. They should be scraped, boiled in very little water, taken out and drained when just tender and placed in a hot vegetable dish. Pour melted butter over, season with salt and pepper, and sprinkle generously with minced parsley. Older potatoes can be treated in the same way, but are not quite so good as the new ones on which the skin still rubs off. Sweet potatoes baked would also go well with this menu.

Jellied Tomato Bouillon

3 cups tomato juice
1 tsp. salt
½ tsp. celery salt
6 peppercorns
4 cloves
Small piece of bay leaf
1½ tsp. sugar
1 small onion
2 cups canned bouillon or beef stock
2 tbsp. gelatin
¼ cup cold water

Drain liquid from a quart can of tomatoes. Add seasonings and onion cut in small pieces and simmer fifteen minutes. Strain and add bouillon and bring to boiling point. Add gelatin softened in the cold water and stir. Pour into bouillon cups and let stand until jellied. Serve cold.

Tenderloin Fillets

As many fillets of steak, cut ¾ inch thick, as there will be servings. Broil these to a rich brown on the outside and rare on the inside; arrange on a platter and spread with butter which has been blended with minced parsley. At one end of the platter heap small new potatoes, parboiled, brushed with butter and browned in the oven; at the other end arrange small stuffed tomatoes. Garnish with pickled onions, radishes and cress.

Brussels Sprouts

1 qt. sprouts
2 tbsp. melted butter
1 tsp. salt
Pepper

Wash the sprouts well, and take off dead leaves; throw sprouts into boiling water, add the salt and boil uncovered for twenty minutes. Drain through colander and turn into hot serving dish. Pour over the butter and give a dash of pepper over the top.

Peppermint Ice Cream

2 tbsp. flour
¼ cup sugar
Pinch salt
1 egg white
2½ cups scalded milk
5-oz. pkg. after-dinner mints
½ cup cold milk
1 cup cream
Green coloring

Mix flour, sugar and salt together and add cold milk. Blend smooth and add to hot milk in double boiler; cook for twenty minutes, stirring until thickened. Crush mints and add to custard, stirring until dissolved. Cool, fold in egg white beaten stiff, and color a delicate green. Turn into freezer, pack in three parts ice to one of salt and freeze. Serve with chocolate marshmallow sauce, made by adding marshmallows to regular chocolate sauce.

OYSTER COCKTAIL
FINGER STEAKS DUCHESSE POTATOES
SAUERKRAUT WITH TOMATO
CHERRY ANNE

If this menu would be otherwise desirable for a summer day, a fruit could be substituted for the cocktail. Or a jellied consommé, if sauerkraut does not appeal, try Chinese Cabbage. Shred it fine and serve with French Dressing. Or an asparagus salad with Hollandaise Sauce, or another cooked vegetable such as new peas, string beans, turnips, green corn or stewed tomatoes. Or, try, if you never have, cooking radishes. They should be sliced thin and boiled in very little water until tender, then either pour over them a little thin white sauce, or a dressing of melted butter, with salt and pepper. In winter we would suggest a little heavier dessert—perhaps a chocolate or lemon pie.

Oyster Cocktail

Cocktail Sauce

- ¾ cup ketchup
- 2 tbsp. horseradish
- 3 drops tabasco sauce
- 1 tsp. Worcestershire sauce
- 1 tbsp. lemon juice
- Salt, pepper, cayenne
- 1 pt. medium sized oysters

Mix all ingredients together and chill. Serve in small glass in center of oyster plate, or pour over oysters at serving.

Finger Steaks

- 1½ lbs. chuck or flank steak
- Flour
- Salt and pepper
- 3 tbsp. butter or fat
- ½ cup hot water
- 1 tbsp. Worcestershire sauce

Cut steak into strips one inch wide and about three inches long. Roll each one in mixture of flour, salt and pepper. Put in hot fat and brown on both sides in heavy frying pan. Add one-half cup hot water and cook from an hour and a half to two hours, until tender. Remove steaks, thicken the gravy in the pan, add Worcestershire Sauce, season, and pour over meat.

Duchesse Potatoes

- 3 cups hot mashed potatoes
- 3 eggs
- 1 tsp. salt
- 6 tbsp. hot milk
- ¼ tsp. pepper

Beat yolks and whites of eggs separately. Mix all ingredients except whites of eggs and fold these in last. Put mixture in greased baking dish, sprinkle with minced parsley and bake 15 minutes in a moderate oven or until hot through and brown on top.

Sauerkraut with Tomato

- 1 can sauerkraut
- 1 cup tomato soup
- 1 tbsp. sugar
- Bacon

Lay sauerkraut in well-greased baking dish. Sprinkle with sugar. Pour the tomato soup over. Lay four or six strips of bacon across top and bake twenty minutes at 375.

Cherry Anne

- 1 No. 2 can large white sweet cherries
- 1 lemon
- ½ cup chopped nut meats
- ½ cup sugar
- 1 tbsp. gelatin

Drain and chop cherries. Dissolve gelatin in a little of the cold cherry juice. Heat remainder of juice and juice of lemon. Add gelatin and sugar to this. Mix with chopped cherries and nut meats, and chill. Serve with whipped cream.

FRANKFURTERS AU GRATIN

TOMATO ESCALLOP PEPPERS STUFFED WITH CORN

MARSHMALLOW COFFEE

THE humble frankfurter, like the ubiquitous hamburger, must play a frequent part in the economical food budget. But, like the hamburger steak, cube steak, chuck roast, and other of the cheaper kinds of meat, it need not be served over and over in its original state. We do not believe in making what we call "stodges" of food —even these ordinary cheaper cuts of meat. That is, so fussing them up with all sorts of incongruous ingredients that they are neither recognizable nor fit to eat; but we do know that they can be so dressed up as to somewhat change their nature and make them more palatable. Frankfurters are good—as frankfurters—once or even twice in awhile, but by giving them a little thought they can make quite a presentable appearance in other forms.

Frankfurters au Gratin

The quantity of this dish must depend on the number to be served. To serve six people, put a layer of mashed and seasoned potato in the bottom of a deep casserole or baking dish. On top of this arrange twelve small frankfurters that have been browned in butter. Cover with the remainder of potato, which should not be too dry. Sprinkle thickly with grated cheese and finally with bread crumbs buttered. Brown in an oven at 375 until heated through.

Tomato Esscallop

3 cups tomato pulp
3 cups soft bread crumbs
Pepper
¼ cup butter
½ tsp. salt

Season tomato pulp with salt and pepper. Cover the bottom of a well-buttered casserole with the tomato pulp; cover with a layer of bread crumbs and alternate layers, with the last layer of the crumbs. Dot with butter and bake in moderate oven for fifteen minutes. Temperature 360.

Peppers Stuffed with Corn

6 green peppers
1 dozen ears of corn
1 tbsp. butter
1 tbsp. evaporated milk
2 eggs
Salt, pepper

Remove seeds from peppers and parboil in salted water for ten minutes. Grate corn from cob, add butter, milk, well beaten eggs, salt and pepper. Fill peppers with this and bake in moderate oven (375) for thirty minutes. Six servings.

Marshmallow Coffee

½ lb. marshmallows
½ cup hot coffee
½ pint whipped cream
Maraschino cherries

Cut marshmallows in pieces and dissolve over hot water; add hot coffee. Let cool; then beat and add whipped cream. Put in sherbet glasses, let stand in refrigerator several hours and serve with dab of whipped cream on top decorated with a cherry or candy.

PEANUT BUTTER SOUP

FISH FILLETS ROLLED FRIED SUMMER SQUASH

MOLDED PEAR AND CHEESE SALAD

THIS would be a good menu to use while summer squash is at its best and fresh fruit is available for the salad which is dessert as well. The soup would be a little heavy for a hot day, but either a cold consommé or hot thin soup could be substituted. Since there is so much fruit in the salad, and fish is the main course, neither a sea food nor a fruit cocktail would be appropriate. If this soup is used another vegetable might be substituted for potatoes—boiled new onions, Brussels Sprouts, tomatoes, leeks or carrots. Escalloped potatoes are suggested, or rice.

Peanut Butter Soup

6 cups milk
2 bouillon cubes
3 tbsp. butter
2 tbsp. flour
6 tbsp. peanut butter
1 tsp. celery salt
¼ tsp. Worcestershire Sauce
½ tbsp. grated onion or onion juice
Salt and pepper

Heat the milk in a double boiler. Add the bouillon cubes. Add butter, flour and peanut butter mixed to a paste, and cook until it thickens, stirring constantly. Add seasonings and serve very hot.

Fish Fillets Rolled

Small fish fillets
2 slices bacon
4 chopped olives
1 chopped onion
Salt and pepper
1 cup bread crumbs
As many firm tomatoes as fillets

Chop bacon and onion together and fry; add a small amount of water, the chopped olives, salt, pepper and bread crumbs. Split and bone any small fish (or get fillets at market), spread with dressing and roll. Cut tops from tomatoes and dig out insides. Set rolled fish inside tomatoes, and bake until tender. Make a sauce of the tomato pulp highly seasoned. Set each tomato fillet on a piece of toast, garnish with quarter slice of lemon and parsley and serve with tomato sauce.

Fried Summer Squash

Wash, dry and slice summer squash in pieces about one-half inch thick. Roll in flour and fry in butter until tender and slightly brown.

Molded Pear and Cheese Salad

1 4-oz. pkg. cream cheese
6 stuffed olives
6 pear halves
1 tbsp. gelatin
¼ cup cold water
⅔ cup sugar
⅓ cup lemon juice
1 cup pear juice and water
Strips of pimiento

Mix the cream cheese with the chopped olives and fill the cavities of the pears. Garnish with strips of pimiento. Soften the gelatin in the cold water; heat the pear juice and if necessary add hot water to make one pint. Cover the bottom of individual molds with this liquid and let it cool and set. Then lay half a pear on this jelly, cover with remainder of liquid and let stand until firm. Turn out on lettuce leaf and serve with mayonnaise or boiled fruit dressing. If fresh pears are used, hot water takes the place of pear juice.

TANGERINE APPETIZER

RUSSIAN STEAKS NEW BRUNSWICK POTATOES

COMBINATION SALAD

MENUS at best are merely suggestive. We have tried in those which are given in this book to make them not only simple and economical, but with the various dishes so chosen that neither fruits nor vegetables will be unseasonable according to the meat or main dish. In fact most of the menus have actually been used as they are given and have been found logical and satisfactory except where a matter of personal taste enters. Some do not like onions, others cannot abide parsnips. Therefore, the user of the menu must judge by what is given, what substitute could be made that would be similar in quality, taste and nutriment.

Tangerine Appetizer

Peel tangerines, separate sections and arrange on small glass plates in circular form with a mound of powdered sugar in the center. Sugar may be made into mound by pressing in a large thimble. The tangerine is to be eaten with the fingers.

Russian Steaks

1 lb. round steak ground
¼ lb. butter
Frying fat
Salt and pepper

Season the ground meat and work into it with a wooden spoon the fourth of a pound of butter. Form into fat balls and fry on both sides in very hot fat. Allow three minutes to each side. Serve with the following sauce:

2 tbsp. oil
1 tbsp. butter
1½ tbsp. flour
Salt and pepper
1 tsp. lemon juice
2 tsp. onion juice
1 tsp. grated horseradish
¼ tsp. prepared mustard
1½ cups meat stock
¼ cup cream

Mix together the oil and butter, blend into it the flour, add the onion juice, horseradish, mustard, salt and pepper. Add gradually the meat stock (or hot water) and cook three minutes; take from fire and add cream and lemon juice, stirring until smooth.

New Brunswick Potatoes

Allow one good sized potato for each serving and as many small onions as potatoes. Peel potatoes and onions. In one end of each potato bore a small hole with apple corer. Insert a small onion in this hole and roll both in flour. Brown in hot frying pan in water. Then lower the heat, cover and cook very slowly until tender. Add salt and pepper just before covering. The fat and steam should cook them without water.

Combination Salad

4 tomatoes sliced
1 sweet pepper chopped
12 stuffed olives
Small pickled onions
Clove of garlic
Lettuce leaves

Rub salad bowl with the clove of garlic and line with white lettuce leaves. Arrange the sliced tomatoes on these. Sprinkle over these the chopped sweet pepper, the olives thinly sliced and a bottle of small pickled onions drained. Over all pour this dressing:

2 tbsp. lemon juice
6 tbsp. oil
1 tbsp. chili sauce (highly seasoned)
½ tsp. Worcestershire Sauce

Shake these ingredients to an emulsion and pour over salad. Add one teaspoonful of sugar if desired.

ROAST GOOSE, APPLESAUCE
MASHED POTATOES GIBLET GRAVY
CRANBERRY SALAD
FLOATING ISLAND

ROAST goose has been forever immortalized in the Cratchit's Christmas Dinner, but even so, it has with us an unvanquishable foe in roast turkey for holiday dinner. The goose, nevertheless, is a delectable fowl if eaten young and should make at least one change in our holiday dinner repertoire throughout the year. Geese are a long-lived fowl and do not grow tenderer as they grow older. Past three years of age a goose is good only as a pet or to furnish relief for congested lungs. A young goose has down on its legs, and the legs are a fresh yellow and the webbing between the toes tender. The under bill is soft. Try, sometime, stuffing the goose with mashed potato and sauerkraut.

Roast Goose

Scrub the goose with hot soap and water to remove surface fat and accumulated dirt, rinse well first in hot water, then in cold. Goose is likely to be fatter than other fowl, and unless young (under a year) is improved by parboiling. After parboiling (from half to three-quarters of an hour according to age) wipe dry with a flannel cloth. While the bird is parboiling, prepare a dressing of bread crumbs. Moisten the bread crumbs with hot applesauce seasoned with salt, pepper, sage and chopped onion. Stuff the bird with this, sew up apertures, and rub the outside with a mixture of salt, pepper, celery salt and sage. Put the bird in the roaster, cover, and allow twenty minutes to the pound for a young bird, thirty minutes if older. Cook until quite tender, then drain off all grease, brush with melted butter, sage, pepper and a little salt; dredge lightly with flour, and return to the oven to brown.

When done remove the goose to a hot platter, thicken the juice in the pan with flour and add the giblets, chopped, and the water in which they were cooked. Season to taste. Serve with applesauce.

Cranberry Salad

1 qt. raw cranberries
1 orange
2½ cups sugar
2 pkgs. lemon gelatin

Grind cranberries and orange. Drain, to the juice add enough water to make two cups of liquid. Bring liquid to a boil and pour over the sugar and the lemon gelatin. Stir thoroughly, let cool, then add the fruit. Put in salad mold, or individual molds, and chill. Serve on lettuce with mayonnaise.

Floating Island

1 qt. milk
3 eggs
½ cup sugar
½ tsp. salt
1 tsp. vanilla
1 tbsp. cornstarch
Jelly

Heat milk in double boiler. Separate eggs. Mix salt, sugar and cornstarch; beat yolks of eggs and beat into them the dry ingredients. Stir this gradually into the hot milk and cook until thick, stirring continuously. Cool and add vanilla. Pour into a wide topped glass serving dish or onto a handsome platter and chill. When ready to serve beat whites very stiff and make little "islands" of them on the custard. In the center of each put a small cube of red jelly, or a cherry.

BAKED STEAK WITH BANANAS
COOKED CHICKORY
TOMATO-CHEESE SALAD
QUICK DUTCH APPLE CAKE

No first course is suggested with this menu because it is quite heavy in itself. If a first course is desired it should be no more than a thin, hot soup, or a jellied bouillon if used in warm weather. Chicory, or American endive is a vegetable all too little used. It is in most markets in early spring and for a long season. We cook it just as we do dandelion greens and consider it a good substitute. If chicory is unavailable, substitute another vegetable—spinach, chard, wilted lettuce, beet greens.

Baked Steak with Bananas

2 lbs. round steak
6 strips bacon
3 large bananas
2 tsp. brown sugar
Lemon juice
3 tbsp. water
½ tsp. salt
⅛ tsp. pepper

Have the round steak cut one inch in thickness. Split it open through the center, leaving one side uncut. Spread it open like a book, and on one-half sprinkle salt and pepper, and lay on the bananas cut in lengthwise slices. Sprinkle the sugar over these and a few drops of lemon juice. Fold the other half upon this, and lay the strips of bacon over it. Fasten the two halves together with steel skewers. Place in a buttered baking dish and bake for forty minutes at 400.

Cooked Chicory

Wash one or two bunches of chicory (according to required amount) thoroughly. Shake dry and plunge into boiling water in which three or four slices of bacon or salt pork have been boiling for fifteen minutes. Boil for 25 to 40 minutes according to tenderness of chicory. Drain, season with salt, pepper, a few drops of vinegar and serve hot. If preferred, dress with a plain French dressing of oil and vinegar. Cooking with bacon or pork is making it an equivalent of "greens"—dandelion or mustard. We recommend it highly.

Tomato-Cheese Salad

Cut the tops from as many small, firm, red tomatoes as are needed. Scoop out the insides and fill with cottage cheese that has been highly seasoned with salt, pepper, paprika and cream, and rolled in chopped parsley. Sprinkle over with chopped chives, green onion tops or a little green pepper and serve on lettuce with French Dressing.

Quick Dutch Apple Cake

4 apples
½ cup sugar
Rich biscuit dough
2 tsp. cinnamon
1 egg yolk

Make a rich biscuit dough (using 4 tablespoons of butter for shortening to the regular recipe calling for 2 cups of flour) and spread this dough one-half inch thick in the bottom of a deep oblong biscuit tin. Peel, core and cut apples into eighths. Press the pieces of apple down into the dough thickly, sprinkle with sugar, cinnamon and dot generously with butter. Bake 30 minutes in an oven at 350. Serve with cream.

INDIVIDUAL HAM PATTIES
BOILED RICE   SOUR CABBAGE
RHUBARB AND BANANA PUDDING

CANNED tomato soup is certainly a boon to the busy housewife in more ways than one. As a soup it is probably the most popular of any. But as an ingredient for moistening meat dishes, rice, dressings and stuffings; as a foundation for meat sauces and as a sauce in itself, as well as in dozens of other uses it is one of the most versatile of commercial foods. It would pay to buy it by the dozen—or gross, if you could get it any cheaper that way. Considering the price at which it can be bought, however, even by the single can, it may be better economy to let the grocer stock it for you. But by all means keep a dozen cans on hand at a time.

Individual Ham Patties

½ lb. ham
½ lb. fresh pork
½ cup cracker crumbs
1 onion
1 green pepper
1 egg
½ cup evaporated milk
1 tbsp. prepared mustard
Salt, pepper
Mushrooms
Tomato Soup

Have the ham and pork ground together; add cracker crumbs, onion and pepper chopped, beaten egg and seasonings. Mix thoroughly and moisten with a little of the soup. Put in well greased muffin tins, large size, but do not fill quite full. Over the top of each put a tablespoonful of tomato soup highly seasoned. Sprinkle a half teaspoonful of brown sugar over the top and a dot of butter. Bake in moderate oven (350-375) for forty-five minutes. Take from oven, put a teaspoonful of cream and a large mushroom on each, return to oven and bake ten minutes longer at 400. Serve boiled rice as a vegetable.

Sour Cabbage

1 medium sized head cabbage
2 tbsp. butter or fat
½ cup sugar
1 tbsp. flour
1 onion
⅓ cup vinegar
¼ cup sour cream
Salt, pepper, paprika

Shred the onion and the cabbage. Put butter in frying pan and melt. Add cabbage and onion and barely cover with water. Cook one-half hour, covered. Add vinegar, sugar, and flour mixed with cream. Bring to boiling point. Serve hot.

Rhubarb and Banana Pudding

1 qt. diced rhubarb
2 bananas
¼ cup butter
2 cups sugar
1 tbsp. water
¼ tsp. cinnamon
1 cup bread crumbs

Melt butter in frying pan and sauté bread crumbs until brown. Put a layer of rhubarb in bottom of buttered baking dish, sprinkle with sugar, moisten with water, add bread crumbs; alternate layers until all is used, bread crumbs last. Dust lightly with cinnamon. Bake in moderate oven (350-375) forty-five minutes. This same mixture makes excellent pie. If more moisture is needed, add water.

CREAM OF MUSHROOM SOUP
ROLLED ROAST OF LAMB
GREEN CORN ON COB   NEW POTATOES
HUCKLEBERRY PIE

For use in late summer when corn is at its best a hot soup may be too hearty, in which case, serve chilled watermelon balls with a few mint leaves scattered over. In order to save space for more important recipes we have not mentioned a salad, but one should by all means be included, especially with tomatoes and cucumbers fresh from the market. These vegetables, when at the height of their natural maturity, need but little dressing up into aspics or other combinations. There is plenty of time for such salads when canned fruit and vegetables have to be used, or when forced into ripening and so lacking in the flavor which is theirs when they come to us direct from the garden.

Cream of Mushroom Soup

½ lb. fresh mushrooms
1 cup milk
1 cup chicken stock
1 sliced onion
2 tbsp. butter
½ cup flour
1 cup cream
Salt and pepper

Chop mushrooms fine; chop onion; add both to stock and milk combined. (All stock may be used instead of part milk.) Cook twenty minutes in double boiler. Melt butter in saucepan and blend flour with this; add to stock and then put in the mushrooms; heat thoroughly but do not boil. Add cream and season to taste.

Rolled Roast of Lamb

5 lbs. lamb roll
4 cups stale bread crumbs
1 onion minced
Garlic clove
Hot water
Pickled onion
Tomato
Radishes
2 tbsp. melted butter
1 tsp. salt, pepper
1 tsp. sage
Pears
Mint Jelly

Mix bread crumbs, minced onion, salt, pepper, and sage with melted butter and moisten with milk, stock or any fruit juice. Spread this on the meat, roll up and tie. Rub outside of roll with a garlic clove and sear in hot fat in roasting pan. When browned, add one cup of hot water and bake in a moderate oven for two hours, or until tender. Fifteen minutes before meat is done lay as many halves of pears as there will be servings (or more) in the roaster around the meat. Do not let them cook soft. Remove meat to platter and garnish with the pears, the cavities of which should be filled (after placing on the platter) with mint jelly. Place a small white pickled onion on top of each square of jelly. Between the slices of pear lay a slice of tomato or a radish rose. Not more than six pear halves should be used.

Huckleberry Pie

2 cups fresh berries
¾ cup of sugar
2 tbsp. butter
¼ tsp. cinnamon
Pinch of salt

Pick over and wash berries; line a pie tin with rich pastry and fill with berries. Sprinkle the sugar and cinnamon over them with the smallest pinch of salt and dot with butter. Cover with pastry and put in the oven at 500 degrees for fifteen minutes, then reduce the heat to 450 and bake twenty minutes longer.

FRESH FRUIT COCKTAIL

SPANISH STEAK BOILED POTATOES

CREAM PIE WITH MERINGUE

THIS is a good cold weather menu, easy to prepare. The cream pie can be made in the morning, the cocktail requires but a few moments' time in preparation. The main dish is one of the most appetizing and complete that we have ever tested. It may be made in the oven or in a roaster on top of the stove. If a thick piece of round steak (two and a half inches) is used instead of the chuck, it will make a handsomer dish, and would be a real treat for an informal dinner. We have sometimes used as much as a seven-pound piece of round to serve a party of twelve generously, in which case more vegetables are required.

Fresh Fruit Cocktail

- 1 grapefruit
- 2 oranges
- 1 cup diced pineapple
- 1 pint strawberries

If neither fresh pineapple nor strawberries are available, use canned pineapple and either canned peaches or large sweet cherries. Separate grapefruit and oranges into sections and dice. Mix and chill. Sprinkle over it a few drops of lemon juice before serving and a teaspoonful of confectioners' sugar. Pour a very little of the mixed juice from fruits over, and garnish with a mint candy or sprig of mint.

Spanish Steak

- 4 lbs. chuck or round of beef
- Small piece of suet
- 1 green pepper
- 1 parsnip
- 5 stalks celery
- 3 small carrots
- 6 onions
- Flour
- 1½ tbsp. mixed spices
- 2 tsp. salt
- ¼ tsp. black pepper
- 1 qt. tomatoes, strained

Melt suet in heavy roasting pan or Dutch oven; sear meat on both sides; take out of pan and dredge both sides heavily with flour, about ½ cup. Take out suet and put meat back into the fat. Cover with all vegetables chopped. Add strained tomatoes and sprinkle the mixed spices over. Dredge with ⅔ cup of flour. Add one cup of boiling water and blend vegetables and flour together with a spoon. Cover and cook very slowly for three and a half to four hours, or until very tender, adding water if necessary. Take up the meat and vegetables, and to the sauce left in the pan add one cup of hot water and thicken with flour if necessary. Pour over and around the meat.

Cream Pie with Meringue

- 2 cups hot milk
- 5 tbsp. flour
- ½ cup sugar
- 2 eggs, separated
- 1½ tsp. vanilla
- Plain pastry

Mix sugar and flour; add hot milk, blending smoothly; cook until thoroughly done. Beat egg yolks slightly; pour first mixture into eggs. Add flavoring; pour into pie tin lined with plain pastry. Bake 35 minutes in moderate oven. Cover with meringue made of stiffly beaten whites slightly sweetened and continue baking for 20 minutes.

VEAL CASSEROLE

BEET GREENS AND BACON

RAISIN BREAD PUDDING

VEAL is a meat that is lacking in fat and therefore some fat should be added in the cooking. Cutlets are not satisfactory either broiled or fried because the meat is too dry. They are best first browned and then cooked in some kind of liquid. Veal must be well cooked and cooked slowly or it is not easily digested. Mashed potatoes, rice or some form of macaroni may be added although with the bread in the pudding no great amount of starchy food should be needed. Most people, however, would want something to accompany the cutlet, and potatoes in some form seem most suitable.

Veal Casserole

- Veal flank
- 1 tsp. salt to each qt. of water used
- 1 small onion with clove
- 2 cupfuls soft breadcrumbs
- 1 clove
- 2 cupfuls tomato
- 6 small onions
- 1 cupful celery diced
- Dash of mace

Trim all bone, fat and gristle from flank. To the salted water add one small onion with a clove in it. Simmer the meat in this for 30 minutes. (Cook the day before it is to be used.) Remove the onion and clove and simmer until tender. Cut meat into small pieces and flour heavily. Brown in hot fat. Remove the meat and toss into the hot fat the bread crumbs, tomato, clove and bring to a boil. Remove the clove, add onions, sliced celery and mace. Add one-half cup veal stock (made the day before and strained). Mix all ingredients together, put in greased casserole, and bake at 350 for two and a half hours. Cover casserole for last 30 minutes.

Beet Greens and Bacon

- 2 bunches beet greens with beets
- 3 thin slices bacon
- Salt, pepper, vinegar
- Sugar

Clean beets and tops. Do not cut root end to bleed. Cook beets and bacon together. When beets are tender rub the skin off them, and chop beets and tops together, adding the bacon or not as preferred. Heat half a cupful of vinegar, a teaspoonful of sugar, salt and pepper together and pour over the beets. Or serve French Dressing with them.

Raisin Bread Pudding

- 9 slices of bread buttered and sugared
- Currants (dried)
- 1½ pts. milk
- 4 beaten eggs
- Pinch salt
- Vanilla

Butter the bread generously and sprinkle sugar over. Put a layer of bread in the bottom of a casserole or baking dish, sprinkle with the currants and repeat. Beat the eggs well, add the vanilla and milk, with sugar to sweeten slightly and pour over the bread. Bake in a moderate oven for one hour. Let stand two hours before using. Serve with cream if desired.

ROLLED BEEF ROAST
GLAZED CARROTS
CHERRY SALAD

THESE meat recipes that call for long, slow cooking are economical in more ways than one. They are the most inexpensive cuts of meat, but amongst the most nutritious. They require but little attention. There is a gravy with them which makes a rich dressing for potatoes, rice or noodles. Or even bread. For there are still people on earth so unsophisticated and unspoiled by an overdose of propriety, as to like gravy on their bread. And this method of cookery uses but little fuel. They are homely meals, but the great majority of us who have to worry about meals are still homely folks—and proud of it. The main thing with us is to learn how to cook our plain food well. It is not difficult to broil a porterhouse steak; almost any persons with reasonable intelligence and a hot fire can do that. But it requires skill, imagination and a cultivated taste to take a piece of brisket, chuck or flank and cook and season so that even an epicure will smack his lips over it. But it can be done, and even the average woman who is willing to put her mind to it can accomplish the feat.

Rolled Beef Roast

3 lbs. rolled beef, chuck, flank or brisket
2½ tbsp. flour
2 tsp. salt
⅛ tsp. pepper
1 medium onion
2 tbsp. fat
Garlic

Wipe the meat with a damp cloth, lay it out flat and rub both sides with garlic clove. Dredge with a mixture of flour, salt and pepper. Make slits or pockets in the meat and rub the dressing into them. Cover with dressing, roll up and tie and place in roasting pan. Rub the outside with a little of the dressing, slice the onion over it, put a few pieces of suet over the top, cover and bake for two hours at 350 degrees. When tender remove the meat, thicken the juices in the pan with flour, thin with water, season and serve separately.

Glazed Carrots

6 to 8 carrots
1 cup stock
1 tbsp. sugar
2 tbsp. butter
Salt
Pepper

Scrape, wash and cut carrots in two lengthwise; boil in salted water until slightly tender; drain; put in saucepan with stock, sugar, butter, salt and pepper. Cover and cook ten minutes. Uncover, shake the carrots about to coat with syrup, and cook until liquid is gone and carrots glazed.

Cherry Salad

1 can white cherries
1 can sliced pineapple
Small stuffed olives
Lettuce, mayonnaise

Remove pits from cherries and insert a stuffed olive in the cavity. Lay one cherry in the center of a slice of pineapple placed on a lettuce leaf. Arrange others around, and serve with mayonnaise in which cream has been whipped.

GRAPEFRUIT COCKTAIL

ROAST DUCK—ORANGE STUFFING

BROWN RICE BOILED ONIONS

CARDINAL SALAD

Most women marketers trust docilely to the judgment and chivalry of the salesmen when selecting meat. Where one trades always at the same store and with a reliable and sympathetic merchant such practice is well enough. But since marketing is one of the chiefest of the homemaker's several duties, and one most pertinent to the pocketbook, there would surely be no harm in acquainting one's self with a few of the principles of selection. In this matter of choosing a duck, now: One that is young and fit for the roasting pan will have an underbill that bends with pressure; the breast will be plump and fat—but not too fat. The breast bone will be pliable. There is no way in which you can tell whether the meat will be full flavored and yet not strong *but* to trust your man. And he knows only by where he bought it. The good poultry raiser does not allow his fowls to become scavengers as ordinary barnyard fowls are, but confines them to a certain location and feeds them on what will contribute to the flavor of their flesh. The answer then, it would seem, would be first to know your poultry man, and from him learn as much as you can about poultry. Brown rice is cooked as any other.

Grapefruit Cocktail

1 large grapefruit
1 tbsp. orange juice
1 tbsp. grape juice
Sugar
1 tbsp. maraschino cherry
Juice from grapefruit juice
Cherries

Cut grapefruit in two crossways and remove pulp in sections. Mix fruit juices and sweeten to taste. Place grapefruit sections in cocktail glasses and sprinkle with finely cut maraschino cherries. Pour the juice over, and let set several hours, chilled.

Roast Duck

Clean the duck, wash, rinse, and dry. Sprinkle inside and out with salt and pepper. Dredge lightly with flour. Make the following

Orange Stuffing

3 cups dry bread crumbs
1 cup dried apple
½ cup seedless raisins
4 tbsp. sugar
⅔ cup orange juice
Salt, pepper
Butter

Mix ingredients and add liquid to make a moist and easily handled but not wet stuffing. Stuff the duck with this and sew up opening. Tie the wings tightly back to the body with the skin drawn down over the neck and fastened under the wings, and the legs to the side.

Lay the duck in a roasting pan and put in a hot oven (500), uncovered. At the end of twenty minutes put half a cup of water in the pan, cover, and baste frequently, allowing 25 minutes for a duck a year old or more, 15 for a younger fowl. If the duck is more than a year old, steam one hour before roasting.

Cardinal Salad

2 heads lettuce
Bunch watercress
2 boiled beets
6 small radishes
6 hard cooked eggs
1 cucumber
Mayonnaise

Clean and chill all vegetables; cut the beets in slices; chop eggs fine; arrange lettuce leaves in salad bowl; mix cress, radishes, beets, eggs and sliced cucumber together. Mix with mayonnaise to which a small amount of beet juice has been added. Put in salad bowl and serve at once cold and as a separate course.

CRANBERRY COCKTAIL

CREAM-CODFISH GRAVY BOILED POTATOES

BAKED TOMATOES

CHERRY FRITTERS

CODFISH gravy as it is often made, skimped in butter, minus cream and egg, is a none too palatable dish justifying the opprobium of "poor man's dish." But "Cream-codfish gravy" such as I knew it in my mother's home, and in the farm homes where, in my school-teaching days, I learned more about good cookery than any cooking school I have ever seen could teach, codfish-gravy was something to smack your lips over. Ask any prominent business men you know whose boyhood was spent on a farm—especially a farm in Michigan where I learned *my* codfish gravy, or York State where most Michiganders came from. It will stir up memories and he will begin to talk about salt pork gravy and buckwheat cakes, but pin him down and he will tell you a thing or two about codfish. But a salt codfish *must* have his butter and cream.

Cream-Codfish Gravy

Break salt cod into reasonably small pieces. Pour warm water over and let stand half an hour. Drain, pour cold water over and bring to simmering point but do not boil. Drain. Make a rich medium white sauce and add to it one tablespoonful of butter for each cup of sauce. When the butter is melted stir in a slightly beaten egg, season with salt and pepper and serve hot.

Baked Tomatoes on Toast

Choose firm tomatoes of uniform medium size, not overripe, and cut in two crosswise, unpeeled. Place in shallow baking pan and sprinkle with salt and pepper, add half a teaspoon of sugar and a good "dot" of butter to each piece. Put in a moderate (375) oven and bake slowly about 45 minutes, or until tender. Serve on small squares of bread and garnish with cress, endive, chicory or parsley.

Cherry Fritters

1 cup canned cherries, drained
1 egg
1 cup milk
1 cup flour
1 tbsp. sugar
1 tsp. baking powder
Rind of half lemon, grated
1/4 tsp. salt

Drain the cherries and place in bottom of well buttered glass baking dish. Add the egg, well-beaten, to the milk, and mix the dry ingredients which have been sifted together to this. Pour this batter over the cherries and mix all together carefully. Drop by spoonfuls into hot fat and fry a golden brown. Drain on paper toweling. Dust all over with powdered sugar. Serve with cherry sauce or plain. Other fruits may be substituted for cherries.

GRAPEFRUIT HAWAIIAN

DUCK FRICASSEE WITH PEANUT BUTTER SAUCE

ORANGE SALAD

PECAN CREAM PIE

For those who like dark meat of fowl there is nothing more delicious than duck or duckling. It is not, however, an economical fowl even when the price is low for there is but little meat on it. Once in awhile, especially when you want to entertain some person of epicurean taste, it will be worth while to undertake. Roast duck is a handsomer dish than this fricassee, and elsewhere we have a roast duck dinner, but this particular dish is a favorite with some. The flavor of orange is suitable to duck and in the roast fowl, orange flavors the meat and gravy. In this case it is simply the accompaniment. If preferred, a simple salad of sliced orange and sweet onion on lettuce may be substituted for that given. Buttered asparagus and parsley potatoes are recommended as accessories to the main fact.

Grapefruit Hawaiian

Cut grapefruit in half crossways. Loosen and remove membrane. Mix crushed pineapple with grapefruit pulp, return to the shells and put either a maraschino or a green cherry in the center or a section of canned tangerine. Serve cold.

Duck Fricassee with Peanut Butter Sauce

1 young duck
1 onion chopped
Fat for frying
2 tbsp. peanut butter
1 sweet red pepper or pimiento
⅛ tsp. cayenne
½ cupful mushrooms
1 tsp. salt

Separate duck into serving portions and cook in just water to cover until slightly tender. Take from kettle, drain, roll lightly in flour and fry in butter with a tablespoonful of finely chopped onion, until very tender and slightly browned. Mix two tablespoonfuls of peanut butter with the stock in which the duck was cooked, add one sweet red pepper, seeded and chopped (or pimiento), ⅛ teaspoon cayenne and one teaspoon of salt. Pour this over the fowl and let simmer until well heated through. A half cupful of cut mushrooms will further improve the flavor.

Orange Salad

3 oranges
2 tomatoes
1 green pepper
Lettuce
French Dressing

Peel oranges, divide in sections and cut sections into thirds. Scald tomatoes, peel and chill; cut in halves crosswise, then into wedge-shaped pieces. Remove seeds and white fiber from pepper and cut in rings. Arrange orange and tomatoes on lettuce, cress or chicory, with pepper rings overlapping around each mound.

Pecan Cream Pie

Yolks of 4 eggs
Whites of 2 eggs
1 cup heavy cream
1 cup sugar
1 cup pecans chopped fine

Beat the yolks of eggs to yellow foam. Beat whites stiff. Combine the two and add cream, nuts and sugar. Put in double boiler and cook until thick, stirring constantly. Put in a previously baked pastry shell, cover with the stiffly beaten whites of two eggs sweetened, and put in slow oven (350) to brown meringue.

MINESTRONE SOUP

JELLIED VEAL WITH SAUCE FRESH STRING BEANS

CANTALOUPE CUP

THIS is an excellent menu for company on a hot Sunday. The meat dish can be prepared the day before—in fact, it should be. The dessert is practically nothing to do, and so only the soup and the beans have to be done at the time. For that matter, this particular soup can be made some other time and a canned soup substituted here. The Minestrone, however, is a good nourishing soup, and should not be neglected. If the menu is used when new peas are at their best, or when fresh native asparagus is cheapest, either of these vegetables may be used instead of the beans, a salad added if wished.

Minestrone Soup

1 qt. beef stock
4 medium onions
3 medium carrots
2 cups shredded cabbage
½ cup macaroni
2 tbsp. butter
Salt, pepper
Grated Parmesan Cheese
1 cup tomatoes

Chop the onion, slice the carrots thin, shred the cabbage fine. Cook the vegetables in butter and add to the stock. When boiling, add the tomatoes and macaroni and boil until macaroni is done (about twenty minutes). Serve in soup plates with a teaspoonful of Parmesan cheese sprinkled over the top of each serving.

Jellied Veal with Sauce

3 lbs. veal or veal knuckle
1 large onion
2 tsp. salt
Worcestershire Sauce
Tabasco

Wipe the meat with damp cloth and cut into small pieces; cover with cold water and cook with the onion and salt until meat is very nearly tender. Set to one side until cool enough to handle. Remove the bones and onion and any undesirable portions. Cut the meat into fine pieces. Add to this meat the stock which should have boiled down to about two cupfuls. Season to taste with salt and pepper, two or three drops of tabasco sauce and a teaspoonful of Worcestershire sauce. Pack into a buttered (or oiled) bread pan about 3 inches deep, 9x5 inches at the top. Chill. If desired for better appearance, the bottom of the pan may be covered with thin slices of stuffed olives and gherkins (drained) before putting the meat mixture in. When ready to serve, unmold and serve, sliced, with this sauce:

1 pt. cream whipped
1 cupful mayonnaise
1 tsp. chopped onion
2½ cups chopped celery
¼ lb. blanched almonds coarsely chopped
2 hard cooked eggs chopped
Salt, pepper

Mix together and serve with the meat.

Cantaloupe Cup

Cut cantaloupes open crosswise and remove seeds and loose pulp. With small vegetable cutter, cut out balls, put in a bowl and chill. When ready to serve fill the cantaloupe shells with melon balls, white grapes and red cherries, either fresh or Maraschino. Pour the juice from a can of Maraschinos mixed with an equal quantity of sherry or claret over the fruit, and put a sprig of mint on top. The cantaloupes should be small in size.

FRENCH ONION SOUP
SALT PORK WITH CREAM GRAVY
MASHED TURNIPS AND POTATOES
ORANGE AND ONION SALAD
COCOANUT BREAD PUDDING

HERE is a farmer's menu for certain, but we urge that it be tried just *once*. Men who were raised on a farm are sure to like it, not only because it will recall youthful days (always so much pleasanter in retrospect than when passing), but because they really *will* like it. And try the potatoes and turnips mashed together too. The cream gravy will go as well with the one as the other and excellently with both. The orange and onion salad is nothing new but gives just the right tang to the salt pork dinner. And, since the potato is mixed with turnip the bread in the dessert will not provide too much starch for once.

French Onion Soup

3 medium sized onions
3 tbsp. butter
2 qts. of stock
Salt and pepper

Peel and slice onions thinly. Heat butter in saucepan and add onions. Cover and simmer over a slow fire until the onions are tender and not browned. Add to stock in soup kettle (hot water and bouillon cubes will do but meat stock is better) and simmer for half an hour. Then add salt and pepper, and put through a purée sieve or not as desired. Serve hot with toast or thick slices of French bread.

Salt Pork with Cream Gravy

1 lb. thinly sliced salt pork
2 cups top milk
Salt and pepper
Flour

Put the slices of pork into cold water and let stand one hour. Drain and wipe dry. Have frying pan very hot. Dip each slice of pork in flour and fry until crisp. Place on hot platter while gravy is being made.

Cream Gravy

Leave two tablespoonfuls of the fat in frying pan and into this blend two tablespoons of flour, mixing smooth. When blended add the milk very slowly, stirring continuously. When the gravy is smooth, cook gently for 5 minutes, season, and either pour over the meat or serve separately.

Mashed Turnips and Potatoes

Yellow turnips are best. Peel, wash and slice them. Cook in a kettle of water until tender. Drain and mash; season with salt, pepper and plenty of butter. To these add the same amount of mashed and seasoned potatoes. Dress with a tablespoonful of melted butter and a dash of black pepper.

Orange and Onion Salad

Thinly sliced Bermuda or Italian onion, alternated with half slices of orange, served on lettuce with French Dressing.

Cocoanut Bread Pudding

1 slice of bread for each serving
Cocoanut shredded
Evaporated milk or top milk
Cream

Dip each slice of bread in diluted evaporated or top milk. Take out and roll in shredded cocoanut and lay in well buttered baking dish. Bake in oven at 450 for fifteen minutes. Serve with cream whipped.

TOMATO JUICE COCKTAIL
FRIED SMELTS BAKED HOMINY
CUCUMBERS WITH SOUR CREAM DRESSING
LEMON SPONGE PIE

SMELTS are not always in season but when they are they are a very delicious and economical fish. Dr. David Starr Jordan, famous ichthyologist of Stanford University, described smelt as "the finest food fish in the world—tender, fragrant, digestible." It is best known in the region of the Columbia River, but can be had at times in the east and in middle states. It is found in the spring in rivers and brooks where it runs to spawn. Then is when it is cheapest. The smelt is small and tiresome to fry but well worth it. A sour cream dressing for sliced cucumbers will be found in page 196.

Fried Smelts

Choose the largest, wipe them dry and roll them in flour. Put two or three tablespoonfuls of oil (according to size of skillet) in frying pan, bring it to a heat, but do not let it brown. Lay the fish in, not crowding, and brown on both sides. If a second pan is to be cooked, wipe the pan clean with paper, put in fresh oil and repeat. Do not try to fry a second batch in the floury fat left from the first. This method also keeps the fish from breaking. Serve on a hot platter garnished with lemon slices, slices of beet, and with plenty of tartar sauce. (See Page 206.)

Baked Hominy

1 cup hominy (cereal)
1 qt. milk
2 tbsp. butter
2 eggs
Salt

Heat the milk, stir the hominy in and cook together in double boiler for one hour. When done, stir in the butter and salt and cool. Then add two eggs well beaten, put in a buttered baking dish and bake for twenty minutes with oven at 350. Serve as a vegetable.

Cucumbers with Sour Cream Dressing

Peel and slice chilled fresh cucumbers and place in glass salad bowl. Make a dressing as follows:

½ cup sour cream
1 tbsp. vinegar
1 tsp. sugar
¼ tsp. paprika
Salt, pepper

Mix cream, vinegar and seasonings thoroughly together and pour over the cucumbers.

Lemon Sponge Pie

Juice of 1 lemon
1 cup sugar
3 tbsp. flour
Yolks of two eggs
¾ cup sweet milk
1 tbsp. melted butter
Egg Whites

Stir all ingredients together; add the stiffly beaten whites of eggs; put in a pastry-lined pie plate and bake forty minutes in oven at 350, until the pie is a golden brown.

BONED LAMB MINT ICE
PEAS AND LETTUCE
NEVER FAIL GINGERBREAD AND WHIPPED CREAM

THIS is a good menu for a summer Sunday when peas are at their best. Of course in cities peas can be had for many months out of the year, but since we are planning for those who must be economical in their purchasing, we suggest using the menus as near the season in which various foods are found in home markets as can conveniently be done. Having an ice to accompany the meat makes a cold appetizer undesirable, so if any first course is desired, we suggest a clear tomato soup. No salad is needed with the ice and the two vegetables. With the rice on the meat dish and the gingerbread for dessert, neither potatoes nor bread are needed.

Boned Lamb

3 lbs. boned lamb
1 onion
1 small clove of garlic
1 tsp. paprika
1 green sweet pepper
½ cup orange juice
1 tbsp. vinegar
Sale and pepper
Butter
Boiled rice

Cut lamb into small pieces and brown them in hot butter; add minced onion and seeded green pepper chopped; add orange juice, vinegar, salt, pepper and enough boiling water to cover; cook slowly until meat is tender. Heap dry boiled rice on a platter and lay the meat around it. Thicken the gravy and pour over or serve in a boat.

Mint Ice

½ lb. After dinner mints
1 qt. bottled or diluted evaporated milk

Pour the cold milk into the freezer can. Pack and freeze slightly. Then add the mints which have been thoroughly crushed with rolling pin. Add a tablespoonful of minced mint leaves, or a very small amount of vegetable coloring. Freeze.

Peas and Lettuce

2 cups shelled peas
2 tbsp. butter
1 large head lettuce
1 cup water or bouillon
3 small onions
Sprig parsley
½ tsp. salt
⅛ tsp. pepper

Melt butter in saucepan, and add raw peas and stir. Add hot water or meat stock, shredded lettuce, onion and seasonings. Simmer until tender and serve in same juice. This is a Southern method of cooking peas and very delicious.

Never Fail Gingerbread

1 cup molasses
½ cup sugar
½ cup shortening
2 eggs
2 cups flour
½ tsp. ginger
¼ tsp. allspice
1 tsp. cinnamon
2 tsp. soda
1 cup boiling water
½ tsp. salt

Mix ingredients as listed, dissolving soda in boiling water. Bake in a moderate oven—350 degrees—for forty minutes. Serve with whipped cream.

CHIPPED BEEF—CORN CASSEROLE
PEACH SALAD
AUNT CORDELIA'S JELLY ROLL

THE old-fashioned jelly roll is nowadays seldom seen. Why do you suppose this is? Is it because there is no preserve closet to which to go at a moment's notice for jelly? Or is it because you really do have to go to a little trouble in making the cake? Or is it because we used to have jelly cake for supper, and we no longer have suppers? No matter what the reason it seems a pity. And whether you follow the suggestion of having the jelly roll as dessert for dinner, or whether you substitute a custard, cream or apple pie and serve the jelly roll with a cup of tea in the afternoon—at any rate, and for old time's sake, some morning when the kitchen looks particularly attractive and outside interests are not too many, try Aunt Cordelia's Jelly Cake.

Chipped Beef Corn Casserole

¼ lb. chipped beef
1 can corn
1 onion
1 green pepper
Salt, pepper
2 cups fresh or evaporated milk (diluted)
3 tbsp. butter
4 tbsp. flour
1½ cups bread crumbs

Cut beef into small pieces. Mince onion and pepper. Melt butter in skillet and sauté pepper and onion until tender. Add beef and cook until it frizzles at edges. Stir in flour and milk alternately and slowly until smooth and thick. Butter a casserole and partly fill with mixture. Add layer of bread crumbs, then remainder of beef and corn mixture, and finally the remainder of bread crumbs. Bake in 400 oven for twenty minutes.

Peach Salad

1 can halved peaches
½ lb. cottage cheese
Stuffed olives
Mayonnaise
Chopped nuts
Parsley

Drain the peaches. Season cheese with salt, pepper and paprika. Build a small ball of cheese around one stuffed olive. Roll each ball of cheese in minced parsley and set in cavity of half a peach. Lay on a lettuce leaf, and serve with a tablespoonful of mayonnaise into which some of the peach juice has been beaten. Sprinkle with chopped nuts.

Aunt Cordelia's Jelly Roll

2 eggs, separated
¾ cup sugar
4 tbsp. cold water
1 cup flour
2 tsp. baking powder
½ tsp. salt
1 tsp. vanilla
1 cup currant jelly

Beat yolks. Add sugar, gradually beating after each addition. Add water and beat. Sift baking powder and salt with flour. Add to sugar and egg and beat. Add vanilla. Fold in egg whites beaten stiff. Pour in shallow oblong greased tin to fill one-fourth of an inch. Bake for twenty minutes at 325. Sprinkle a clean towel with powdered sugar, and lay the hot cake on it. Spread with jelly and roll.

STUFFED PICNIC HAM

SWISS CHARD SPAGHETTI

PEACH PICKLES

APRICOT LEMON ICE

For a first course, we recommend a fruit cocktail of whatever is in season. There is starch in the stuffing for the ham and in the spaghetti and although there is fruit in the dessert, a rather tart first course to start off with will be found appetizing—fresh cherries, strawberries, grapes, or grapefruit. If the menu is used when chard is not to be found, spinach can usually be had, or chicory. In summer other greens, such as beet, turnip top, dandelions may be substituted. Young radish tops, mustard tops before they grow harsh, are all worth trying if you have access to a garden. Cowslips, just when they are in bud, are a rare treat, but both rubber boots and enterprise must be engaged in getting them. Peach pickles are appropriate and tasty but others may be used instead.

Stuffed Picnic Ham

1 large picnic ham

Stuffing

Soak the ham overnight. Then, with a sharp knife cut the meat entirely away from the bone and remove. (Use the bone for pea soup another day.) Fill the cavity with regular bread stuffing such as is used for poultry (or an apple stuffing given below) and sew up. Take a strip of cloth and bind tightly around the ham to preserve shape and fasten. Boil the ham slowly for three or four hours or until tender. Take out and cool. Remove any skin and excess fat, fill with apple stuffing, cover with a mixture of brown sugar and 1 teaspoon mustard, decorate with cloves and preserved or dried cherries, and bake until sugar has browned.

Apple Stuffing

1 cup chopped apples
4 slices of bacon
2 cups bread crumbs
Salt, pepper
¼ cup onion

Cut bacon into small pieces and fry to brown in frying pan. Add apple, onion, bread crumbs and seasoning. Simmer a few minutes to blend and then use as stuffing. Should be firm to handle.

Swiss Chard

Shred the leaves from the white center rib, wash and cook in a very small amount of water. When tender, drain, cut criss-cross, and dress with butter, pepper, salt, a few drops of lemon. Or serve with French Dressing.

Apricot Lemon Ice

1 No. 3 can of apricots
1 lemon
1 cup sugar
1 cup water

Drain, mash apricots and put through coarse sieve. Add juice of lemon. Bring sugar and water to a boil and when cool add the apricot pulp. Pack in ice and salt and freeze, or freeze in refrigerator, stirring every half hour for first two hours. Allow three hours. When ready to serve, cut angel food cake into rings size of large cookie and hollow out center. Fill this with the Apricot Ice.

SOUTHERN COCKTAIL
ROAST LOIN OF PORK—APPLE RINGS
SWEET POTATO FLUFF
DIVINITY LEMON PIE

PLENTY of fruit and green or raw vegetables should accompany pork. To this menu a plain lettuce salad with Russian dressing would act as an excellent appetizer, or one of tomatoes and lettuce. A "dish of greens"—chard, beets, chicory or any of the other tops would go well with it. The sweet potato soufflé is rich, and perhaps you would prefer riced potatoes here, and serve the soufflé some day with broiled ham. The Divinity Pie is a light dessert, and since there is fruit in the cocktail, and apple with the meat, this seems a reasonably good finish. However, an ice may be preferred, such as raspberry sherbet or cherry ice. Certainly nothing heavy should be added.

Southern Cocktail

¼ cup cantaloupe balls
¼ cup white grapes
¼ cup ginger ale
Mint leaves

Chill cantaloupe and grapes. Arrange them in sherbet glasses and pour ginger ale over. Garnish with mint leaves and a green or red cherry. This is one serving.

Roast Loin of Pork—Apple Rings

Wipe meat with damp flannel cloth. Rub with salt, pepper and one-half teaspoon of sage mixed together. Dredge with flour. Place in roasting pan with one-half cup of water and cook in a moderate oven (350) allowing twenty-five minutes to the pound. Baste every fifteen or twenty minutes. Garnish with apple rings, alternated with sprigs of parsley.

Apple Rings

Wipe the cored unpeeled red, tart apples. Slice in half-inch rings and sauté until tender in hot butter. Serve the pork roast on a platter surrounded by apple rings. In the cavity of each ring place a ripe olive.

Sweet Potato Fluff

2 cups mashed sweet potato, hot
1 cup hot milk
2 tbsp. sugar
2 tbsp. butter
2 eggs
1 tsp. nutmeg
½ cup raisins chopped
½ cup nut meats
½ doz. marshmallows

Heat milk, add sugar and salt, add butter and stir until well blended. Add this mixture to potatoes and beat until light and fluffy. Add nutmeg, raisins and nuts. Fold in beaten whites of eggs. Pour the mixture into a buttered baking dish. Arrange marshmallows one-half inch apart over the top. Bake in moderate oven (375) until the fluff is set and the marshmallows are a delicate brown.

Divinity Lemon Pie

3 eggs
1 cup sugar
4 tbsp. lemon juice
½ tsp. grated lemon rind
3 tbsp. hot water

Beat egg yolks until thick. Gradually add one-half cup of sugar and mix thoroughly. Add lemon juice and rind. Add hot water and cook in top of double boiler to a thin custard or when mixture coats the spoon. Add one-half cup sugar gradually to beaten egg whites and fold into custard. Fill previously baked pie crust and brown in moderate oven. Temperature 325. Time in baking thirty minutes. Use ten-inch pie-plate.

BEEFSTEAK SMOTHERED IN ONIONS

STUFFED EGGPLANT

MOLDED PEAR SALAD

FROSTED STRAWBERRY PIE

THIS is not a dinner to be eaten before going to the opera or to a bridge party, but on a cold rainy night when a man is justified in watching the clock from three-thirty in the afternoon with a vision of a nice long evening at home, it will probably just about throw him into a fever of anticipation from the moment his nose gets through the door. He probably would like porter house better, but round or flank, well pounded, well seasoned and buttered and *smothered* in onions will give you an opportunity to get a little ahead of the budget.

Beefsteak Smothered in Onions

Peel and slice thin as many onions as will be needed. Throw them into cold water for an hour or longer. Drain very dry and then cook them until tender in hot pork fat or butter and season. Broil or pan-broil steak until done on the outside and slightly rare inside. Remove to a hot platter and cover with onions. Set in oven for a minute or two to heat through. Have everything else ready and serve at once. Garnish platter with slender strips of dill pickle.

Stuffed Egg-plant

1 medium sized eggplant
¼ cup tomato sauce
¼ cup sweet corn
¼ cup minced ham
1 tbs. butter
Paprika
Buttered Crumbs

Cut eggplant in half and cook until tender in salted water. Drain, scoop out the pulp, chop this fine and mix with tomato sauce, corn, ham, butter and paprika. Fill shells with this mixture and cover with crumbs. Bake in hot oven until well browned.

Molded Pear Salad

1 can Bartlett Pears
Juice of 1 lemon
Sugar
1 tbsp. gelatin
Pear juice
Ginger Snaps

Cut each pear half into 3 sections. To the pear and lemon juice add enough of any other juice, if necessary, to make 1 pint. Soften gelatin in a little cold water. Heat the fruit juice and add gelatin to it. Sweeten to taste. Lay the fruit in a rinsed mold and pour juice over it. Put away to set and chill. To serve, turn the mold onto a serving plate and cover it with rolled ginger snaps; cover this with whipped cream, and sprinkle ginger snap crumbs thickly over this.

Frosted Strawberry Pie

Plain Pastry
3 cups strawberries
1 cup sugar
3 tbs. flour
Pinch salt

Line a pie plate with plain pastry; put in 3 cups of hulled strawberries; mix flour, sugar and salt together and sift over the berries. Cover with crust. Bake in hot (450) oven for 20 minutes; reduce heat to 400 and bake 10 minutes longer. Remove from oven and cool. Make a stiff boiled frosting and cover pie unevenly.

VEGETABLE SOUP WITH FANCY NOODLES
CASSEROLE OF PORK AND POTATOES
FRIED APPLES AND ONIONS
BANANA GINGER ALE PUDDING

EGG noodles can now be had in fancy shapes—shells, bow knots and other figures. They are very interesting and worth hunting up. The glass casserole is another invention of the present day for which we should give housekeeping thanks since it can be brought to the table without disturbing the food which is cooked in it. Some have silver or other metal rings to further enhance their beauty and protect the table. Even chicken can be roasted in a casserole but for turkey we still prefer the old roaster and platter. A turkey could never, without great loss to his dignity, be brought to the table on anything but the platter and preferably one belonging to some forbear of the family in whose service he now lies in state.

Casserole of Pork and Potatoes

2 lbs. lean pork shoulder
6 medium potatoes
2 cups milk
2 tbs. butter
1/4 tsp. sage
Salt, pepper

Cut the meat into individual servings; brown in hot fat in frying pan; season with salt, pepper and sage. Slice half the potatoes very thin into a well greased baking dish, sprinkle with salt and pepper, dot with butter and sift flour over. Lay the pieces of pork on this bed of potatoes and cover with remainder of sliced potatoes; repeat seasonings and butter, dredge with flour. Pour the milk over and bake in moderate oven until potatoes are very tender—about an hour or a little more. Smoked ham may be used instead of pork and without the sage.

Fried Apples and Onions

Wash and core without peeling, well flavored apples. Peel and slice half as many onions as apples. Heat bacon or other cooking fat (using half butter with any) in a frying pan and cook the onions until slightly tender. Season with salt and pepper, stirring until they are all cooked alike without browning. Now cover with the sliced onions, season these with salt, pepper, a sprinkling of sugar, some dots of butter, put a cover over and let cook until apples are tender. Enough fat should be added to keep the bottom from burning. Stir as little as possible. The amount of onions used depends on individual taste.

Banana Ginger Ale Pudding

2 tbsp. gelatin
1 tbsp. cold water
1 1/2 cups ginger ale
2 tbsp. sugar
1 tbsp. lemon juice

Soften the gelatine in cold water and dissolve over hot water. Add the ginger ale with sugar and lemon juice. Fill molds half full of this mixture and let harden, then add the following mixture.

3/4 cup milk
1 egg
2 tbsp. sugar
1 tbsp. gelatin
2 tbsp. cold water
1 banana
1/2 cup cream

Heat the milk, add the beaten egg and sugar and cook until thickened. Add the gelatin softened in cold water. Let stand until partly stiff and then fold in the mashed banana and whipped cream. Place in molds on top of ginger ale jelly. Let harden. Serve with whipped cream and bits of preserved ginger with some of the juice.

CHESHIRE CHEESE SPECIALTY PIE
BAKED ONIONS AND RICE
CRANBERRY-RAISIN TART

Now here is a dish named with reason, plausibility and even veracity. This is really a dish that is—or was—served at that famous old Inn in London called the Cheshire Cheese. Pigeons are not always available and so we tried it with veal. The Cheshire Cheese would probably renounce the whole dish and cut it off without a shilling, but to our way of thinking, never having tasted it in its natural environment and haunted by the spirit of Ben Jonson and other immortals who have graced that noted hostelry with their presence, it was pretty good. Young chicken would have probably been better but we were just fresh out of chickens that day too. The person who presented us with this recipe had actually eaten it in London, under the sacred roof of the Cheshire Cheese and so we did not invite her in when we tried it out. Sometime when we get our country place with a barn for which we have no other use than raising pigeons we shall try it again as it ought to be. In the meantime, we hand it on to you to do with as you will—and can.

Cheshire Cheese Specialty Pie

1½ lbs. fine round steak
Fat salt pork
2 lamb's kidneys
Salted flour
Minced onion
2 or 3 pigeons
½ lbs. mushrooms
½ tbsp. butter
1 tbsp. ketchup
1 tsp. sauce
Pastry

Cut the steak into inch wide strips, roll each strip around a short strip of salt pork and fasten with toothpicks; dice the kidneys and toss all in salted and peppered flour, adding a pinch of dry mustard. Cook onion in fat for five minutes; when very hot add the meat and stir until all is brown; add the pigeons quartered, cover with boiling water, cover and simmer until the meat is all tender. Remove picks from meat, add the broken mushrooms which have been stewed in butter for five minutes, also the liquid, ketchup, brown gravy or any sauce. Place all in a deep glass baking dish, cover with a rather thick, rich pastry crust and bake until richly brown.

Baked Onions and Rice

2 cups cooked rice
8 onions
1 green pepper
2 tbsp. flour
1 cup milk
1 cup grated cheese
3 tbsp. butter
1 tsp. salt
Pepper

Boil onions until tender in salted water. Melt butter, add flour, seasonings and milk. Cook until smooth. Add half the cheese and stir to the boiling point. Lay onions, broken up, and rice alternately in a buttered casserole and pour sauce over. Cover with bread crumbs and cheese. Bake 15 to 20 minutes in 350 oven.

Cranberry-Raisin Tart

Line individual pie tins or patty pans with pastry; put in a generous layer of washed cranberries and cover with sugar to sweeten. Over this place seeded raisins to completely cover cranberries. Sprinkle with rather coarsely chopped walnut meats and cover with pastry top. Bake in moderate oven 25 to 30 minutes, or until crust is golden brown. Serve hot with or without whipped cream.

SAVORY MEAT CAKES GOLDEN ONIONS
BANANA WHIP CREAM PIE

By this time we are not deceived by any of these fancy names. Therefore, under no flag but our own we present our old friend hamburg with a plain title, the soundness of which we can vouch for. Hamburg *can* be made savory by a skillful hand. And how we ever got along before we had hamburger I cannot imagine. *I* didn't have hamburger when I was a young housekeeper. I had to ask the butcher to grind me up a pound and a half of beef, a pound of veal and half a pound of salt pork when I wanted to make a meat loaf for the picnic. And neither did I have tomato soup all tinned and ready to make tomato sauce. As a matter of fact, if it was out of the tomato season I went to the shelf where my own canned tomatoes were and made my own sauce. (And I still think it was better than I can make with the prepared material—although it took me longer.) But, having our steak already ground (so long as you can depend on your meat-man) is a great convenience and we still maintain that it is not only a convenience but an economy worth practicing in all the ways we recommend and others which you may know and we have not yet found out.

Savory Meat Cakes

1 lb. hamburg steak
1 lb. raw chopped potatoes
1 egg
Tomato sauce
Chopped onion
Salt, pepper

Mix the meat and potato together; beat the egg and to it add about a tablespoonful of milk. Mix all together adding more milk if necessary but just enough to bind the mixture. Form into small cakes not larger than an egg. Sear on both sides in hot fat, then put them in a greased casserole and pour over them a thick tomato sauce seasoned with the chopped onion according to taste. The sauce should come only about halfway up on the meat. Do not cover. Cook in moderate oven for 20 minutes.

Golden Onions

Boil or steam large onions. When soft, but not falling to pieces, season with salt and pepper, place them in a pie dish well greased. Pour over them a very little of the water in which they were cooked (or hot water) and generous quantity of butter. Cover with equal parts of fine bread crumbs and grated cheese. Bake for about half an hour in moderate oven.

Banana Whip Cream Pie

3 medium sized bananas
Whites of 2 large eggs
Pinch salt
1 cup sugar
1 tsp. vanilla

Make a rich pie crust and bake it for 10 minutes. Remove from oven and cool. Mash bananas, beat whites of eggs and mix with banana. Beat all together, put in crust and bake 20 to 30 minutes in moderate oven. Cool and cover with whipped cream.

ROAST LEG OF VENISON

RUSSIAN SALAD

PEANUT BRITTLE-PEACH DESSERT

MOST meats, especially mutton, beef and venison are better for aging a little. Venison is a dry meat and should either be larded with salt pork, or frequently basted while cooking with fat. The leg, a saddle or a haunch are cooked the same as mutton. Venison, like lamb, should be of fine grain and pink in color. As the animal grows older the color becomes less pronounced. Larding is a method of introducing fat into meat which is naturally dry. Salt pork or bacon are the meats used for this purpose. Pork is usually preferred. It must be young firm pork, and cold. The thin line of muscular flesh that lies between the rind and fat is the part used. A larding needle is threaded with these narrow strips (after they have stood on ice or in ice water to harden) and then drawn through the outer surface of the meat to be larded. These slits of pork are called lardoons. A very sharp knife must be used to cut the lardoons. The stitches should be about an inch deep and nearly an inch in length. Sweet potatoes are good with venison.

Roast Leg of Venison

A leg of venison is cooked the same as a leg of lamb, allowing a little less time because lamb must be well done while venison is better slightly rare. A saddle or haunch of venison is cooked the same as shoulder of mutton. To cook the leg, wipe it with a damp cloth, then sprinkle with salt and pepper, and spread with melted butter or lard with pork. Venison is a rather dry meat and fat must be added. Cook in a hot oven (450) for half an hour, then reduce heat to 350 and allow fifteen minutes to the pound. Turn over when half done, sprinkle lightly with flour, salt and pepper. When the meat is nearly done and begins to brown, spread with currant jelly, add a little water to the pan and baste frequently. Serve with Currant Jelly Sauce (page 203).

Russian Salad

½ cup cooked string beans
½ cup small lima beans
½ cup cauliflower flowerlets
½ cup green peas
½ cup diced beets
½ cup chopped celery
French Dressing
Mayonnaise
Hard Cooked Egg

Mix all ingredients and marinate in French Dressing for two hours. Drain, put in a salad bowl that has been rubbed with cut garlic clove, lay a mound of thick mayonnaise on top, garnish with slices of hard cooked egg.

Peanut-Brittle and Peach Dessert

1 small can sliced peaches
½ lb. peanut brittle
½ pt. heavy cream

Boil liquor of peaches to heavy syrup and chill. Put peanut brittle through grinder using medium fine knife. Whip the cream. Arrange slices of peaches in bottom of individual serving dish. Divide ground brittle in two parts. Add one-half to the syrup and fold the remainder into whipped cream. Cover sliced peaches with syrup mixture and top with whipped cream mixture. This should be served with a salty cracker.

IRISH LAMB STEW—TORETTA STYLE
SAVORY PEAS WITH RICE
APPLE-CABBAGE SALAD
LEMON SPONGE

DON'T ask us what "Toretta" means. If we are ever again privileged to dine at the Algonquin, and we find that Irish Lamb Stew is still being served every Monday, perhaps we may screw up sufficient courage to ask. But Algonquin waiters are pretty haughty, and since the ingredients, so far as we can see, sound reasonably familiar, we have thought best so far, to let it go. Moreover, where it says "boquet garnie"—while we have an idea what it means, we found it answered just about as well to use our old standby Kitchen Bouquet. We did not learn just how they make their dumplings, but our own are good enough and we use them, for ourselves, whether with lamb, or beef or chicken or veal. And the whole thing boils down to using our biscuit dough with two cups of flour, two teaspoons of baking powder, one teaspoon of salt, one tablespoonful of lard and two of butter. This we mix to a batter just stiff enough to drop and then drop it onto the meat about twenty minutes before it is done. Other folks steam it to make sure it doesn't fall.

(Served every Monday at the Algonquin)

Irish Lamb Stew—Toretta Style

2 lbs. neck, shoulder and breast of lamb
½ doz. small onions
Boquet garnie, or Kitchen Bouquet
1½ tsp. salt
6 small carrots
12 raw potatoes
1 lb. riced potatoes
Chopped parsley
1 tbsp. Worcestershire Sauce
Dumplings

Cut the meat in two-inch squares; put in pot in salted water and bring to boil. Drain meat and cool. Put back in pot with fresh water to cover; add the bouquet, onions, carrots, potatoes and salt. Cook until vegetables are soft. Prepare extra riced potatoes for thickening and add to the stew and boil for five minutes. Add the chopped parsley, Worcestershire. Serve with hot biscuits or dumplings.

Savory Peas with Rice

1 cup rice
2 cups canned peas
½ cup minced ham
1 tsp. grated onion
1 tbsp. butter
Salt and pepper

Boil rice in salted water, drain and rinse. Add peas, then liquor; add ham, onion, butter and seasonings. Cook 10 minutes slowly and serve hot.

Apple-Cabbage Salad

Shred fine firm head of cabbage very fine and throw in cold water. Peel and core well flavored apples and throw in cold water as peeled. Drain both and mix together with mayonnaise dressing. Sprinkle with chopped nut meats on top. Serve on lettuce.

Lemon Sponge

6 eggs
1 cup sugar
2 lemons
¼ cup butter
2 tbsp. cream

Beat the egg yolks with sugar, juice of lemons, grated rind of one, butter and cream. Line a pudding dish with stale sponge cake and pour the mixture in. Bake 20 minutes in moderate oven. Cover with meringue made from whites of eggs and confectioners' sugar and brown in slow oven.

CREAM OF TOMATO SOUP
BAKED PORK CHOPS—FRIED CREAM OF WHEAT MUSH
TURNIPS AND APPLESAUCE
CHERRY COBBLER

THIS would make a good menu for a late fall day when turnips are fresh and especially since pork is more of a cold weather meat. Yellow turnips or rutabagas have a stronger, but also a sweeter flavor than white turnips. The latter are sometimes bitter, and also watery. When very young these are good sliced and dressed with either French Dressing or vinegar, salt and pepper, but for the cooked dish, we prefer what farmers refer to as "beggies." They should be carefully washed, sliced to about a quarter of an inch or a little more, peeled and thrown into cold water. They require longer boiling than white turnips—about forty to forty-five minutes; mashed and seasoned with plenty of butter, salt and pepper they are a delicious vegetable. The gravy from baked or roast pork, a brown gravy highly seasoned, is good on them. Since pork chops are a lean and dry meat, a little water should be added to the pan in which they are baked—not more than two tablespoonfuls, but just enough to keep them moist. A bay leaf in the pan, or a *very* little shaved garlic adds to the flavor.

Baked Pork Chops–Fried Mush

Trim number of chops required and arrange in shallow baking pan; sprinkle with salt, pepper and powdered sage. Put in hot oven (450) and bake for ten to fifteen minutes (or until done) basting with hot water in which a tablespoonful of butter has been melted. When done, lay chops on platter, arrange slices of fried mush around the edge and garnish with ripe olives, radish roses and parsley. The mush should have been made, moulded and allowed to get cold beforehand. A gravy can be made from the drippings in the pan.

Turnips and Applesauce

3 cups mashed turnips
1 cup hot applesauce
2 tbsp. butter
½ tsp. salt
Buttered Bread Crumbs

Mix together the turnips and applesauce (unsweetened), butter, salt. Turn into a well buttered baking dish, cover with bread crumbs and bake in 400 oven for 10-12 minutes, just to heat through.

Cherry Cobbler

1 cup flour
1½ tsp. baking powder
½ tsp. salt
Milk
2 tbsp. butter
1 cup sugar
2 cups cherries (unsweetened)

Mix flour, baking powder, and salt and sift together. Blend the butter into this and add enough milk to make a soft dough—just soft enough to stir. Put the drained, unsweetened cherries in the bottom of a buttered baking dish and sprinkle with sugar. Spread the dough over and bake three quarters of an hour in a 375 oven. Serve with sweetened cream or

Cherry Sauce

1 cup cherry juice
½ cup sugar
1½ tbsp. corn starch
1 tbsp. butter

If there is not a cupful of juice from the can, add other juice to it to make that amount. Heat this in a double boiler. Mix cornstarch and sugar in a little water and add to juice. Cook until it thickens, stirring all the time. Serve warm with the Cobbler.

PEACH AND MELON COCKTAIL
HAM ESCALOPED WITH POTATOES
VEGETABLE SALAD
CRANBERRY FRAPPÉ

If this menu is used at a time when cantaloupe is out of season, avocado can be substituted, or canned pears although with the latter it will be more insipid and less unusual. In that case, a little preserved ginger might be added. The scallop of ham and potatoes is a very tasty dish and may be made with or without onions depending upon the family's taste. Its perfection depends upon getting the amount of milk and flour to result in exactly the right consistency. We suggest using a glass casserole through which it can be seen whether the potato is browning too much, or if it is getting too dry in which case more milk can be added. The glass baking dish may be used as a serving dish as well.

Peach and Melon Cocktail

1 can halved peaches
1 melon
Confectioners' Sugar
Lemon juice
Ginger Ale

Cut balls from melon from which seeds have been removed. Cut peach halves in cubes. Both should be chilled. Arrange equal quantities of each in cocktail glasses and sprinkle one tablespoonful of confectioners' sugar, one tablespoon of peach syrup and one teaspoon of lemon juice over each. At serving, fill glasses with chilled ginger ale. Garnish with a mint leaf or red cherry on top.

Ham Escalloped with Potato

The following will serve six generously. One small Daisy ham, about one and a half quarts of sliced potatoes, four medium sized onions. Choose a ham that has not too much fat, or buy the end of a ham and cut pieces suitable for serving from it. (The bone can be used for bean or pea soup or a boiled dinner.) Put a layer of ham in the bottom of the dish and cover with a thick layer of sliced potatoes and over these a layer of onion. Sprinkle with salt, pepper and a dredging of flour and dot with butter. Repeat this until the dish is full, and over it all pour either diluted evaporated milk or whole milk to cover. Bake in a moderate oven for an hour or until potatoes are tender.

Vegetable Salad

Grate raw carrot, shave raw cabbage, and heap inside a green pepper ring placed on a lettuce leaf. Top with mayonnaise.

Cranberry Frappé

1 qt. cranberries
2 cups water
1 cup sugar
Juice of 2 lemons

Cook cranberries in water eight minutes and then force through sieve. Add sugar and lemon juice, and freeze to a mush using equal parts of salt and ice, or freeze in refrigerator tray for three hours. Stir three times during the first hour and a half.

CRANBERRY COCKTAIL
PORK SAUSAGE IN RICE
APPLE RINGS AND COTTAGE CHEESE
QUAKER PUMPKIN PIE

CLEAR tomato soup is suggested on account of its tartness. A cream soup would be too heavy. With this menu neither bread nor potatoes are necessary since rice furnishes the starch. For another vegetable, mashed turnips or some kind of greens are recommended. If half pork and half beef is used, the meat should be more highly seasoned. The Quaker Pumpkin Pie may be made in individual patty shells if desired.

Pork Sausage in Rice

1 lb. pork sausage
1 cup rice cooked
1 sweet pepper
Milk

Cook rice one half hour in double boiler. Cool and add to it the pepper chopped fine. Form sausage into small cakes and fry on both sides until brown but not done. Line a well greased baking dish with half the rice and pepper. Put in the sausage cakes and fat from the pan. Cover with remainder of rice and add milk enough to just cover, no more. Sprinkle with paprika and bake 30 minutes at 400 degrees.

Apple Rings with Cottage Cheese

4 red apples
½ lb. cottage cheese
¼ lb. cinnamon candies
1 cup sugar
1½ cups water
1 tsp. lemon juice
1 tsp. gelatin
Lettuce

Boil water, sugar and cinnamon candies together until candies have dissolved. Core (do not peel) apples and cut in about three thick slices. Put slices of apple in syrup and boil until tender, not soft. Cool in the syrup and then drain on paper toweling. Add the teaspoonful of lemon juice to the syrup and the teaspoonful of gelatin to a pint of liquid. Dissolve gelatin first in a small amount of cold water. Let this set. When ready to serve place a ring of apple on a white lettuce leaf, fill with seasoned Cottage Cheese and garnish with cubes of the jelly from the jellied juice in which the apple has cooked. Serve mayonnaise separately.

Quaker Pumpkin Pie

4 eggs
1 cup sugar
2 tsp. cinnamon
½ tsp. ginger
½ tsp. nutmeg
¼ tsp. salt
2 cups evaporated milk
1 tbsp. melted butter
7 tbsp. cooked pumpkin

Beat the yolks of the eggs, add sugar, salt, spices, milk, pumpkin and butter. Fold in beaten egg whites last. Fill crust as full as possible and bake in oven at 500 degrees for ten minutes; then lower heat and bake at 325 for fifty-five minutes. This makes a large pie.

FILLET OF SOLE
TOMATOES WITH BREAD STUFFING
STRAWBERRY CHARLOTTE

Fillet of Sole is one of the most popular and most delicious kinds of fish that comes to our markets. As a matter of fact, a fillet is a particular cut of fish—a steak, as it were. And as still further matter of fact, what we usually find in our markets masquerading under the name of fillet of sole, is really a fillet of flounder and none the worse for it either. The real "sole" is not common. Fillet of sole is usually a rather expensive fish because it *is* a steak so to speak, and you have to pay for the discarded bones and waste that you usually buy in other fish. However, you do not have the bother of such waste. Fillet of sole is usually rolled and fried in deep fat—a most delicious way of cooking it. This particular recipe is the contribution of one of the best known home economists in the commercial field.

Fillet of Sole

2 lbs. butter
1 large onion finely chopped
2 tbsp. chopped parsley
1½ lbs. fillet of sole
Salt and pepper
1 bay leaf
1½ cups milk
Whole cloves

Melt butter in frying pan and sauté the onion and parsley in it. Sprinkle the fish with salt and pepper and put in frying pan with onion and parsley. Lay half a dozen whole cloves and the bay leaf on the fish. Add milk, cover and bake in hot oven (400) for 20 minutes. Serve with the following sauce:

2 tbsp. butter
3 tbsp. flour
hard cooked egg yolk
1 tbsp. parsley chopped
3 tbsp. India Relish
1 tsp. Worcestershire Sauce

Melt butter in saucepan, add flour and blend. Strain and add the liquid that is in the pan in which fish was baked (about 1¼ cupfuls). Cook, stirring constantly until thick. Then add crumbled hard boiled egg yolk, chopped parsley, India Relish and Worcestershire Sauce. Place the fish on a hot platter, pour the sauce over it and garnish with eighths of lemon and parsley.

Strawberry Charlotte

1 pt. milk
2 tbsp. cornstarch
½ cup sugar
2 egg yolks
1 tbsp. gelatin
2 tbsp. cold water
½ pint cream
1 pint fresh strawberries
1½ doz. lady fingers

Heat milk in double boiler, add cornstarch previously softened in cold milk, and sugar. Cook until thickened, stirring constantly. Beat egg yolks and add to milk; cook a few minutes longer. Add gelatin softened in cold water. Cool and when it begins to harden, fold in the stiffly beaten cream. Cut strawberries in quarters, sweeten and allow to stand for half an hour. Line the bottom of the mould with parchment paper. Cut off one end of each lady finger, stand the long pieces around the sides of the mould and arrange the small ends just inside these. Put half the custard mixture in the mould, then add the strawberries and rest of custard. Chill and turn out of mould to serve. Ten servings.

HAM CROQUETTES WITH PEANUT BUTTER SAUCE
NORMANDY CARROTS—SPANISH RICE
WINE JELLY

PEANUT BUTTER is a richly flavored food product put up in convenient form for use, but too seldom used as a flavoring. As a sandwich filling its presence is felt (and smelt) in every, or almost every home, especially where there are children. It is full of character and has a striking personality. Sometimes it strikes you almost too hard, especially if you are not very fond of peanuts. Combined, not too generously with other and less pronounced articles of food, however, it is a pleasant addition to the variety shelf. Mixed with banana it makes a tasty sandwich filling for tea or evening refreshments. Mixed with finely chopped pickle is another way of using. In a cream sauce it often meets with favor as a dressing for cauliflower, carrots and, as in this instance, meat. It is worth experimenting with—if you like peanut butter. This is another menu that would benefit by the addition of a green salad.

Ham Croquettes with Peanut Butter Sauce

1 cup milk
2 tbs. fat
4 tbs. flour
2 cups chopped cooked ham
Cracker crumbs
1 cup mashed potato
1 tbs. chopped onion
1 tsp. prepared mustard
Dash of pepper
¼ tsp. Worcestershire Sauce

Make a white sauce of the milk, flour and fat, mix with the remaining ingredients and spread out on a flat dish to cool. Form into croquettes, roll in flour, egg and cracker crumbs and fry in deep fat at 360 degrees.

Normandy Carrots

2 cups carrots cut in 2 inch slivers
½ cupful sugar
½ cup vinegar
¼ tsp. salt
¾ tbsp. cornstarch
2 tbsp. butter

Parboil the carrots in salted water until tender, and drain. Stir the cornstarch into the vinegar, add sugar and salt and boil for five minutes. Add butter and stir until melted. Reheat carrots in mixture and serve.

Spanish Rice

3 cups cooked rice
1 onion
3 slices bacon
2 cups tomatoes
Salt, pepper

Cook bacon and onion in frying pan until brown. Add rice, salt, pepper and tomatoes. Mix thoroughly and cook 30 minutes or longer; or place in a baking dish, cover with buttered crumbs and brown in moderate oven (350).

Wine Jelly

1 pt. cold water
1 tbsp. gelatin
Juice of 3 lemons
Rind of one lemon
2 lbs. granulated sugar
1 qt. boiling water
1pt. Madeira or Sherry Wine

Dissolve gelatin in water; add lemon juice and rind. Let stand 1 hour. Add sugar and boiling water, stir until dissolved, strain through fine sieve or cloth into rinsed mould. Chill in refrigerator.

FLANK STEAK—SPANISH STYLE
CAULIFLOWER POLONAISE
BROWNED POTATOES
BUTTERSCOTCH PIE

JUST exactly what justifies the implication that the Iberian peninsula is in any way responsible for this meat dish, is more than we know. No study of ingredients, no intimate acquaintance with the succulent qualities of the dish, points the way. It may as well, for all the characteristics of its flavor, have originated in Utah (and perhaps did). We disclaim all responsibility for the name but we have demonstrated its homely virtues as a food. And if you think you have met the same plebeian flesh before, perhaps under the guise of a product under the championship of Switzerland, you will be right. Spanish Steak or Swiss Steak, or whatever flag covers it, a flank steak is pretty much a flank steak. But it can be given different treatment, generally devised by some good Yankee cook. Such as ourselves.

Flank Steak—Spanish Style

1 flank steak (1½ to 2 lbs.)
2 tbsp. cooking fat
2 tbsp. vinegar
1½ tsps. salt
¼ tsp. pepper
1 onion chopped
1 tbsp. minced parsley
1 tbsp. minced celery
1 small green pepper chopped
2 cups tomato soup

Wipe the steak with a damp cloth and score it on both sides with a sharp knife. Cover with a dressing made of the fat (or oil), vinegar, onion and other seasonings. Soak the meat in this for an hour or longer. It may be left all night without harm to marinate. Heat cooking fat in a frying pan, take the meat from the marinate and wipe the liquid from it with paper toweling and sear it in the fat, on both sides. Place it in a shallow baking dish. Pour the remainder of the marinate dressing over it, the tomato soup (can of soup, can of rinsing) and bake in a moderate oven (325) until the meat is tender—about two hours. Six servings.

Cauliflower Polonaise

1 cauliflower head
1 cup white sauce
⅓ cup grated cheese
Buttered bread crumbs

Soak the cauliflower, head down, in cold water to cover for 20 minutes; put in boiling water and cook until almost tender. Drain and put in a buttered casserole; pour over it one cup of white sauce, then sprinkle with buttered bread crumbs and finally with the grated cheese. Bake until crumbs are brown. Sprinkle with one tablespoonful of chopped parsley mixed with one tablespoonful of chopped pimiento. Serve in same dish.

Butterscotch Pie

1 cup brown sugar
1 cup evaporated milk
½ cup water
1 tsp. vanilla
½ tsp. salt
2 tbsp. flour
2 tbsp. butter
2 egg yolks
2 egg whites

Beat together the egg yolks, brown sugar, butter and salt; add flour and milk (half evaporated milk, half water) and cook in double boiler until thick. Add vanilla. Put in an unbaked pastry shell and bake in a 375 oven for twenty-five minutes. Make a meringue of the whites of eggs and confectioners' sugar and cover the pie. Return to slow oven to brown.

ALEATHA'S CREAM OF VEGETABLE SOUP

CURRIED LAMB—BOILED RICE

APPLE STUFFED WITH SWEET POTATO

APRICOT TRIFLE

ALEATHA is a dusky Jamaican cook who was trained in an English school of cookery, and who has catered to Back Bay appetites for a good many years. She was greatly interested in this book on which I was working while visiting where her spoon and skillet provide delectable food and she kindly offered me some of her choice recipes. The Cream of Vegetable Soup is one. "The secret of making good soup," she said, "is in cooking all the good *out* of what you put in the soup into the soup." A cryptic remark, but the sense of which is obvious. And that, she assured me, can only be done by long and slow cooking, and by watching over things. "You can't just throw things onto the stove," said Aleatha, "and then go off and 'tend the movies. You got to watch 'em." But that is the difference between a born and bred cook like Aleatha and the woman who hasn't time for long and slow cooking, or for watching. A *good* cook must give her mind to it—at least some of her mind, and quite a little of her time. Aleatha scorns canned soups and always has a jar of stock in her refrigerator, replenished daily from the tag ends of celery, vegetables, meats and the water in which they are cooked. The garbage man looks at Aleatha's contributions to his livelihood with contempt.

Aleatha's Cream of Vegetable Soup

This is an economy soup made mostly from tag ends and left overs. Wash the leafy ends of celery, pick off dead leaves, scrape the root and add that. Throw all this into a soup kettle with 2 quarts of cold water. Add three or four medium sized potatoes, two onions, a few sprigs of parsley, the trimmed off tops of scallions—or any other vegetable scraps. Simmer slowly for two hours, covered, then put through the purée sieve or colander. Season with salt, pepper, add a cup of top milk heated or half cup of evaporated milk and half a cup of water, and a tablespoonful of butter.

Curried Lamb

3 cups cold cooked lamb
1 large onion, chopped
1½ cups celery chopped
¾ cup brown sauce
3 tbs. butter
⅛ tsp. curry
3 drops Tabasco Sauce
½ tsp. salt

Sauté the onion and celery in butter; add the meat cut in small pieces, and seasonings. Mix and heat through with brown sauce, gravy or stock. Arrange a mound of boiled rice on a chop plate or platter and pour the curried lamb around it. Sprinkle with coarsely chopped parsley.

Apple Stuffed with Sweet Potato

6 medium sized apples
4 sweet potatoes
Butter
Salt
Marshmallows

Cut a slice from stem end of apples and remove core and flesh, leaving a shell thick enough not to break. Boil sweet potatoes, put through ricer and season with salt, pepper and butter. Stuff apple with potato; put in a baking dish with very little water—just to cover bottom of pan—and bake in 375 oven until tender. Just before removing from oven, place a marshmallow on top of each apple and return to oven to toast.

WHOLE MEAL PORK CHOPS
CORN AND TOMATO RABBIT
MAPLE CUSTARD SOUFFLÉ

THIS Whole Meal Pork Chops dish would make a good wash-day dinner—if anybody had wash-day any more. Or, if wash-day meant what it used to—a long day over the tub with the kitchen to clean up afterward. Nowadays, however, with a washing machine that practically goes around from room to room picking up the wash and afterwards hanging out the clothes, wash-day means no more than the day the club meets. In fact, the club can meet on wash-day as well as any other. Nevertheless, there are days when things get kind of cluttered up and it's nice to put a dish into the oven that you know will at least keep the family alive until you can get around to the usual soup and fish. And another thing about this dish, when it is done the pork chops won't be so dry and hard that you can't get your teeth into them without danger to your dentistry. Pork chops can be ruined by poor cookery about as thoroughly as anything. On the other hand, no meat is more savory and toothsome, if correctly treated. Neither broiling nor pan broiling are really successful ways of cooking pork any more than veal. Oven baking one way or another is best. If they are pan broiled (fried in the frying pan), use plenty of butter or pork fat.

Whole Meal Pork Chops

Have lean pork chops cut about one and a half inches thick and place in baking dish. Dredge with flour and brown in hot fat. Place a slice of onion on each chop, then a tablespoonful of raw rice on top of this, and on top of the rice a slice of tomato, and top that with a ring of green pepper. Season with salt and pepper, put a dot of butter on each one. Add hot water to come up onto the chop but not to cover. Cover closely and bake in a slow oven (350) for an hour.

Corn and Tomato Rabbit

2 tbsp. cooking fat
1 small green onion
1 green pepper
1 qt. canned tomatoes
1 pt. canned corn
2 eggs
1 tsp. salt
1/8 tsp. white pepper
Toast
Grated cheese

Heat the fat and in it brown the onion and pepper minced. Add tomatoes and cook until the bulk is reduced one-half. Add corn and cook ten minutes longer. Add the unbeaten eggs and stir carefully for a minute. Add seasonings. Heap the mixture on rounds of toast, sprinkle with grated cheese and brown in hot oven.

Maple Custard Soufflé

2 cups top milk or cream
3 beaten eggs
1/2 cup grated maple sugar
1/8 tsp. salt
1 tsp. vanilla
2 egg yolks
Nutmeg
1/4 cup scraped maple sugar
1/4 cup minced pecans or almonds
1/4 cup whipped cream

Beat three eggs and two extra yolks together and mix with cream, half a cup of grated maple sugar, salt, vanilla and a dash of nutmeg. Beat all together and turn into buttered custard cups; set in a pan of hot water and bake in 325 oven until done. (A knife point will come out clean when the custard is done.) Cool. Turn out on dessert plate, cover with shaved maple sugar, nut meats and whipped cream last.

THIN SOUP OR COCKTAIL

ROAST TURKEY—BREAD STUFFING

CAULIFLOWER AND ONION SALAD—CRANBERRY JELLY

PUMPKIN PIE

THIS is the kind of dinner that has served American people for a good many generations and it is too good to tamper with. It is now practically an institution. A fowl weighing from twelve to fourteen pounds is, for a family of five or more, more economical than a smaller one, unless the family is so small that it will mean eating turkey for a week. In a young turkey the legs will be black and a globbler will have small spurs. The younger fowls will have shorter necks than the old ones. The skin should be white—not blue—and the breast bone tender. An old bird will have hairs on the body while a young one has pin feathers. The flesh should be firm, the breast broad and plump. A turkey should be stuffed at least twenty-four hours before roasting to allow the flavorings in the stuffing to permeate the meat.

Roast Turkey—Bread Stuffing

Have the butcher cut off the head and feet. You will have to pay for them but you do not have to carry them home. He will also draw the bird. The first step after you get the bird home is to singe him. This you can do by holding him over a gas jet, or a burning paper over the open griddle of a coal stove. This removes hair and down. Next, remove pin feathers with a sharp knife and tweezers, the giblets—heart, liver and gizzard should have been taken out of the bird and laid aside. Now wash the fowl thoroughly with warm water. We use soap and hot water for large birds, rinsing them well with hot and then cold water. Now make a bread stuffing as follows:

1 loaf stale bread
1 cup chopped onion
Salt, pepper
½ cup melted butter
Poultry dressing
Chicken stock, milk or water

Break the bread into small pieces and pour over it enough liquid to moisten thoroughly. Let stand until soft. Drain and mix with it the salt, pepper, and the butter, and poultry seasoning to taste. Onion, too, should be regulated to suit the taste. It should be well seasoned with sage. The more highly seasoned the stuffing, the better the bird will be flavored. Stuff the cavities where the crop and entrails were and sew up with darning needle and cord. Lay the bird in a roaster and, with the hand, rub some of the dressing over the outside. Additional salt and pepper may be needed. Lay very thin strips of salt pork over the neck and wings (which have been trussed back and tied to the body). Put the bird away in a cold place until ready to roast. Trim off ends of veins, remove the lining from the gizzard, wash the giblets and put in refrigerator. When the bird is being roasted, boil the giblets, chop them and add to the gravy. Allow a temperature of 450 for the first 20 or 25 minutes, then lower the heat and allow 25 minutes to the pound for roasting. Baste frequently.

Cauliflower and Onion Salad

Peel two Italian (or other sweet) onions, slice and let stand in a weak vinegar and salt solution for an hour. Boil a small, hard head of cauliflower and chill. When ready to serve, break the cauliflower into flowerlets and arrange in a salad bowl with the sliced onion, and pour French Dressing over. Garnish with slices of radish cut very thin.

BOILED LEG OF MUTTON WITH CAPER SAUCE
BOILED RICE—PICKLED BEETS
PEACH SNOW

EITHER a Julienne, tomato or chicken soup would properly introduce this menu, or a fruit juice, depending upon the temperature of the day and the occasion. If another hot vegetable is desired, either boiled onions buttered, peas, spinach or carrots would agree with the mutton. In that case a relish might be substituted for the salad; for instance, pickled pears or peaches, or ripe cucumber, sweet gherkins; or currant or mint jelly. If the storeroom boasts none of these—so much the worse for the storeroom, but they can be found at the grocery store. The housewife who never "puts up" anything such as pickles and relishes, misses a lot of fun. Hard work? No, not if you have a cool pleasant kitchen (and there *are* those who have found it a satisfaction in a hot kitchen), and the love of being a "good pervider" for her family.

Boiled Leg of Mutton with Caper Sauce

6 or 7 lb. leg of mutton
Flour-butter
Capers
Vinegar
Salt, pepper

Trim the leg of mutton, wipe with damp cloth, and boil in water to cover for one and one-half hours. Drain the water off. Do not take the meat out with a fork as that allows the juices to escape. Take one pint of the broth and thicken with 4 tablespoonfuls of flour mixed with 2 tablespoonfuls of butter; add salt, pepper and about a teaspoonful of vinegar. Strain this through a double cheesecloth and add to it a tablespoonful of drained capers. Thin with stock if too thick. Serve this sauce with the meat in a separate dish.

Pickled Beets

Wash and cook small beets until tender. Pour cold water over and rub the skin off with the fingers. Slice and make a sweet-sour sauce as follows:

2 tbsp. butter
2 tbsp. flour
½ tsp. salt
2 tbsp. sugar
¼ tsp. pepper
¼ cup vinegar
½ tsp. paprika
1 tbsp. chopped green pepper

Melt the butter and sauté the pepper in it. Add the flour and stir until it is slightly browned and well blended. Add the vinegar, sugar and other ingredients. Thin to right consistency with stock or water. Pour this over the beets and let stand for several hours.

Peach Snow

1 qt. canned peaches
2 tbsp. cornstarch
2 whites of eggs
½ cup cream

Blend cornstarch to smooth paste with small amount of cold milk. Drain syrup from peaches, stir the cornstarch paste into the syrup and cook in double boiler until clear; add the peaches which have been drained and mashed to a fine pulp; add the stiffly beaten whites of eggs and then carefully fold in the cream whipped to a stiff froth. Pour into a mold and chill. Garnish with maraschino cherries. If peaches are not sweetened, add sugar to taste.

WHITE SOUP STOCK

PLANKED STEAK

SWEET AND SOUR CABBAGE

DELICATE PUDDING

It is an excellent plan to keep a jar of soup stock in the refrigerator, either to serve as an emergency soup or as a base for sauces. White stock makes an excellent base for white sauce, and beef stock for brown sauce. Instead of cooking a fowl on purpose to make white stock, the broth may be saved when one is boiled for frying or fricassee. The broth from boiled beef should be saved in the same way. These with any left-over gravies, water in which vegetables are cooked (if cooked, as they should be, in the least possible amount) strained, should be added to the stock jar. There is great satisfaction in practicing these little economies when once one gets into the way of it. There are so many urgent needs for money that it seems futile to throw away any food that can be utilized. It is neither good management nor good sense.

White Soup Stock

1 3 lb. fowl
1 veal knuckle
2 lbs. beef marrow bone
1 celery stalk
1 carrot
1 onion
Bunch of parsley
Salt and pepper

Cut up fowl and cook with veal and beef-bone in a kettle with water to cover. Let come to boil and simmer gently for four hours. Add the vegetables chopped, and simmer for another hour. Strain and season. When cold, skim off the fat and serve hot with chopped parsley on top. Most of the nourishment will have gone from the meat into the soup, but if chopped and highly seasoned it will make a fairly good loaf. The stock will serve also as a base for White Sauce.

Planked Steak

Porterhouse Steak 1½ inches thick
Mashed potatoes
Fried onions

Broil the steak on both sides. Heat the plank very hot, butter it and place the steak on it. With a pastry tube arrange mashed potatoes (seasoned) around the outside of the plank, with delicately fried onions next the steak. Put in a hot oven (500) and heat until potatoes are a light brown. Spread the steak with butter, season with salt and pepper, garnish with sprigs of parsley, radish roses, and serve very hot.

Sweet and Sour Cabbage

1 qt. red (or white) cabbage
2 sour apples
2 tbs. bacon fat
4 tbsp. brown sugar
2 tbsp. vinegar
2 tbsp. flour
Salt, pepper

Cut the cabbage in quarters; remove the core and shred very fine. Peel and slice the apples, add these to the cabbage and season with salt and pepper. Heat the fat in a frying pan very hot and put the cabbage and apples in it. Pour over them just enough boiling water barely to cover and let cook until tender. Sprinkle the sugar over and the flour and vinegar mixed together. Cook 15 minutes longer and serve hot.

Delicate Pudding

1 pt. stale bread crumbs
1 qt. evaporated milk diluted
Yolks of 4 eggs
2 tbsp. butter
1 cup sugar
Grated rind of lemon
Pinch of salt
5 tbsp. confectioners' sugar

Beat the egg yolks and add them to the bread crumbs and milk alternately; add grated rind of lemon, salt and sugar. Put in buttered baking dish and bake in moderate oven for 45 minutes. Cool, and spread over the top a layer of currant jelly or raspberry jam. Beat the whites of the eggs to stiff froth with confectioners' sugar and brown in hot oven. Serve with cream.

ROLLED FLANK STEAK
WILKESBARRE CARROTS
BUTTERSCOTCH PUDDING

If flanked steak had a first name we should be calling it that by this time. The flank is sometimes called the "skirt" and lies below the loin. It is not one of the choice cuts but if properly cooked it can be made tender and juicy and it has a very good flavor. It is best cooked after one of the recipes given in this book, but is sometimes liked pan broiled. It is either pounded with a meat tenderer or a wooden potato masher or cut in criss-cross fashion for tendering. Of course to treat a sirloin or porterhouse steak after this fashion would ruin it because it would release all the juices, but the flank is likely to be tough without just such rough treatment as this. It also requires that long, slow cooking that we have heard about before. It is an economical cut of meat and worth the little attention and study required to make of it a respectable member of the meat family. Put in a heavy casserole or baking dish without pounding, browned on both sides with hot fat, and cooked with onion, carrot and tomatoes, it makes a good pot roast and a legitimate excuse for dumplings and gravy.

Rolled Flank Steak

Flank steak
2 cups bread stuffing
4 tbsp. fat
Flour
Salt, pepper
1 can tomato soup

Make a bread stuffing of 2 cups bread crumbs, 1 chopped onion, 1 chopped pepper, 1 beaten egg and water to moisten and hold together. Wipe the flank with a damp cloth and score in criss-cross squares with sharp knife; season with salt and pepper; Spread the bread stuffing over the flank, roll and tie at ends and middle. Roll in a mixture of flour, salt and pepper. Heat the fat in a baking pan and lay the roll in it to brown all sides. Then pour the tomato soup over (rinsing out the can) put in oven and bake one hour. Accompany with mashed potatoes.

Wilkesbarre Carrots

1½ tbsp. butter
1½ tbsp. flour
1 cup milk
½ cup cream
12 small carrots
¼ tsp. mustard
Salt, pepper, cracker crumbs

Make a sauce by melting butter to which add the flour and blend to smooth mixture; add milk and cream (not hot) slowly until thickened. Season with salt and pepper and mustard. Scrape young carrots, wash, slice and place in buttered casserole. Add barely enough water to show in bottom of casserole and cook in moderate oven (375) until tender. Then add sauce, sprinkle with cracker crumbs, return to oven and brown.

Butterscotch Pudding

⅜ cup brown sugar
3 tbsp. butter
1 cup milk
2 tbsp. cornstarch
⅛ tsp. salt
½ tsp. vanilla

Put butter and brown sugar in saucepan together, stir and boil one minute. Add milk and put in double boiler. When hot add cornstarch dissolved in a little cold milk (extra). Stir until smooth. Cover and cook 15 minutes stirring occasionally. Cool, add vanilla, chill and serve with whipped cream.

LAMB STEW WITH DUMPLINGS
CABBAGE AND CHEESE CASSEROLE
PEAR-PEANUT SALAD
COTTAGE PUDDING

WITHOUT putting too much strain on our minds in recalling whether milk comes under A or D, we might try to remember this: that for growth and general good health we need milk, butter, cream, cheese and vegetables. The particular nutriment attributed to these is classed as Vitamin A. Vitamin B does not differ so much from A since it also contributes to our general good health. It is found especially in green vegetables such as lettuce and cabbage. C is not outclassed by these others since it is needed for variety and is found in fruits, such as oranges and lemons, and in tomatoes. E is found in milk and eggs and makes bone. All of them are found in many of the meats we frequently use.

Lamb Stew with Dumplings

2 lbs. breast of lamb
8 medium potatoes
3 onions
2 carrots
1 cup tomatoes
1 tsp. salt
Pepper

Have the lamb cut into small pieces. Put it in a heavy kettle with water to cover, onion (sliced) and seasonings. Cover and cook slowly for one hour. Add potatoes and carrots, sliced, and tomatoes and cook 30 minutes longer. Put dumplings in on top of stew 20 minutes before it is done and cook, closely covered. Add very little water if necessary to keep from sticking. Thicken any juice left and pour over the meat. For dumplings see recipe on Page 000.

Cabbage and Cheese Casserole

1 qt. cooked cabbage
1½ cups buttered bread crumbs
1 cup evaporated milk diluted
1 cup grated cheese
Salt
Pepper
Paprika
1 tbsp. minced parsley

Mix cooked and chopped cabbage with 1½ cups bread crumbs and cheese; season with salt, pepper and parsley. Moisten with one cup evaporated milk diluted one-third. Put in well buttered casserole and heat through—twenty minutes—at 400.

Pear-Peanut Salad

Drain canned Bartlett pears from syrup. Roll in freshly roasted peanuts that have been crushed fine with rolling pin. Place on lettuce leaf (two halves to each serving) cavity side down, and beside each half place a small mound of cottage cheese sprinkled with paprika. Serve with mayonnaise.

Cottage Pudding

¼ cup butter
⅔ cup sugar
1 egg
1 tsp. salt
1 cup milk
2 cups flour
4 tsp. baking powder

Cream butter, sugar, egg. Add dry ingredients which have been sifted together, then milk. Bake in moderate oven 35 minutes. Serve warm with

Sauce

1 cup sugar
½ cup water
1½ tsp. lemon juice
2 tsp. butter

Boil sugar and water to a syrup. Remove from fire and add lemon juice and butter. Beat well and serve hot.

BAKED STUFFED SPARERIBS
STEWED TOMATOES MASHED TURNIPS
FRUIT MOLD

SPARERIBS! The very word calls up visions of my childhood home and the good smelly kitchen where much plain homely food was cooked. It is not easy to get the kind of spareribs nowadays that we had then. There was *meat* on those spareribs. Part of the tenderloin was allowed to adhere to them, and when dressed with sage and coated with stuffing—well, the recipe below tells you how—but it cannot tell you how to get the ribs! No rule is given for the mashed turnips, for the rule is very simple. Yellow turnips (we called them "beggies") are better with pork than white. It takes about an hour to cook them. Mash them fine and shut your eyes when you put in the butter. Some of the fat from the spareribs lends additional flavor. And plenty of salt and pepper.

Baked Stuffed Spareribs

Whole fresh (not corned) spareribs. Trim off thin skin covering. Make a bread stuffing with plenty of onion, sage, savory, and highly seasoned with salt, pepper and butter. Moisten the bread with applesauce very slightly sweetened. Rub the spareribs with salt and pepper, put in roasting pan with half a cup of water. Bake in 400° oven for three-quarters of an hour, then spread over with stuffing and bake for half an hour longer.

Stewed Tomatoes

1 qt. tomatoes canned
1 onion
2 tbsp. butter
Salt, pepper, sugar

Melt the butter in a saucepan and sauté the thinly sliced onion in it. Add tomato and stew for twenty minutes. Season with salt, pepper and one tablespoonful of sugar. Pour over small squares of toast in a vegetable dish.

Fruit Mold

1 cup broken pineapple
1 cup maraschino cherries
1 small can sliced peaches
Juice from fruit to 1 pt.
1 tbsp. gelatin

Dissolve gelatin in ¼ cup cold water. Heat fruit juices (water added if necessary to make 1 pint) and add dissolved gelatin. Arrange fruit in mold, pour juice over and set away to chill. Serve on lettuce with mayonnaise to which a small amount of whipped cream has been added.

CINNAMON APPLES SAUSAGE STUFFED
CREAMED POTATOES
RAINBOW SALAD

VARIOUS uses for apples tinctured and colored with cinnamon or cinnamon candies are given in this book, but that is because they make a most attractive accompaniment to certain meat dishes, especially pork. They also help out on the fruit content. This menu would be the better for the introduction of another vegetable, either cooked or raw as a salad. The dessert is in the form of a salad, but the meal could stand either stewed tomatoes, raw tomatoes, cabbage salad or cole slaw, or any of the other salad greens. A recipe for creamed potatoes may be thought superfluous since this is a common dish. But because it is common is no reason to assume that a mixture of cold potatoes, milk and flour is really *creamed potatoes* as they have a right to be understood. Some of the most familiar—and aggravating—evils which befall this dish are: too much flour making a substance not widely different from that used by paper hangers in their profession; not enough flour, resulting in a viscous mess that only the eating methods of a cat can properly manage. Tastelessness is another sin committed against a dish which seldom lives up to its name. This is one of the dishes where evaporated milk is used to advantage.

Cinnamon Apples Sausage Stuffed

6 red apples
2 cups sugar
1 cup water
¼ lb. cinnamon candies
12 small sausages

Boil water, sugar and candies to a syrup over a slow fire. Cut the tops squarely off stem end of apples and core. Do not peel. Cut once across the middle. Cook for five minutes in the syrup, covered. Take from syrup with strainer or slotted spoon and drain on paper toweling. Run one or two small sausages through the cavity of each piece of apple and lay in glass baking dish, one slightly overlapping the other. Pour syrup over and bake in moderate oven (350) for 30 to 40 minutes or until tender. Serve hot in same dish.

Creamed Potatoes

3 tbs. flour
3 tbs. butter
1½ cups milk or evaporated milk diluted
½ tsp. salt
Pepper
3 cups boiled potatoes diced

Melt butter in saucepan; add flour and stir until well blended. Then pour the cold milk in a little at a time, stirring constantly. Bring to the boiling point, add seasoning and the diced potato. Heat over a very low flame using a fork to stir. Serve in vegetable dish, sprinkled with paprika.

Rainbow Salad

This is one of the most attractive salads we have ever made, and takes the place of a dessert as well. It is somewhat expensive if made in any quantity, but if planned for only four or six people such parts of the melons as are not used in the salad can be served as a fruit course for the next meal. Cut cantaloupe, honey dew and watermelons in half. Remove seeds and then with small round vegetable cutter, scoop balls from each. Add sections of orange, white grapes, and a few green minted raisins; mix all together and pour French Dressing over. Let stand and chill. Line a salad bowl with small crisp lettuce leaves and fill with fruit.

LAMB ON SKEWERS
BOHEMIAN SPINACH
HUCKLEBERRY PIE

WE suggest boiled rice with this menu, with perhaps a curry sauce (See Page 136). There are both wooden and steel skewers. The latter are best for this purpose. Mint jelly would also be a pleasant addition to the meal. For a first course, something a bit acid, like grapefruit (in fact, a sherbet glass filled with grapefruit sections and garnished with a cube of mint jelly to serve right along with the meal would be both attractive and tasty). Or a brown sauce (See Page 205) with currant jelly. For a salad (and even if we do have spinach we should find a raw vegetable salad a suitable addition) cabbage and celery chopped together, or lettuce and cucumber. There is little danger of our overdoing the vegetable content of our meals, and particularly the raw vegetable. In making berry (or any other kind of pies for that matter) cut some kind of a figure in the middle of the top crust to act as a vent for steam. My mother always made a figure S and embroidered it with eyelets on either side. I always supposed it was purely ornamental until later years showed its more practical use.

Lamb on Skewers

Cut lamb steaks into pieces about one and a half inch square and season with salt and pepper; run a steel skewer through the middle of a piece of lamb, then through the center of a large mushroom. Allow three or four of each to a skewer. Do not put them close together. Brush very lightly with melted butter, lay them on the broiler or on a baking tin in a very hot oven and cook until done—about 15-20 minutes.

Bohemian Spinach

Boil spinach in as little water as possible. Drain it and save the juice. Chop the spinach fine. Take one tablespoonful of butter to 2 cups of spinach, melt it in a saucepan, add some finely chopped onions according to taste, and sauté until golden brown; blend in one tablespoonful of flour and some of the spinach juice to make a thin gravy. Season with salt and pepper and mix with the spinach. Garnish with slices of hard cooked egg. Serve with rice.

Fresh Pineapple Salad

Choose a large and quite ripe pineapple; cut it squarely down through the center lengthwise and including the spine and leaves at the top. Scoop out the center, leaving a shell. Cut the pulp into small pieces and place in a bowl with diced ripe peach, a few blackberries, red raspberries or strawberries. Chill both the pineapple shell and the mixed fruit. When ready to serve, pour French Dressing over the fruit, toss together gently not to bruise the berries, and fill the halves of pineapple shell. Decorate with a few sprigs of mint. Lay the two halves of pineapple on a large salad plate or suitable dish, and serve to individual salad plates.

INDIVIDUAL TENDERLOINS
CURRY OF MUSHROOMS AND PEAS
CUCUMBER SALAD IN PEPPERS
APPLE CRUMB

THE tenderloin is one of the choice steaks and is rich and full of flavor if properly cooked. The best way of cooking is to broil; the next best way is to pan broil. To pan broil have a heavy frying pan just as hot as it can be made. Lay the meat in without any fat and sear it on both sides, then cook until done. Such steaks as tenderloin, porterhouse and sirloin are so full of flavor themselves that they do not need—in our opinion at least—any additional sauce than the butter with which they are dressed, and their own released juices. We have often given as directions from the preparation of meat, "wipe with a damp cloth." Never *wash* meat. Use a piece of heavy flannel, or flannelette dampened with which to wipe the meat.

Individual Tenderloins

Slice the tenderloin one-half inch thick. Sear on both sides in hot pan; then put butter in another pan and fry thin slices of onion in that (number of tenderloins and amount of onion depending on servings) and fry to delicate brown. When steak is done—brown on outside and slightly rare in middle, place on hot platter and dot thickly with butter. Lay the fried onion at one side, and set in hot oven for five minutes. Serve a dill pickle with each tenderloin.

Curry of Mushrooms and Peas

1 tbsp. chopped onion
3 tbsp. cooking fat
2½ tbsp. flour
1 cup mushroom broth
1 tsp. curry powder
½ tsp. salt
1½ cups mushrooms
½ cup cream
1 cup canned peas
3 hard cooked eggs

Cook onion in 2 tablespoonsful of fat until yellow. Add flour and blend thoroughly. Add mushroom broth (liquid from can of mushrooms, or, if fresh mushrooms are used, use meat stock) adding a little water if necessary to make required amount. Add curry powder, salt, and simmer 10 minutes. Add mushrooms, fresh or canned, sautéd in the remaining tablespoonful of fat (butter preferred); add peas. Just before serving add cream and bring to the boiling point. Serve on triangles of buttered toast, and garnish with slices of hard boiled egg. An excellent luncheon dish by itself.

Cucumber Salad in Peppers

Green peppers
2 cucumbers
Salt
¼ cup minced onion
½ cup minced celery
½ cup minced pecans
French Dressing
Mayonnaise

Wash and seed the peppers and put a tablespoonful of French Dressing in each. Chop the cucumbers (not too fine) and mix with the onion, celery and salt. Cover with French Dressing and let stand to chill. When ready to serve, drain the peppers and the vegetable mixture. Fill the peppers with the mixture, sprinkle with nut meats, lay on lettuce on salad plates and on each serving put a teaspoonful of thick mayonnaise. Sprinkle with paprika.

Apple Crumb

4 sour apples
½ cup butter
1 cup brown sugar
1 cup flour

Butter a baking dish and cover the bottom with a thick layer of sliced, well-flavored apples. Work butter, sugar and flour together until mixture is like granulated sugar. Spread over apples. Bake in hot oven (400) for 10 minutes, then reduce heat and bake until apples are soft and crumbs are brown. Serve with cream whipped or plain.

TRIPE WITH MUSHROOMS
STUFFED BEETS
CARAMEL CUSTARD

It is surprising how many people do not know what tripe is—except a convenient and expressive word by which to designate certain things that offend credulity. Tripe is what might be called the interior drapery of ruminants of the cow family. It is the lining to the stomach. There *have* been people who thought it was a fish. Tripe is considered a great delicacy by some people and there are a number of ways to cook it. The recipe given is our favorite way of serving it, although fried in batter it is of delicate texture and flavor. The way vegetables are getting their own insides taken out and matter entirely foreign to their individual personalities introduced, must be a great surprise to them. Here, for all these years, a beet has been just a beet as a turnip has been a turnip and a tomato a tomato. And now we ruthlessly tear the very heart from a beet and put cottage cheese in its place. And a very good substitute we think it, too.

Tripe with Mushrooms

2 lbs. boiled tripe
¼ lb. bacon
Salt, pepper
Flour
12 large mushrooms chopped fine
½ pt. stock or water
1 tbsp. flour
2 tbsp. sherry

Cut the tripe into 1 inch squares; cut bacon into strips and fry out all fat in frying pan. Discard the bacon; season the tripe with salt and pepper, dredge with flour and brown on both sides in the bacon fat. Remove tripe from pan to hot dish. Add one tablespoonful of flour to the fat, blend, and then add the stock or hot water to it, stirring until smooth. Then add the mushrooms and stir to the boiling point. Season with salt and pepper, add the sherry and pour over the tripe. Serve with boiled rice.

Stuffed Beets

6 medium sized young cooked beets
½ cup cottage cheese
1 tbsp. chopped green olives
Mayonnaise

Hollow out centers of beets. Add olives to cheese and mix with mayonnaise. Fill beet cases and let chill in refrigerator 30 minutes. Serve on lettuce leaves and garnish with spot of mayonnaise.

Caramel Custard

1 pt. milk
3 tbsp. burned sugar
1½ tbsp. cornstarch
1 tsp. vanilla
Sweetened cream

Cook the milk and sugar together in a double boiler. Moisten the cornstarch with a little cold milk and add it to the hot milk and sugar. Cook until thick and smooth, stirring constantly. When done, flavor with vanilla. Chill and eat with sweetened cream.

To make the burnt sugar (or carameled sugar) put the sugar in a saucepan over a low fire and stir it with a spoon until melted and of a light brown in color. Do not let it get too burned and do not allow it to stick to spoon or pan.

BAKED LIVER AND BACON
ESCALLOPED CORN
APPLE-CRESS SALAD
RED CHERRY SPONGE

THIS is a good busy-day menu because both main dishes can be baked at the same time, the salad is extremely easy to prepare, and the dessert can be prepared ahead of time. Speaking of temperatures, of course the modern ovens—gas, electric and oil, are equipped with thermometers, and the first two with time controls as well. Where there is no thermometer on the stove, however, the portable answers very well. A thermometer for deep fat frying is also a valuable addition to the devices for accurate cooking. Other latter-day indispensables are a pastry blender (mixing pastry with the fingers is likely to melt the shortening and make less flaky pastry), a pastry brush, several of them in fact, for brushing melted butter over meats, for greasing pans, and many other uses. These must be washed and dried after each using. A cake tester—to take the place of the questionable straw from the broom; a rubber scraper for cleaning the mixing spoon, scraping batter out of a bowl (and thus depriving the children of one of their inalienable rights), and a roll of paper toweling.

Baked Liver and Bacon

¼ cup flour
½ tsp. salt
¼ tsp. pepper
3 slices onion
¾ lb. sliced liver
1 cup cracker crumbs
¼ cup melted butter
½ cup water
6 slices bacon

Soak liver five minutes in cold water, wipe dry and roll in flour. Sprinkle with salt and pepper. Mix crumbs and melted butter. Sprinkle a layer of crumbs in baking dish, then add the layer of liver. Top with the onions and remainder of crumbs. Add the half cup of water; place the bacon on top and bake 25 minutes in moderate oven (350), removing the cover for the last ten minutes.

Escalloped Corn

1 No. 2 can corn
2 cups milk
1 cup chopped cheese
1 cup bread crumbs
½ cup chopped celery
1 green pepper, chopped
2 tbsp. butter melted
1 tsp. salt
Dash pepper
2 tbsp. Worcestershire Sauce

Mix all ingredients together and bake in moderate oven (350) for 40 minutes.

Apple-Cress Salad

Peel apples, slice and throw into cold water to prevent discoloring. Wash crisp water cress and shake dry. Lay cress on salad plates. Drain apple and pour French Dressing over; drain again; place slices of apple on each plate, top with slice of Roquefort cheese and Cooked Salad Dressing No. 2 (Page 196).

Red Cherry Sponge

1½ tbsp. gelatin
2 tbsp. cold water
1 can red cherries pitted
2 eggs

Soak the gelatin in the cold water for five minutes. Drain the syrup from the cherries and bring to a boil. Pour hot syrup over the gelatin and when it is dissolved add the cherries. Allow this to cool, and when beginning to stiffen add the well beaten whites of eggs. Mold in individual dishes and chill. When ready to serve, unmold onto dessert plates with a custard made of the egg yolks.

MEAT PASTRY ROLL GREEN CORN PUFFS
POTATO SOUFFLÉ
APPLE Á LA MODE

THIS dish, "Meat Pastry Roll" as you read it over, may *sound* like meat pie—met with elsewhere. But, while it has all the fundamental ingredients of a meat pie, still it isn't. And it is worth trying. And the Green Corn Puffs are good too. If you use canned corn (which is quite suitable) drain it through a colander, then run it through a meat chopper with fine knives. In that gusty novel which recently won the Pulitzer Prize, "Honey in the Horn," Mr. Davis, in relating what the frontiersmen had to eat, speaks of "yellow corn mowed off the cob and boiled in milk." Almost contemptuously he refers to what he seems to consider a ruthless method of separating the succulent seed from its parent stem. Nevertheless, in making certain dishes, you *have* to "mow" the corn from the cob. Doubtless Mr. Davis prefers his on the cob and so do we. But sometimes a change is desirable. Green corn oysters or patties are delicious but you have to mow the corn off the ear to make them.

Meat Pastry Roll

1½ lbs. ground beef
1 lb. ground veal
½ lb. pork
4 hard cooked eggs
½ cup chopped onion
½ cup chopped celery
1 tsp. salt
Dash of pepper

Cheaper cuts of beef and veal are chosen for this Roll. Put through the meat grinder twice, season with salt and pepper, add chopped onion and celery. Line a loaf pan with a damp cloth (flannelette is good), pack half the quantity into the pan, cover with sliced hard cooked eggs, sprinkle these with salt and pepper and spread over them a thin coating of ketchup mixed with prepared mustard. Then cover with the remainder of the meat and let stand overnight. When ready to use, transfer it (without the cloth) to a greased roaster, brush the top with melted butter and put in a hot (500) oven for 20 minutes to sear. Reduce the temperature to 350 and bake for one hour. Then raise the temperature to 450, drain the juices from the loaf and cover with a biscuit dough rolled to about ¼ inch in thickness and return to oven to bake for 15 minutes at 400.

Green Corn Puffs

2 eggs beaten stiff
1 cupful milk
1 pint grated corn
Grated cheese
¼ tsp. paprika
½ tsp. salt
Few grains cayenne

Add one cupful of milk to the beaten egg, add the corn to that and the seasonings. Grease six custard cups and fill half full with this mixture. Add 1 tablespoonful of grated cheese to each cup and set in a baking pan with hot water nearly to top of cups. Bake in moderate oven until firm. Serve with tomato sauce.

Apple à la Mode

6 red apples
½ cup sugar
½ tsp cinnamon
½ cup water
Red vegetable coloring
Vanilla ice cream

Wipe, core and pare an apple for each serving, leaving ½ inch band of peel around the middle. Bring to a boil the sugar, cinnamon, and water. Add the coloring matter to just the right shade. Put the apples into this syrup, cover and simmer slowly until they are cooked tender but not until the flesh is soft. Turn frequently. When done, remove the apples to plate, boil the syrup down until very thick. Put a serving of vanilla ice cream on each dessert plate and make a depression in the center. Place a warm (not hot) apple in the center and pour a little of the syrup on top. Cinnamon candies may be used instead of the cinnamon and coloring matter.

FILLET OF SOLE FRIED
VEGETABLE CAKES
CUCUMBERS WITH HORSERADISH SAUCE
PEAR TAPIOCA

QUICK cooking Tapioca is another one of the recent—or reasonably recent developments of the food industry that makes life simpler and pleasanter for the housewife. There are probably those who still cling to the old pearl kind—viscous globules that slid around in the mouth seeking escape, but in the main, the quick cooking kind is practically the only kind you will find on the shelves of the modern housewife. Its uses are manifold. It thickens a soup to just the right consistency; it keeps the fruit pies from running over and without giving any flavor of its own. A teaspoonful will do the trick. (And think of how we used to bind a piece of tape or Fruit of the Loom or something around the edge of a pie, making it look like a sore thumb.) And for an almost instant dessert to knock together when unexpected company comes, it can't be excelled. Just poured over bananas, peaches, berries, oranges sliced it makes a nutritious, delicate dessert beloved by children and despised by none unless it is the beafsteak-and-onions man.

Fillet of Sole Fried

Sprinkle the fillets with salt and pepper, roll up and fasten with toothpicks. Roll in flour, cracker crumbs or corn meal, dip in beaten egg, roll in crumbs again and fry in deep fat at 360 degrees until nicely browned. Serve with Tartar Sauce.

Vegetable Cakes

- 2 cups chopped cabbage
- 4 onions minced
- 2 cups mashed potato
- 1 egg
- ½ can tomato soup
- ¼ cup water
- Salt, pepper, paprika

Cook cabbage and onion in water until soft, drain and add to mashed potato. Season with salt, pepper and paprika, form into little cakes and fry or bake on greased pan until brown. Serve with Tomato Sauce (page 205).

Cucumbers with Horseradish Sauce

- 2 cucumbers
- 1 cup sour cream
- 1 tbsp. vinegar
- 3 tbsp. horseradish
- ¼ tsp. paprika
- ½ tsp. salt

Peel and slice cucumbers very thin. Stir the horseradish into the sour cream, add vinegar and seasonings and pour over cucumbers. Serve on a bed of lettuce.

Pear Tapioca

- ½ cup quick cooking tapioca
- 1½ cups boiling water
- ¼ tsp. salt
- 3 tbsp. lemon juice
- 1 tbsp. orange juice
- 2 tbsp. syrup from maraschino cherries
- ¾ cup sugar
- Bartlett pears
- Maraschino cherries

Cook the tapioca in a double boiler with the water and salt until clear. Add lemon and orange juice and syrup from cherries and sugar. Peel pears, remove cores and place in baking dish, cut side up. Place a cherry in each cavity. Pour the tapioca mixture over and bake in moderately hot oven until the pears are done. Serve hot or cold with whipped cream.

BAKED GRAPEFRUIT

ROAST GUINEA HEN RAISIN STUFFING

STRING BEAN SALAD

GUINEA HENS will *not* be one of the feathered tribe to inhabit our country place. We once lived within sound of a poultry farm where there was a flock of these speckled fowl, and while there were probably not over thirty altogether, they sounded like an enthusiastic Democratic convention. Moreover they are a bird of early rising habits. They begin to clatter about four in the morning and keep it up until the neighbors are too exhausted to compute time. But, as a contribution to the pleasure of epicurean man they leave little to be desired—if he doesn't have to encounter them otherwise. If you are fond of dark meat the guinea is your bird. If not, and you are invited as a special treat to a dinner of guinea hen, you better be taken sick. For the guinea fowl is all dark meat. And a strong meat at that, more like that of wild fowl than of tame. In fact, the guinea is not a domesticated bird. He just stays around from force of habit. He never hob-nobs with other fowl (except to torment and make their lives miserable), he wanders all over Kingdom Come and would rather hunt his own food than be fed. But once in the oven and subsequently on the table, he becomes docile enough and succumbs with reasonable grace to stuffing and currant jelly.

Baked Grapefruit

Cut large juicy grapefruit in half and loosen membrane as for serving raw. Spread each one with a little butter, then with brown sugar and sprinkle cinnamon over the top. Set in a 400 oven and bake until the sugar has melted and the skin is soft. May be used also as a dessert.

Roast Guinea Hen with Raisin Stuffing

Guinea hen is prepared for cooking as any other fowl. This is a small fowl and two young hens would be needed for a dinner of six. When the fowl is ready for roasting, stuff with the dressing given below, sew up the openings and rub the outside with salt, pepper and a few drops of lemon juice. Lay in a roasting pan with two cups of water and cover. Steam (in the oven) for half an hour or until slightly tender, then drain off the juice, keeping it to baste with, uncover the birds and roast until tender. Serve any desired vegetable with this dinner—carrots cut in narrow strips and buttered; artichokes; broccoli or onions. And currant jelly.

Raisin Stuffing

2 cups dry bread crumbs
1/3 cup seeded raisins
1/3 cup walnut meats ground
1 tsp. salt
1/8 tsp. pepper
1 tsp. poultry seasoning
Dash of mace
1/4 cup melted butter
About 1/3 cup hot milk or
Chicken stock

Combine bread crumbs, raisins, nuts and seasonings: then add melted butter and hot liquid. Let stand 15 minutes over a low fire stirring occasionally. This may also be used as stuffing for duck.

String Bean Salad

1 qt. young string beans
6 narrow rings of pimiento
French Dressing
Mayonnoise

Wash and string the beans and cook them whole in salted water until tender. Drain and cool. Marinate in French dressing for an hour or two in the refrigerator. Arrange on salad plates on small white lettuce leaves in small mounds, in small bundles held inside pimiento rings. Serve with mayonnaise.

ONION SOUP WITH MILK
NUT LOAF
FRIED PARSNIPS   STUFFED CAULIFLOWER
WINE JELLY CAKE

THIS is a good dinner for the vegetarian or for those for whom red meat is prohibitive. The nut loaf is delicious and came from a famous Battle Creek sanitarium where meat is not served, and which is noted for its delicious food. Of course this particular institution would not approve of the wine jelly cake, but neither do we approve an all vegetarian diet. Any other light, simple dessert would do as well. In cooking vegetables, remember that the secret of flavor lies in short, quick cooking with a minimum of water. Brussels Sprouts require more water than spinach and carrots, but they should not be overcooked. Parsnips are better if dug fresh from the ground in the spring than if gathered in the fall.

Onion Soup with Milk

2 cups milk
3 cups water
6 onions
Pimientos
2 tbsp. butter
1 egg yolk
Salt, pepper
Parmesan cheese

Chop the onions fine and sauté in one tablespoonful of butter until soft but not brown. Add water, simmer for twenty minutes, then press through a sieve. Melt the other tablespoonful of butter, blend in the flour, add the milk (scalded) and cook for five minutes; mix with the onion broth, add the beaten egg yolk, a few chopped pimientos, season and serve with grated Parmesan cheese on top.

Nut Loaf

2 cups dry bread crumbs
2¾ cups milk
1¼ cups nut meats (chopped)
½ tsp. salt
1 egg
1 tsp. Kitchen Bouquet
½ tsp. pepper
1 tbsp. butter or bacon fat melted

Mix all together, put in greased bread tin and bake in 400 oven for 25 or 30 minutes.

Stuffed Cauliflower

Soak a hard, close head of cauliflower in salted water for 20 minutes, then parboil in clean salt water for ten minutes. Drain and cool. Make a bread stuffing of 3 cups bread crumbs, 2 eggs, 2 tablespoonfuls butter, ½ pound pork sausage, and season to taste. Moisten the stuffing with milk. Stuff this in between the flowerlets and tie up in a cheese cloth; steam for half an hour. Serve with white sauce.

Wine Jelly Cake

2 tbsp. gelatin
½ cup sugar
½ cup cold water
1 cupful sherry
½ cup orange and lemon juice
1½ cups boiling water
1 cup chopped nuts

Soak the gelatin in ½ cup cold water and add to the boiling water; stir until it dissolves, then add sugar, fruit juice and sherry. Set aside to mold. Cut the top squarely off a sponge cake and dig out center, leaving substantial bottom. Fill the cavity with wine jelly. Add a tablespoonful of chopped cherries and half a cupful of chopped nuts. Put the top back on and chill. When ready to serve cover with whipped cream.

BAKED BEEF HEART
POTATOES AU GRATIN
STUFFED ALLIGATOR PEAR SALAD

THE so-called "organs" of food animals are, we are told by nutritionists, rich sources of vitamins and iron and should be used oftener than they are. Liver, of course, has within the last few years come to be known as one of the surest cures for anemia, and that knowledge has put it almost out of reach of the slim purse. Calves' liver is the most delicate, but pigs' liver is tender and good and so is that of young beef. Beef heart, baked, is quite as good cold as hot. Boiled and pickled in sweetened vinegar it is another kind of delicacy. Calves' hearts are even better, being more tender. Boiled without stuffing but well seasoned and sliced cold, they make an excellent supper dish.

Baked Beef Heart

1 beef heart
1 green pepper
⅔ cup milk
½ cup brown sugar
½ cup vinegar
½ cup boiling water
1 tsp. prepared mustard
2 cups bread crumbs
1 egg
½ tsp. paprika
1½ tbsp. butter or fat
Salt

Wash the heart, trim off veins, split open and let stand in cold water half an hour. Mix bread crumbs, seasonings, beaten egg, milk, chopped green pepper and cooking fat (butter, bacon or pork fat). Stuff the heart with this and sew or tie together. Put in baking pan with one-half cup of boiling water and bake in slow oven (350) until tender. Allow three hours. Let water evaporate but add enough to baste with from time to time.

Potatoes au Gratin

½ pt. milk
Yolks of 2 eggs
2 tbsp. butter
6 boiled potatoes
1 tbsp. flour
½ pt. of stock
4 tbsp. grated cheese
Salt, pepper, paprika
Bread crumbs

Slice the cold boiled potatoes and lay in casserole. Melt butter in saucepan and blend the flour with it. Add the milk (cold) gradually, and the stock (hot). Stir continually until blended and thickened. Add beaten egg yolks and seasonings. Pour over the potatoes. Mix bread crumbs and cheese and sprinkle over top. Put in 450 oven for fifteen minutes to heat potatoes and brown crumbs.

Stuffed Alligator Pear Salad

Alligator pears
½ can tomato purée
1½ cakes cream cheese
1 tbsp. gelatin
2 tbsp. cold water
½ cup mayonnaise
Tomatoes

Cut half as many pears as will be required for serving in two, remove seeds and fill with the following mixture: Mix tomato purée, cream cheese, gelatin softened in cold water and dissolved over hot water, and mayonnaise. When this is firm, slice pears in reasonably thick slices and peel. Place on thick slices of peeled ripe tomato, and serve on lettuce with French Dressing.

BARLEY SOUP
VEAL DRUMSTICKS
APPLE-PEPPER SALAD
PEACH PUFFS

THE recipe given for Veal Drumsticks is not only a very savory one but, considering that veal is never a cheap meat, and often quite an expensive one, is economical under almost any conditions. In testing the recipe in our own kitchen we found that the cost of the meat was fifty-six cents, and that it served six people generously. Half the recipe would do for four. The original recipe calls for only a tablespoonful of onion, but we used a whole small onion and found it none too much for our taste. Skewers, in case you might not have them on hand, should be found at the ten-cent store, possibly a hardware store. They are a convenience in various ways and should be kept on hand, both steel and wooden. Green peas would make the menu more complete.

Barley Soup

1 qt. beef stock
1 cup barley
1 tsp. onion juice
Salt, pepper

Cook barley in double boiler until soft, with just enough water to cover. Add to beef stock and bring to boiling point. Season to taste.

Veal Drumsticks

1 lb. veal
1 lb. lean fresh pork
2 tsp. salt
½ tsp. pepper
1 egg
1 cup cracker crumbs
2 tbsp. melted butter
2 tbsp. flour
1 cup milk
1 minced onion

Scald and wipe skewers. With a meat tenderer or wooden potato masher, pound salt and pepper into the meat until it is flat and thin. Cut into two-inch squares (or pieces) and insert a skewer into the middle of each piece, alternating veal and pork, with five or six pieces on each skewer. Mold the meat onto the skewers in "drumstick" shape, then dip in beaten egg diluted with a teaspoonful of milk and then in cracker crumbs. Brown the "drumstick" to a delicate shade in hot fat and place in a baking dish. To the hot fat add flour to make a paste and to this add the remainder of milk and stock and stir until thickened. Pour this gravy over the drumsticks, cover, and bake in moderate oven (375) one hour. Serve with hot biscuits.

Apple-Pepper Salad

Cut large firm green peppers in two crosswise; take out seeds and ribs. Use the lower half as a salad cup and chop the remainder. Peel, core and dice very tart, nicely flavored apples. Mix chopped pepper with diced apple and very highly seasoned mayonnaise and fill pepper cups. Put a teaspoonful of mayonnaise on top of each and sprinkle with chopped nuts. Celery may be added. This should not be made long in advance as the apples discolor.

PEACH PUFFS

In each half of a canned peach place a marshmallow. Roll the whole in shredded cocoanut and set in hot oven (500) for the marshmallow to toast. Two halves to each serving, on small slices of sponge cake.

BAKED PORK BUTTS OR CHOPS WITH DRESSING
CREAMED CABBAGE
RHUBARB-PEACH-TOMATO PIE

LET your hand open wide in the use of butter. Not to be needlessly extravagant, of course, but be generous. This is especially essential where there are children. Butter is rich in food values. It also makes things taste good. Fancy desserts are likely to put up the food costs and are not vital to the health of the family. Plain junket for the children, or a custard, and plenty of butter in the spinach is good economy. Butter, milk, eggs and cream will do more for the delicate or fussy child, or the anemic adult, than expensive meats. In making a dressing or stuffing for any kind of meat or poultry, be generous with melted butter unless, as in the Pork Chops recipe, another fat is called for. Even in this instance our personal preference would be for half pork fat and half butter in which to fry the onion and pepper.

Pork Chops or Butts with Dressing

3 lbs. pork chops or butts
2 large onions
1 green pepper
1 tsp. celery salt
1 qt. bread crumbs
1 cup boiling water

Chop onions and pepper and fry in pork fat or oil until soft and brown. Put a layer of chops in baking dish, cover with layer of chopped vegetable, then layer of bread crumbs. Alternate until all are used, bread crumbs on top. Cover with the hot water seasoned with salt, celery salt, and pepper. Bake in moderate oven (350-375) for two hours and serve with applesauce.

Creamed Cabbage

1 head new cabbage
½ pt. cream
2 tbsp. sugar
1 egg
¼ cup vinegar
2 tbs. olive oil (or melted butter)
Salt, pepper, paprika

Cut a hard head of new cabbage into halves, then into quarters. Boil in salted water for twenty minutes and drain. Beat the egg to a froth and add to cream. Put vinegar, oil (or butter), sugar, salt and pepper into a sauce-pan and bring to boiling point. Add the cream, and egg, stir thoroughly but do not boil. Add the cabbage and heat. Serve hot.

Rhubarb-Peach-Tomato Pie

1 cup cooked and sweetened rhubarb
1 cup cooked or canned tomatoes well sweetened
1 can sliced peaches and juice (small)
½ cup seeded raisins
½ cup flour

Mix all ingredients and heat but do not cook. Fill two-crust pie and cook until done.

ASPARAGUS SOUP
CHILI VEAL
HAWAIIAN CARROTS
APRICOT PIE

ONE of the advantages of having cream soup, especially where there are children is adding that much more milk to the daily diet. With a richer meat dish, cream soup would be too hearty, but with a light menu such as this it seems entirely suitable. A raw vegetable in the form of salad should accompany this menu, or a cooked vegetable such as sauerkraut or a sweet-sour cabbage, cole slaw, wilted lettuce. No potatoes are needed if the carrots are used, but a bowl of rice to supplement the veal would be good. Plenty of green vegetables and vegetables in which there is but little starch should be one of the standards on which a day's rations are planned. With a generous allowance of vegetables, some cooked and some raw, and plenty of fruit, with milk, meat or egg once a day, and cereal in some form (this includes bread), we shall not need to worry much about "balanced" meals.

Asparagus Soup

1 No. 2 can asparagus
2 cups thin white sauce
1 tbsp. butter
Salt, pepper, paprika

Drain the asparagus and chop rather coarsely. Mix juice from can with white sauce and bring to boiling point. Add asparagus, butter, salt and pepper. Serve in cups with dash of paprika, or a spoonful of whipped cream and a dash of cayenne.

Chili Veal

3 tbsp. butter
4 tbsp. flour
2 cups veal stock
2 cups cooked veal diced
1 onion
1 cup cracker crumbs
2 tbsp. chopped green pepper
1 hard cooked egg
4 tbsp. melted fat
2 tbsp. chopped olives
½ tsp. chili powder

Melt butter and add flour and cook slowly, stirring constantly until the mixture is brown. Add the stock and cook slowly until it thickens. Add veal, onion, olives, green pepper and egg chopped. Put into a buttered baking dish and cover with bread crumbs mixed with the melted fat—bacon, butter or oil. Bake in a moderate oven for 25 minutes. Serve in same dish.

Hawaiian Carrots

1 qt. diced carrots
2 tbsp. butter
1 tbsp. flour
1 cup water
½ tsp. salt
4 tbsp. sugar
4 tbsp. vinegar

Parboil carrots and then cook in butter in a frying pan until brown. Remove from pan and add flour to the fat that is left (should be about a tablespoonful). Add water gradually and bring to the boiling point, stirring constantly. Add salt. Drain over the carrots and cook in uncovered pan until the liquid is almost evaporated and the carrots tender. Add sugar and vinegar and cook until slightly reduced. Serve hot.

Apricot Pie

½ lb. dried apricots
¾ cup sugar
1 tbsp. butter
¼ tsp. salt
2 tbsp. cornstarch

Wash apricots and soak over night in just enough water to cover. Cook in the same water until soft. Put through a coarse sieve and heat. Add other ingredients and enough water to fill medium sized crust. Bake, cool and cover with whipped cream.

CHICKEN—CORN IN CASSEROLE
CUCUMBER JELLY SALAD
FROZEN RICE PUDDING

GREEN string beans are to be had almost throughout the year in city markets, but if fresh ones are not to be had, canned beans are not to be despised by any means. Some brands are better than others, and when you have found one that suits you, it is well to stick to it, although there is no harm in trying several until you find what you consider the best. When cucumbers are not available for the salad, an apple and celery combination, or just lettuce with Russian or Thousand Island Dressing, would be suitable. Or—if you are so fortunate as to have them, some of your own home-made pickles and relishes. Pickled pears or peaches, for instance, although the green vegetable would be better.

Chicken—Corn in Casserole

1 small chicken
1 pt. grated sweet corn
1 onion sliced
1 large tomato chopped
1 large green pepper
2 tbsp. butter
Salt, pepper
Cayenne

Cook the chicken (or young fowl) in as small a quantity of water as possible so that there will be but little broth left. When chicken is done, cool and cut in pieces for serving. In a frying pan melt the butter and when hot sauté the thinly sliced onion, chopped tomato and pepper. Add the pieces of chicken to this and the grated corn. Season and put in a well buttered casserole to cook about 15 minutes or until the corn is done.

Cucumber Jelly Salad

3 cucumbers
1 onion
1 tsp. chopped chives
2 tbsp. gelatin
1 tbsp. chili sauce
1 cup French dressing
Salt, pepper
Radishes, lettuce

Peel cucumbers. Chop two cucumbers and put in a saucepan with chopped onion, salt, pepper and two cups of water. Cook ten minutes. Dissolve gelatin in 4 tablespoonfuls of cold water and add to cooked cucumber and water. Cool. Line a mould with slices of cold cucumber and paper-thin slices of radish. Pour a little of the cooked cucumber liquid into the mould and let set. See that cold slices stay in place. As it sets pour in a little more until all is in with slices of cucumber and radish in place. Chill. Unmold on a bed of lettuce, and serve with French Dressing mixed with Chili Sauce and chives and thicken over a lump of ice.

Frozen Rice Pudding

½ cup rice
1½ cups cream
¼ cup powdered sugar
1 tsp. vanilla

Boil ½ cup of rice until tender. Whip 1½ cups of cream stiff. Add powdered sugar and vanilla. Mix all together and put in ice tray. Freeze 4 hours, stirring every half hour for first two hours.

ROAST BEEF—YORKSHIRE PUDDING
GERMAN SALAD

CERTAINLY nothing could be less unusual than a roast of beef but no book of menus for an American home would be complete without it. We do not seem to feel that a Yorkshire Pudding is absolutely essential to a dinner of roast beef as the English do, but that may be due to our growing disinclination to do no more than we have to, and it may be because there seems to be a pernicious idea skulking about some kitchens that it is difficult to make. Both objections can be overrode in a moment if the ear will be attentive. It takes but a few minutes to make the pudding—not longer than biscuits, it cooks at the same time the meat is roasting, and it is no more difficult to manage than pop-overs. In fact, we use the same recipe for the pudding that we use for the pop-overs.

Roast Beef–Yorkshire Pudding

Rib and back of rump are the least expensive cuts suitable for roasting. The rib roast is rolled by the meat man after the bones have been removed. Sirloin makes a delicious roast but costs more. Rump or rolled rib is best for a large roast, and small roasts are not as satisfactory as the heavier cuts. With the small roast it is more difficult to get that stage of rareness which meat lovers crave. A roast weighing from four to six pounds is best, and what is left over can be used in many ways. Wipe the meat with a damp cloth and lay in the roaster, rub over with salt and dredge with flour. Place it in a hot oven (500) for about twenty minutes to sear the outside and restrain juices. Let it cook on all sides. When the surface is seared and the flour in the pan has browned, lower the heat to 375 and baste with fat. This may come from any excess fat there was from the roast, or, if it was very lean, from some suet tried out in a frying pan. Baste every ten minutes on one side for half the time, then turn and dredge the other side with flour and baste in the same way. This will make the meat juicy and tender. Allow twenty minutes to the pound for medium rare and twenty-five for well done. If the flour begins to get too brown, add a half cup of hot water, but no more than necessary; the less water added, the better.

Yorkshire Pudding

2 eggs
1 cup milk
½ cup flour
½ tsp. salt

Beat the yolks and whites of eggs separately. Mix salt and flour and stir the milk in to make a smooth consistency. Add the beaten eggs, whites last. Bake either in very hot iron muffin irons well greased, as pop-overs, or in shallow bread or biscuit tin. In either put a good coating of fat from the roaster. Pour over a little of the beef fat when the pudding is half done. Serve with the roast and gravy.

German Salad

1 pt. sauerkraut
1 medium large onion
Endive, chicory or lettuce
1 pt. shredded red cabbage
1 tbsp. horseradish grated
French dressing

Cook a pint of sauerkraut in boiling water for five minutes. Drain and rinse in cold water. Shred red cabbage to make one pint and mix with the sauerkraut. Chop one medium large onion very fine, and add to it a tablespoonful of grated horseradish. Arrange endive, chicory or lettuce around inside of a salad bowl, put sauerkraut mixture in center and pour French dressing over.

BUFFET SUPPER MENUS

For Sunday Night or Any Other Time

THE custom of entertaining on Sunday evening is one so universally observed that the problem of what to have to eat that will be just a little different from what the hostess of last Sunday night had, is almost as acute as that of daily meals. It need not, however, be either an expensive or burdensome form of entertaining if we hold to the rule of simplicity on which we have based our menus for other occasions. Not too much should be left to the last minute and neither does one want to spend too much time and energy on preparation during the–supposed–day of rest. The solution, therefore, is to make the meal as simple as possible, and, so far as can be done without confusion, to let the guests help. Men are not at all averse to taking a hand at a grill, a toaster, a coffee pot, or even a pancake griddle, and the more successful their efforts the better time they will have.

Certain equipment (by no means essential only to entertaining) of modern invention will add much to the ease and also to the pleasure of such occasions. An electric coffee percolator, electric grill on which bacon can be fried, eggs scrambled, ham broiled; electric toaster, waffle iron and pancake griddle, and an electric mixer are amongst those devices that come most readily to mind. All of these will earn their cost many times over during the year, and will lend a special air of business-like efficiency to the party meal. Nor should the chafing dish be left out. The old-fashioned one with the alcohol lamp is not at all bad, or it may be electrified at not too great a cost.

Without any of these, however, and with nothing more modern than a stove in the kitchen, an enterprising hostess (or host) can get up a party that may earn an everlasting reputation for hospitality. In fact, some of the best parties we have ever given have emanated from a coal or oil stove in the kitchen. So do not let the absence of fancy contrivances deter you from opening your door to your friends and giving both them and yourself a good time.

Modern equipment, however, has its place in the modern home, and we suggest that such pieces as we have listed along with the plank for cooking meat, fish and vegetables, elsewhere mentioned, the salad bowl, the casserole and similar devices would make appropriate gifts to any proper minded house. In fact, we propose that all members of the family who no longer have use for their birthdays and would be glad to get rid of them, turn them ovei to the house and make suitable oblation to commemorate the event. This custom of giving away birthdays may be a new—and welcome—idea to some who have tried various means of ridding themselves of what has become an unwanted institution, but is heartily endorsed by those who have tried it. I have, myself, just recently presented mine to a young member of my family to whom birthdays are still welcome.

In serving the informal company supper, the simpler it is the better. For large parties the dining room table suitably dressed (the coarse lace cloths which are inexpensive and seldom need laundering are best) and decorated with fruit, flowers or candles, should act merely as a base of supplies. Plates, cups, silver, napkins and food are placed on it (in order and symmetry) and guests help themselves. Here, too, are soup tureen or pitcher, coffee, tea—hot or cold. Electric and other cooking devices may be placed on auxiliary tables if the dining table is not large enough to hold them.

For the large supper, nothing is easier to arrange than the buffet, or plates of assorted meats, cheese, sandwiches with relishes and bowls of salad. All one has to do is to provide enough and invite the guests to "come and get it."

For the smaller, more intimate party, the set table over which one can linger or a table drawn up to the fire on a cold evening or out onto the porch, weather permitting, will inspire more genial spirits, better talk, and more of it, than the large party.

The menus and recipes given in the following chapter are all simple of preparation and merely suggestive in nature.

WAFFLES AND SAUSAGE
APPLESAUCE OR MAPLE SYRUP
VEGETABLE SALAD

Waffles, Plain

2 eggs
1¼ cups milk
2 cups flour
1 tbsp. sugar
5 tbsp. melted butter
4 tsp. baking powder
½ tsp. salt

BEAT eggs very light. Mix and sift dry ingredients. To the eggs add the milk and dry ingredients alternately, stirring to keep free from lumps. Beat until smooth, then add melted butter and beat again. The electric mixer is a great time and energy saver in such processes as this but care must be taken not to beat too long. Bake the batter on a hot waffle iron that has been well preheated. Pour the batter into the center of the griddle and let it spread to the edges. One of the secrets of success in making waffles is to be generous with butter. This recipe makes five average waffles. Maple syrup may be substituted for the applesauce.

Vegetable Salad

A mixed salad of shredded lettuce and tomatoes in French Dressing makes a suitable accompaniment for the waffles and sausage, or one of tart fruits.

BUFFET PLATE OF FISH AND MEAT
RYE BREAD SANDWICHES
MOLASSES GEMS

Buffet Plate of Fish and Meats

Small sardines
Small smoked herring
Sliced bologna
Sliced corned beef
Deviled eggs
Relishes, pickles, etc.

ARRANGE a large plate artistically with these various articles of food, dividing the varieties from each other with water cress. Hollow out halves of tomatoes and fill with pickled onions, halves of small green peppers with tiny gherkins. Put these also on the plate, using some kind of sandwich spread as a center. This will prove a very popular dish. Accompany with potato chips.

Molasses Gems

3 tbsp. shortening
1 tsp. cinnamon
¼ tsp. ground clove
½ tsp. ginger
2 cups flour
2 tbsp. sugar
¾ cup molasses
1 egg
½ cup milk
½ tsp. soda

Mix shortening, spices, sugar and one-fourth of the molasses together and place on the stove to cook, stirring until smooth. Cool and add well beaten egg, milk, flour and the soda mixed with the remainder of the molasses. Flavor with lemon or orange juice and pour into greased gem pans. Bake in a moderate oven for 30 minutes. 12 gems.

HORS D'ŒUVRES

MOLDED CHICKEN SALAD

HOT BISCUITS

RASPBERRY JAM—CHEESE ROLL

Molded Chicken Salad

- 2½ cups cold cooked chicken diced
- ¾ cup diced celery
- ¼ cup chopped green pepper
- 2 cups chicken stock
- 2 tbsp. gelatin
- ½ cup mayonnaise
- ½ cup cream

MIX chicken, celery and pepper. Soften the gelatin in the cold stock and dissolve by bringing to the boiling point. Add to the chicken mixture and let stand until it begins to stiffen. Fold in the mayonnaise and the cream which has been whipped until stiff. Turn into a ring mold and let stand until firm. Unmold onto a bed of lettuce hearts. Fill the center with mayonnaise to which has been added an equal quantity of whipped cream.

Hors d'œuvres

Arrange a plate of radishes, celery hearts, olives, small pickles, and lengths of fresh crisp cucumber to accompany the salad.

Raspberry Jam—Cheese Roll

- 8 ozs. cream cheese
- 1 cup butter
- 3 cups flour
- ½ tsp. salt
- Raspberry jam

Grate cheese and mix ingredients as for pie crust. Chill for four hours. Remove from refrigerator, roll out not too thin and spread with raspberry jam. Roll up like a jelly roll and bake in hot oven. Cut in rather thick slices and top with whipped cream.

SWEDISH SALAD

RYE AND BROWN BREAD SANDWICHES

Swedish Salad

- 1 doz. small sardines
- 1 cup cooked chicken or veal
- 1 large cooked potato
- 1 pickled beet
- 1 onion
- 1 tbsp. minced parsley
- Hard cooked eggs
- French Dressing
- Lettuce, salt, pepper

FLAKE the sardines and stir into the chopped chicken. Cut the vegetables into small cubes except the onion which should be minced very fine. Add the parsley and enough well seasoned French Dressing to make right consistency and flavor. Heap up on lettuce leaves arranged in salad bowl (rub the inside with garlic clove) and garnish with slices of hard cooked egg.

DEEP SEA SALAD
POTATO CHIPS
STEWED RHUBARB SPICE ROLL

Deep Sea Salad

PULL the center from a fine head of lettuce and place it in the center of a round chop plate or platter. Fill with tuna fish salad (half tuna fish, half chopped celery) mixed with thin mayonnaise. On one side of the lettuce head place a mound of crab meat salad and on the other side a mound of shrimp, both dressed with mayonnaise. Garnish with halves of deviled eggs, pickled onions, ripe olives and gherkins placed between the salads.

Spice Roll

1½ tbsp. butter
1 cup sugar
5 eggs
½ cup milk
1 tsp. cinnamon
½ tsp. each cloves, ginger
2 cups flour
3 tsp. baking powder
½ tsp. salt
Currant jam and powdered sugar

Cream the butter and add sugar. Beat eggs until light and add to butter and sugar. Beat thoroughly and add milk and spices. Sift flour, baking powder and salt together and add in small quantities to the cake, beating thoroughly. Bake in a long sheet, turn out on a damp towel, spread with currant jam, roll while warm and when cool sprinkle with powdered sugar.

HOT BOUILLON—MEAT PLATE
POTATO SALAD
BUTTERSCOTCH BISCUITS

Hot Bouillon—Meat Plate

SERVE hot bouillon in cups poured from a silver pitcher or dipped from a tureen in the living room. Arrange on a platter cold baked ham, cold pickled tongue: intersperse with thin slices of Bermuda or Italian onion on lettuce leaves. Put a dish of prepared mustard in the center. Garnish with radishes and celery.

Butterscotch Biscuits

2 cups flour
4 tsp. baking powder
½ tsp. salt
2 tbsp. shortening
⅔ cup milk
½ cup raisins
Brown sugar and butter

Mix the same as baking powder biscuit, roll out and spread with butter and a generous amount of brown sugar, sprinkle with cinnamon. Sprinkle raisins over. Roll up as a jelly roll and cut in one inch slices. Put cut side down on baking tin (greased) and bake 15 to 20 minutes in 375 oven.

MOLDED HAM SALAD
SWEET POTATO OMELET
GINGERBREAD—APPLESAUCE

Molded Ham Salad

1 tbsp. gelatin
¾ cup cooked salad dressing (see page 196)
½ cup chopped celery
¼ cup cold water
6 olives, chopped
½ cup chopped cooked ham
½ green pepper chopped
Water cress

SOAK the gelatin in the cold water; make a cooked salad dressing and while hot combine with the gelatin and cool. When this begins to stiffen add the chopped ham, green pepper, celery and olives. Turn into a mold that has been rinsed with cold water, set in the refrigerator and let stand until firm—about four hours. Turn from mold, garnish with watercress and serve with cucumber sauce. See page 203.

Sweet Potato Omelet

2 cups mashed sweet potato
4 eggs
4 tbsp. milk
¼ tsp. salt

While mashed sweet potatoes are hot add the salt, milk and well beaten eggs. Turn into a well greased frying pan and cook until brown on bottom. Place in a moderate oven until top is set. Fold one half over the other on a hot plate. Serve with tart jelly.

NAN'S FAMOUS CHICKEN SALAD
BANANA GEMS

Nan's Famous Chicken Salad

4 cups diced chicken
1 cup chopped sweet pickles
1 cup chopped celery
1 cup mayonnaise
2 hard boiled eggs chopped
1 tsp. salt
¼ tsp. pepper

MIX all ingredients together, mix with highly seasoned mayonnaise, chill and serve on lettuce.

Banana Gems

3 tbsp. shortening
½ cup sugar
1 egg well beaten
2 bananas
2 cups flour
4 tsp. baking powder
¼ cup salt
1 cup milk

Cream shortening and sugar; add the well beaten egg and mashed banana pulp; add dry ingredients previously sifted together, alternating with the milk. Put in greased muffin tins and bake at 400 for 15 minutes.

SANDWICH PLATE

INDIVIDUAL PUMPKIN TARTS

Sandwich Plate

Cut as many slices of sandwich bread as needed and cut each slice in four squares and toast. Spread with soft butter, then with mayonnaise. Have ready grilled bacon cut in squares, pimiento strips, Swiss cheese cut in squares, sliced olives and wafer-thin slices of onion, ripe olives. Place slices of toast on large platter and on each arrange a slice of cheese, a square of bacon, a slice of tomato and so on, alternating on different slices. Season the ingredients with salt, pepper, paprika. Top each with a ripe olive. These are open-faced sandwiches. Garnish platter with small sweet pickles, parsley, radishes.

Individual Pumpkin Tarts

⅔ cup of sugar
½ tsp. salt
1 tsp. cinnamon
1½ cups milk
1 tsp. ginger
2 eggs
1½ cups pumpkin

Mix sugar, salt and spices. Beat the eggs until light, stir in pumpkin and milk mixed together. Canned pumpkin may be used. Use cheese pastry for shells, or plain pastry with grated cheese in bottom. Cut large rounds and pinch the edges up to form a cup. The edges will be thicker than the rest of the shell. Fill almost to top with pumpkin mixture. Bake in oven at 375 until filling is set and crust browned.

DEVILED EGGS

MACARONI SALAD

ORANGE BISCUITS

Deviled Eggs

4 eggs
½ tsp. dry mustard
1 tsp. salt
1 tsp. vinegar
¼ tsp. Worcestershire sauce
2 drops tabasco sauce
1 tbsp. chili sauce
1 tbsp. mayonnaise

Make a paste of these ingredients and fill egg whites cut in half. Arrange on lettuce and sprinkle with paprika. Use remainder of paste in white bread sandwiches.

Macaroni Salad

1 pkg. macaroni
1 cup chopped olives
2 cups diced celery
2 cups diced green pepper
6 tomatoes cut in pieces
1 cup cheese diced
French Dressing

Boil the macaroni, rinse with cold water and chill. Mix with all other ingredients and marinate with French Dressing in which a garlic clove has stood. Put lettuce leaves on large round plate, arrange salad in center. Garnish edge with the deviled eggs and quarters of small ripe tomatoes.

COLD VEAL LOAF

LETTUCE AND WATERCRESS SANDWICHES

Cold Veal Loaf

2 lbs. raw veal
½ lb. raw salt pork
¼ lb. raw ham
1 cup bread crumbs
2 tbsp. melted butter
1 egg well beaten
Milk
1 tsp. suet
Grated peel and juice of lemon
½ tsp. each pepper, paprika
1 tsp. grated onion
⅛ tsp. each cloves, allspice
Dash of nutmeg

HAVE the meat ground all together very fine, including suet. Soak the bread crumbs in just milk enough to soften; add this to the beaten egg and melted butter and mix all with the meat. Add all seasonings and mix thoroughly with the hands. Pack in a well greased bread tin (glass) and bake one hour basting often with melted butter. Serve cold in slices with cucumber sauce.

HAM AND CELERY SALAD

FRUIT FILLED GINGERBREAD

Ham and Celery Salad

1 cup diced celery
½ cup diced cucumber
1 cup diced cold potato
1 cup boiled ham diced
Pimiento or sweet red pepper
1 green pepper
Hard cooked egg
Mayonnaise

MIX celery, cucumber, potato and ham together; add mayonnaise to right consistency. Arrange lettuce leaves on round plate and place salad in center. Garnish edge with slices of hard cooked egg and rings cut from green and red peppers.

Fruit Filled Gingerbread

1¾ tsp. soda
1 cup sour cream
1 cup molasses
2¼ cups flour
½ tsp. salt
¼ cup melted shortening
2 tsp. ginger

Mix soda with sour cream and add molasses. Sift flour, salt and ginger and add to first mixture. Add shortening and beat well. Pour into two greased layer tins and bake.

Filling

2 pkgs. cream cheese
2 tbsp. chopped dates or seedless raisins
2 tbsps. chopped pecan meats
¼ tsp. salt
1 tsp. cream

Blend cream cheese, chopped dates or raisins (soaked and drained) salt and cream to smooth paste. When the gingerbread is cool spread this between layers. Dust top with powdered sugar.

LOBSTER SALAD
SANDWICH DE LUXE

Lobster Salad

LINE a large salad bowl with small white lettuce leaves and watercress. Arrange on this pieces of boiled or canned lobster, slices of cucumber, sliced sweet onion, halves of deviled eggs, stuffed and ripe olives. Pour French Dressing over and serve with Mayonnaise.

Sandwich de Luxe

6 sour gherkins
1 pimiento
1 pkg. cream cheese
Mayonnaise

Chop gherkins and pimiento; add cream cheese and blend together, softening with mayonnaise. Spread this on buttered slices of white or rye bread (crusts removed) and roll up like jelly roll. Fasten with tooth pick.

CURRY OF CHICKEN
DATE MUFFINS
COTTAGE CHEESE—JAM RING

Curry of Chicken

2 tbsp. butter
1 tsp. minced onion
2 tbsp. flour
1 cup chicken stock
¼ cup cream
Salt and pepper, paprika
1 tsp. curry powder
1 tbsp. sherry (wine or flavoring)
2 tbsp. minced almonds
2 tbsp. minced tart apples
2 cups diced cooked chicken
Patty shells or bread croustades

HEAT the butter and in it cook the onion then add the flour and stir until browned. Dissolve the curry in a little water and add to flour mixture; add also the stock in which the chicken was cooked, the chicken, and lastly the cream, sherry and salt, pepper, paprika and serve in patty shells or bread croustades. Sprinkle with minced almonds.

Cottage Cheese—Jam Ring

Pack cottage cheese, highly seasoned, in a ring mold and chill. When ready to serve, turn out on glass plate and in the center turn out a large glass of raspberry or blackberry jam.

CORN AND GREEN PEPPER
SOUR CREAM SCONES
CURRANT OR GRAPE JELLY

Corn and Green Pepper on Toast

1 onion sliced
1 green pepper minced
1 tbsp. butter
2 cups green corn
1 cup cream
Salt, pepper

HEAT butter, sauté onion and pepper until soft and clear. Add two cups of green corn scraped from the cob and heat; add cream and seasonings last. Serve on toast.

Sour Cream Scones

2 cups flour
½ tsp. salt
2 tbsp. melted butter
1 tbsp. sugar
1 cup sour cream
½ tsp. soda

Mix and sift dry ingredients. Stir soda into the sour cream and mix with flour. Beat well. Let stand 15-20 minutes; roll out on board adding flour to handle if necessary. Cut with biscuit cutter into biscuits one fourth inch thick. Fry on hot griddle both sides and serve with butter.

TASTY BEANS
MUSTARD PICKLES—CHILI SAUCE
BROWN BREAD—BUTTER
CINNAMON COOKIES

Tasty Beans

1 lb. navy beans
1 No. 3 can tomatoes
4 small onions
10 slices bacon
1 cup brown sugar
¾ cup dark corn syrup
1 tsp. salt
1 tsp. black pepper
1 tbsp. dry mustard

SOAK the beans overnight; in the morning drain the beans and rinse them; cover with fresh water and boil until tender. Cut bacon in squares and fry but not to a crisp. Sauté the onions in this until soft; add tomatoes, sugar and corn syrup, salt, pepper and mustard and cook together for about ten minutes. Drain the beans through a colander and put half of them in a bean pot. Cover with half the bacon and tomato mixture. Put in the other half of beans and cover with remainder of the sauce. Cover and cook for three hours in slow (350) oven.

Cinnamon Cookies

2 cups brown sugar
1 cup shortening
2 eggs
1 cup sour cream
2 tsp. soda
Flour
Pinch of salt

Beat one whole egg and the white of another very light. Blend sugar and shortening and beat egg into these. Mix soda and salt with cream and beat into first mixture. Stir in flour enough to roll out in soft dough. Cut with scalloped cooky cutter, brush slightly with white of egg and sprinkle with mixture of sugar and cinnamon. Bake in 400-450 oven.

BALTIMORE CLUB SANDWICHES

JEWEL SALAD

Baltimore Club Sandwiches

1 can crabmeat (1¼ cups)
4 small tomatoes
Lettuce
Mayonnaise

FLAKE crabmeat and mix with mayonnaise. Arrange hearts of lettuce leaves on buttered plain bread, or bread that has been toasted on one side. Put a little mayonnaise on the lettuce and cover with a slice of tomato. Spread the crabmeat over the tomato and cover with a second slice of bread or toast. Serve immediately.

Jewel Salad

1 tbsp. gelatin
¼ cup cold water
¼ cup boiling water
1 cup diced cucumber
1 cup grapefruit pulp
¼ cup sugar
¼ cup tarragon vinegar
⅔ cup grapefruit juice
1 tbsp. lemon juice
Pinch salt
Cherries, green or white grapes
Coloring matter

Soften the gelatin in the cold water and dissolve in boiling water. Drain chopped cucumber and mix with grapefruit pulp. Heat lemon, grapefruit juice and vinegar and combine with dissolved gelatin; add salt. Pour into six different molds rinsed with cold water, and color them different colors with vegetable coloring matter—green, red, etc. Divide the cucumber and pineapple pulp amongst these, stir and set away to set and chill. Turn from molds onto beds of lettuce and serve with mayonnaise. Garnish with cherries and grapes.

SALMON SALAD MAYONNAISE

HOT BAKING POWDER BISCUITS

STRAWBERRY—COTTAGE CHEESE SANDWICHES

Salmon Salad

2 cups cold boiled salmon
2 tbsp. lemon juice
1 tbsp. minced parsley
1 tbsp. minced onion
1 tbsp. gelatin
¼ cup cold water
¼ cup boiling water
1 tbsp. tarragon vinegar
Salt, pepper, paprika

PICK the salmon into small pieces with a fork; add to it the parsley, onion, salt, pepper, paprika and mix together. Soften gelatin in cold water; heat vinegar and lemon juice with boiling water and add to the gelatin. Pour over the salmon, mix and pack into an oblong mold which has been rinsed with cold water, and with slices of hard boiled egg arranged on sides and bottom. Serve with mayonnaise.

Strawberry—Cottage Cheese Sandwiches

Crush fresh strawberries with sugar to taste. Mix with twice the amount of Cottage Cheese well seasoned. Place between thin slices of white or whole wheat bread, buttered. Red raspberries may be used in the same way.

BAKED BEAN SANDWICHES

DILL PICKLES BLACKBERRY JAM

PEACHY SPONGE CAKE

Baked Bean Sandwiches

2 cups baked beans with pork and tomato sauce
8 stuffed Spanish olives chopped
½ tsp. salt
4 sweet gherkins
1 sweet onion chopped
Mayonnaise

PUT beans through purée sieve. Add all chopped ingredients and mayonnaise to make a smooth paste. Spread between buttered slices of Boston Brown, rye or white bread.

Peachy Sponge Cake

Before arranging the plates, make the following syrup: To each serving required take one and a half tablespoonfuls of raspberry or currant jam and three tablespoonfuls of peach syrup from the can. Let stand in hot water to melt jelly. Beat until smooth and chill. When ready to serve, lay either a slice of homemade sponge cake or a small individual sponge cake on a glass dessert plate. On each serving place half a canned peach with the cavity up. Fill this cavity with finely chopped nut meats. Pile whipped cream over the cavity of the peach and then pour the cold syrup over all. Vanilla or peach ice cream could be used instead of whipped cream. Garnish with small pieces of cut peach, or preserved ginger.

ASSORTED CHEESE PLATE

AVOCADO—PINEAPPLE SPIKES SALAD

ARRANGE on a round handsome plate an assortment of cheese, Swiss, cream, American, Roquefort, Gruyère, and in the center put either a pineapple or some other ornamental cheese. Perhaps one of the pottery jars of cheese made with wine. With this serve crackers, small hot baking powder biscuits, or rye bread and butter; also a plate of celery, olives, pickles, radishes with perhaps another of smoked herring or sardines.

Avocado–Pineapple Spikes Salad

Canned pineapple is now put up in another form than either the sliced or the crushed. The apple is sliced lengthwise in long narrow spikes which allows for a new kind of decorative salad. Cut avocados in half. Peel and remove seed. Now cut each half in two and then in narrow strips about the size of the pineapple spikes. Cut rather small, firm small seeded cucumbers in the same way. In a salad bowl arrange lettuce or cress, and then, radiating from the bottom alternate strips of avocado, pineapple and cucumber. In the center place a mound of cottage cheese and sprinkle it with paprika. Fine strips of green and sweet red peppers or pimiento scattered about will add color. Pour French Dressing carefully over, not touching the cheese.

BREAKFAST MENUS

COMPANY BREAKFASTS

THE custom of casually inviting two or three people to "come in and have breakfast with us on Sunday morning" seems to be growing. Perhaps this is because of an occasional atavistic longing for a real breakfast and only outside companionship will give the courage to break over the conventional orange-juice-and-toast habit. At any rate it is a pleasant custom and one to be encouraged because of its simplicity if for no other reason. Even without a maid or other outside help a breakfast for four or five people can be managed without undue exertion and with but little expense.

A company breakfast is usually served anywhere from ten-thirty to twelve-thirty o'clock and so partakes of the nature of a simple luncheon.

The same implements and equipment recommended for use in evening entertainment will be just as helpful earlier in the day. A toaster, a coffee percolator, an electric grill and griddle will enable one to get an entire breakfast at the table, except if hot breads such as muffins or biscuits are included.

Fruits can often be prepared the night before, especially cooked fruits such as apricots, prunes and raisins. Applesauce and rhubarb are both better for being allowed just to cool after cooking. Berries should be cold but not chilled and served, if possible, without washing. Better to risk a little uncertainty about the hands that picked them than to make them mushy or rub off the bloom. If berries must be washed, fill a pan with cold water, toss the berries in lightly, whirl them about by moving the pan, not the berries, and lift them into a colander in order to handle them as little as possible. Berries lose not only appearance by washing but flavor.

Peaches should never be peeled until just before serving if they are to keep their lovely coloring. Peel and cover them with sugar at once. Apples, too, must be handled with care to prevent discoloration. They should be thrown into cold water as peeled.

To the mind of the average American breakfast is made or ruined according to the coffee that is served with it. A good cup of coffee can cover up a number of other sins, but no matter how perfect the rest of the meal may be, poorly made coffee can ruin it.

Two vital factors control the result of coffee making. One is the freshness of the bean itself. The other is the condition of the vessel in which it is made. Not so many years ago people thought they had to buy their coffee in sacks and roast and grind it themselves in order to be sure of blend and flavor. A coffee mill was considered as essential a piece of household equipment as a rolling pin. The wit, skill and business acumen of the modern food merchant have devised ways of doing our selecting, roasting, grinding and storing, and so eliminating all such labor for us and still deliver to us as fresh and fragrant a product as ever came from Grandmother's mill. The packages are small and one is used before it has any chance to deteriorate, or the coffee packed in containers that retain flavor and fragrance to the last.

With fresh well-blended coffee provided, the next step in good coffee making is one for which no one is responsible but ourselves and that is in the brewing. And the first consideration there is the vessel in which the brew is made. An unclean coffee pot, percolator or whatever device is used will taint the flavor of the best coffee in the world. And just an ordinary washing, much less a rinsing out, or even a casual scalding will not insure the kind of cleanliness that is necessary. It must be scoured at least once a week with baking soda or some other cleansing agent to remove any sediment. We have never found anything better than plain baking soda.

With these two precautions, good fresh coffee of well blended beans and a clean pot, we may be reasonably well assured of a satisfactory brew—if it is not spoiled in the brewing.

Again the merchant and the manufacturer have come to our aid in trying to provide us with a fool-proof device for good coffee-making and their efforts have in no inconsiderable measure been successful, but still, carelessness can thwart even the skill of an inventor.

Possibly the best—and surest—method of making good coffee, is by the drip method. There are, however, those who have enough native cunning to frustrate the well laid plans of the man (for of course it was a man, a coffee-loving man) who devised this simple plan, by pouring water a second time over the grounds. The result will be a muddy beverage, bitter and lacking in flavor and probably lukewarm.

Percolated coffee is equally as good as the dripped, if not allowed to percolate too long. Any effort to seep the last drop of strength from the coffee is bound to end in dissatisfaction to those who know good coffee when they taste it.

Boiled coffee is not to be scorned when made over a stone fireplace in the open, and steeped coffee is the most satisfactory method where it must be served in large quantities.

Glass and earthenware vessels for brewing are more satisfactory than those made of metal for two reasons. In the first place they are easily kept clean, and also because there can be no possible taint from the container, even imagined.

Fresh water should always be used in making coffee, no matter what the method. Measurements should be accurate according to the method recommended by the makers of the device used.

Grounds should never be allowed to stand in brewed coffee. The best of the flavor is drawn *off* the grounds.

In using a percolator, make the amount the percolator calls for. If you want a smaller amount–get a smaller percolator. To vary the strength use more or less coffee, not by longer percolating. Slow steady percolating gives better results than furious bubbling. Cold water is used to start with.

In making drip coffee, fresh boiling water is used. The pot should be pre-heated by pouring boiling water into the upper container and letting it drip through. The compartment holding the grounds should be removed as soon as the coffee has finished dripping. If the type of pot that calls for a cloth strainer is used, be sure that it is kept clean. It should be scalded and kept in cold water. We personally like the filter papers that can be thrown away.

To make steeped coffee the proportion is one pound of good coffee to two gallons of boiling water. The coffee is put in a loose bag of double cheese-cloth and dropped into the kettle or pot. The pot is covered and the liquid kept at just under boiling for ten or twelve minutes. Then remove the bag and keep the coffee at the same temperature.

Do not reheat coffee if you want a good flavor. And always serve coffee *hot* if it is meant to be hot, and with ice if it is iced coffee. Lukewarm coffee that is meant to be hot, and hardly cooled coffee when iced is promised is extremely irritating.

To make iced coffee, make a strong infusion of the clear liquid and pour it hot over cracked or cubed ice. After-dinner coffee is made of extra strength and is usually taken clear.

Cafe au lait is made of equal quantities of hot coffee and hot milk.

They are poured together (from different containers) into the cup. The Viennese custom is to put a teaspoonful of cream on top.

Fresh fruit handsomely served or a glass of fruit juice cold, a hot dish, some kind of hot bread and a good cup of coffee makes a breakfast fit for any king yet hanging on to a throne.

Serve your breakfast in the most informal manner. Out of doors if possible in summer, beside a fire on a bleak day, or wherever there is light, color and a pleasant outlook. Use gay cloths and pretty china and glass no matter how cheap. The menus and recipes which follow, like all others in this book, are very simple and easy of preparation. There may not be a single thing suggested that you have not had or seen, but there may be new combinations and ideas that will please and inspire you to carry them out.

We believe that one of the charms in having a home is to share it. Bringing friends and acquaintances together is one way of building up community life, of welding interests, furthering that good old-fashioned neighborliness which was the backbone of rural, town and even city life in those earlier days toward which we often find ourselves turning with homesick fervor. But we believe in a simple interchange of social amenities—not to do more than the strength will stand, the purse approve or the heart dictate. Hospitality must be honest as well as warm. But we believe in doing that little well. A few dishes plentiful in quantity, excellent in quality, nicely served, offered in friendliness is better than—but you know about the stalled ox and the dinner of herbs. It could not be better said.

BAKED APPLE—PRUNE CENTER
ASPARAGUS OMELET
HAM MUFFINS

Baked Apples—Prune Center

CORE but do not peel tart well-flavored apples, and in the center of each put a large prune previously cooked and sweetened and with a nut meat in place of pit. Bake until tender. Serve warm with sugar and cream.

Asparagus Omelet

1 can asparagus tips
1 tbsp. butter
2 tbsp. milk
2 eggs beaten
1 tsp. salt
Dash pepper

Drain the asparagus tips and cut coarsely; season with salt, pepper and a little melted butter. Beat the yolks of the eggs and add the two tablespoonfuls of milk; beat very light. In another bowl beat the egg whites very stiff and fold into the yolks. Season lightly. Put the butter in a frying pan and when melted (do not let it get smoking hot) turn in the egg mixture and cook over a slow fire until the mixture begins to look puffy. It should then be a nice brown on the bottom. Now put the asparagus tips (heated) over one-half the omelet and fold over the other. Set in the oven a few moments to dry. Garnish with cubes of currant jelly.

Ham Muffins

4 tbsp. shortening
1 cup chopped cooked ham
1 egg
1 cup graham flour
1 cup white flour
3 tsp. baking powder
1 cup milk

Cream shortening and add ham to it; add egg well beaten and the dry ingredients mixed and sifted, alternately with the milk. Mix well and put into greased muffin tins. Bake 30 minutes in 400 oven. 12 muffins.

ORANGE JUICE
HEARTY OMELET
CINNAMON ROLLS

Hearty Omelet

1 pt. milk
¼ cup cornmeal
¼ tsp. salt
6 slices bacon
3 eggs
1 small onion

HEAT the milk, stir in the cornmeal and cook for a few minutes stirring constantly. Add salt. Cut bacon into small pieces and fry a light brown; remove bacon. Drain off all but one tablespoonful of fat and sauté onion (chopped) in this until soft, then stir bacon and onion with remaining fat into cornmeal and milk. Separate the eggs and beat thoroughly. Stir the beaten yolks into the mixture and add the whites last. Bake 20 minutes in 400 oven.

Cinnamon Rolls

Make rich baking powder biscuit dough and roll out one-fourth inch thick. Spread with softened butter and sprinkle with mixed sugar and cinnamon. Roll up like jelly cake, cut off three-quarter inch slices, lay these flat down in baking tin (greased) and bake as baking powder biscuit.

APPLESAUCE

CHIPPED PEPPERS

POLENTA WITH CHEESE

Chipped Peppers

6 sweet green peppers
2 large onions
½ tbsp. frying fat
1 cup canned tomatoes
6 eggs
Salt and pepper

CUT peppers lengthwise in large strips after removing seeds. Slice onions in rings. Heat fat in frying pan and when hot put the pepper slices, onion rings and the strained tomato into it and simmer until onions and peppers are soft. Add salt and pepper and enough hot water to nearly cover eggs. When this mixture is hot drop the eggs in one by one very carefully and poach, basting with the liquid. Serve on toast.

Polenta with Cheese

1 pt. boiling water
½ cup cornmeal
Salt
Grated cheese
Melted butter

Sift the meal slowly into the salted boiling water, stirring. Cook until thick, set aside to cool. When cool enough to handle form into pats with a spoon, roll in grated cheese, and put in shallow pan. Pour a very little melted butter over the pats, and set in a hot oven until the cheese has melted. Serve hot.

FRESH PINEAPPLE

MUSHROOM BREAKFAST DISH

MAPLE BUTTERSCOTCH ROLLS

Mushroom Breakfast Dish

Bread slices
Large mushrooms
Minced ham or chicken
Salt, pepper, cayenne
Dash of nutmeg
Butter

SPREAD thick slices of bread (without crusts) with softened butter and sprinkle with paprika. On each slice lay large mushrooms (peeled) upside down. Chop the stems and a small amount of left-over veal, chicken or ham, mix with seasonings and spread this on the mushrooms. Dot with butter and set in a medium hot oven for about 25 minutes. The bread should be toasted, the mushrooms done.

Maple Butterscotch Rolls

2 cups flour
4 tsp. baking powder
½ tsp. salt
3 tbsp. shortening
¾ cup milk
3 tbsp. butter
½ cup brown sugar
1 tbsp. maple syrup scraped
½ cup chopped walnuts

Sift together the flour, salt and baking powder, and work in the shortening. Add milk enough to make a soft dough and roll out into a rectangular sheet about a quarter of an inch thick. Cream together the butter, brown sugar and scraped or grated maple sugar. Spread this mixture on the dough, sprinkle with finely chopped nut meats, roll like a jelly roll, cut and bake as cinnamon rolls.

FRESH BERRIES
BROILED HAM IN CREAM
PECAN ROLLS

Broiled Ham in Cream

HAVE a middle slice of ham cut about half an inch thick. If very salt soak in cold water for two hours. Rinse in cold water, wipe dry with heavy cloth and pan broil in hot frying pan until a light brown; a little brown sugar may be sprinkled over it and a little butter put in the pan. Cook for about 20 minutes, turning frequently. When done, remove to a platter, and pour one cupful of thin cream into the frying pan. Bring to a boil and pour over the ham.

Pecan Rolls

Make a rich biscuit dough (as for Butterscotch Maple Rolls, or Cinnamon Rolls) sprinkle with brown sugar and chopped pecan meats. Roll and cut in slices three-fourths inch thick. Butter patty pans or muffin tins generously, sprinkle with brown sugar and whole nut meats. Put in the slices and bake as biscuits. These may be baked in a large dripping pan; in that case, butter the bottom of the pan, sprinkle with brown sugar, and nut meats. Plain muffins may be made and put in tins treated in the same way.

TOKAY GRAPES
LIVER WITH BACON SAUCE
FRIED HOMINY

Liver with Bacon Sauce

Calves' livers
Minced parsley
Minced onion
Bacon
Salt, pepper
Flour
Stock
Worcestershire Sauce

CUT the livers in slices about a third of an inch thick; cover with boiling water and let stand five minutes. Drain, wipe dry with heavy cloth. Lay them out on a board or shallow pan, dust with salt, pepper, minced parsley and onion (mixed) and let stand an hour. Fry thin slices of bacon (a third as much bacon as liver) in frying pan until done, take from pan and drain on paper toweling. Keep hot. Roll the slices of liver in flour, put in bacon fat and cook until brown on both sides and thoroughly done but not crisp. Place on platter with bacon. Add one tablespoonful of flour to the fat in the pan, blend and brown; add one cup of meat stock, or water with one tablespoonful of Worcestershire Sauce. Bring to boil and pour over liver or serve with it.

Fried Hominy

Make a mush of hominy grits the same as corn meal, and while hot pack it into a greased pan such as bread is baked in. Let stand all night. In the morning slice it and fry in bacon fat, pork fat, or part butter and part oil. Serve with butter and maple syrup.

FRESH PEARS

BROILED FINNAN HADDIE

POTATO PUFF

Broiled Finnan Haddie

COVER a thick fish with cold water and let it stand for an hour. Drain and cover again with fresh water. Drain and cover with hot water at the boiling point but not boiling. (If a stronger flavor is desired, eliminate the last freshening.) Drain and dry; sprinkle over it a few drops of lemon juice, dot with butter and broil for 20 minutes. Or panbroil. Remove to hot platter and pour over it either a thin white sauce or a cup of hot cream. Baked potatoes are good with this.

Potato Puff

2 cups hot mashed potato
3 tbsp. cream
2 tbsp. butter
Dash of nutmeg
Whites of 3 eggs
Salt, pepper
Celery salt
Minced parsley

Add the cream, butter and seasonings to the hot potato and beat until very light. Beat the whites of eggs to stiff froth and fold in. Pile lightly onto a serving dish, brush with some of the egg white, brown in oven. Sprinkle with minced parsley and dash of paprika.

RHUBARB SAUCE

DRIED BEEF WITH SCRAMBLED EGGS

CORNMEAL MUFFINS

Dried Beef with Scrambled Eggs

SAUTÉ one chopped onion in hot fat—butter, oil or pork fat; when soft put into the pan as much dried beef as will be required for serving, picked into small pieces. Stir it until the edges have curled. Remove the beef and onion, add a tablespoonful of flour (and more butter if needed) and blend smooth. Add a cup of top milk and cook until slightly thickened. Beat eggs according to requirement in a bowl, add them to the beef and onion and put all back in the sauce and cook five minutes. Serve on toast or with boiled potatoes.

Corn Meal Muffins

1 egg
½ tsp. salt
2 tbsp. sugar
1 cup flour
1 cup milk
1 tbsp. shortening
3 tsp. baking powder
½ cup yellow cornmeal

Beat egg with milk, add salt and shortening, and lastly the dry ingredients sifted together. Mix to smooth consistency and bake in muffin pans filled two-thirds full for 20 minutes at 375-400.

STEWED FIGS—CREAM
CODFISH SOUFFLÉ
RICE MUFFINS

Codfish Soufflé

1 cup salt codfish shredded
2 cups raw potato, diced
1 tbsp. butter
2 tbsp. catsup
2 eggs

SHRED codfish, and soak in cold water for a short time. Cook fish and potatoes together in water to cover, until potatoes are tender. Drain, mash, add butter and beat to a fluff. Add catsup, stir in beaten egg yolks, and fold in stiffly beaten whites last. Place in greased baking dish and bake for 20 minutes in moderate (375) oven until brown.

Rice Muffins

2 cups flour
5 tsp. baking powder
3 tbsp. sugar
¾ tsp. salt
1 whole egg
1 egg yolk
¾ cup boiled rice
⅞ cup milk
2 tbsp. melted butter

Sift together the flour, baking powder, sugar and salt. Beat the whole egg and the egg yolk together and add to the rice. Mix thoroughly and add the milk. Mix again. Combine the two mixtures, add the melted butter and bake in hot greased muffin pans for 25 minutes at 400.

STEWED APRICOTS AND PRUNES
EGGS IN HAM NESTS
SALLY LUNN

Stewed Apricots and Prunes

PUT one-third prunes to two-thirds dried apricots to soak at night in just water to cover. In the morning stew them in the same water until tender. Add a few drops of lemon juice and sweeten to taste.

Eggs in Ham Nests

Mince left-over ham, mix it with a cream sauce well seasoned; butter custard cups, line with the ham, leaving room in the center to drop an egg. Sprinkle the egg with salt and pepper, put a dot of butter on it and set the cups in a baking tin in which there is a very little water. Place in the oven until the eggs are set.

Sally Lunn

3 eggs
1 cup milk
1 tbsp. melted butter
2 cups flour
2 tsp. baking powder
½ tsp. salt
1 tbsp. sugar

Beat the whites and yolks of eggs separately; add milk and melted butter to the yolks and beat. Sift the flour, baking powder, sugar and salt together and add gradually to the milk and egg. Fold in the whites of eggs and put in shallow baking pan well greased. Bake in a moderate oven from 30 to 40 minutes. Serve hot with butter.

TANGERINES

BEEFSTEAK ROLLS

BLUEBERRY MUFFINS

Beefsteak Rolls

Round steak cut in thin slices
Chopped onion
Chopped parsley
Salt, pepper
Bread crumbs
Beaten egg
Fat

SAUTÉ the chopped vegetables in cooking fat (pork fat or butter) and season with salt and pepper. Have pieces of round steak cut very thin, each piece one serving. Lay these on a board and spread with the sautéd vegetables. Roll up and fasten with toothpicks. Roll in beaten egg and then in bread crumbs and fry in deep fat or put in the oven and broil until the steak is done.

Blueberry Muffins

1 egg
¼ cup sugar
2 cups flour
¾ cup milk
½ tsp. salt
3 tsp. baking powder
2 tbsp. shortening
1 cup berries

Beat egg, add sugar and milk. Sift one and three-fourth cups of the flour with salt, sugar and baking powder and add to egg and milk; have the berries very dry, put them in a paper bag with the remainder of the flour and shake them about, then pour them (with the flour) into the batter. Bake in greased muffin tins in a moderate oven (375) for 20 minutes. Makes 12 muffins.

APPLES BAKED WITH RAISINS

BROILED OYSTERS ON TOAST

CREAMED CUCUMBERS

Apples Baked with Raisins

WASH and core well-flavored apples and put in baking dish. Fill the centers with seeded raisins, put a very little water in the dish and bake until tender.

Broiled Oysters on Toast

Drain from their juice as many large oysters as will be required for serving. Wipe dry, season with salt and pepper and fry in hot butter for a few minutes. Skim them from the fat, lay on a mesh broiler or cooky tin under the broiler, and brown on both sides. Lay them when done, on thin slices of toast, heat a little of the oyster liquid in the hot butter and pour this over. Garnish with slices of lemon, sprigs of parsley and serve hot.

Creamed Cucumbers

3 cucumbers
1 cup white sauce
1 tbsp. minced parsley
Salt, pepper
Yolk of 1 egg
1 tsp. lemon juice
Paprika

Peel small firm cucumbers and cut each into thick slices. Parboil for 5 minutes in salted water. Drain and put in cold water for 5 minutes. Heat 1 cup of white sauce and add the cucumbers to it and cook slowly until tender. Add the minced parsley, the yolk of the egg, the lemon juice, sprinkle with paprika and serve hot.

CLAM BROTH

HAM OMELET HOMINY DROPS

FRUIT

Ham Omelet

6 eggs
1 cup minced cooked ham
1 tsp. minced parsley
Salt, pepper
1 tbsp. butter

BEAT yolks and whites of eggs separately and then fold them together. Season with salt and pepper. Heat the butter in a frying pan (good sized) and pour the egg in; when it has set on the bottom, spread half the ham and the minced parsley over and fold together. Take from the pan and set in a hot oven for a few minutes. Heat the remainder of the ham in the pan and use it to garnish the platter.

Hominy Drops

2 cups cold boiled hominy
1 tbsp. cold water
2 eggs
Pinch salt
1 tsp. baking powder
1 cup flour
1 tbsp. melted butter

Beat the eggs and add to the cold boiled hominy, with tablespoonful of cold water (or milk). Sift the baking powder, salt and a cup of flour together and stir into hominy mixture to make a batter that will drop stiffly from spoon. Drop onto a greased baking sheet and bake in a hot (400) oven.

FRESH CHERRIES

BROILED SALT MACKEREL

LYONNAISE POTATOES

HOT ROLLS—JAM OR JELLY

Broiled Salt Mackerel

REMOVE head and tail, scrape insides and wash. Soak over night in cold water to cover or longer if fish is very salty. In the morning drain, wash in fresh water and wipe dry; brush with melted butter and broil over slow fire until tender. Season with pepper, put on a hot platter, pour melted butter over, sprinkle with minced parsley and garnish with lemon.

Lyonnaise Potatoes

The proportion of onion to potato in this dish should depend somewhat upon personal taste, but about one large onion to three cups of diced potato is a usual proportion. The onion should be chopped rather fine and the potato should be cut in halves lengthwise, then in quarters and eighths and then diced. It should never be chopped fine, neither should it be left in coarse pieces. Allow a tablespoonful of bacon fat, pork fat or butter to each two cups of potato; heat the fat and put the onion in to sauté until soft. Then add the potato, mix them together and let cook over a not too hot fire until slightly browned on the bottom. Then turn with as little stirring as possible until heated through.

FRESH PEACHES WITH CREAM
SALMON STEAK
RICE PANCAKES

Salmon Steak

2 lbs. salmon steak
1 tbsp. minced parsley
Salt, pepper
4 tbsp. butter
1 tbsp. capers
Juice 1 lemon
Flour, salt

MIX flour and salt together and flour the steaks. Fry in hot oil or fat on both sides until cooked through and remove to hot platter. Melt the butter, add the lemon juice, minced parsley and capers and pour over. Serve hot.

Rice Pancakes

1 cup warm boiled rice
1 cup milk
2 eggs
½ tsp. salt
2 tbsp. melted butter
4 tbsp. flour
2 tsp. baking powder

Combine rice, salt, milk, butter and egg yolks. Stir in flour and baking powder sifted together. Fold in stiffly beaten whites of eggs. Bake on hot griddle.

ICED MELON
BAKED HASH QUICK COFFEE CAKE
RASPBERRY JAM

Iced Melon

No matter what kind of melon is served, it should always be cold. Never put it on the table until just before it is to be eaten. Cantaloupe should be washed and put in the refrigerator when it comes from the market, if it is ripe. Otherwise, let it stand out for a few hours or a night before serving. Then put it in the ice box. Never serve ice in or on the melon itself.

Baked Hash

1 cup ground cooked meat
1 cup cold cooked rice
¾ cup milk
1 tbsp. butter
Salt and pepper

Heat milk and rice and blend smooth, mix the meat with it. Season to taste. Add the butter and meat, stir and cook on top of stove for about fifteen minutes, then add the beaten egg, mix. Put in a greased baking pan and set in oven to bake from half to three-quarters of an hour. Test with a silver knife. When it comes out clean the hash is done. Serve with slices of pickle, and ketchup.

Quick Coffee Cake

2 cups flour
4 tsp. baking powder
½ tsp. salt
2 tbsp. sugar
3 tbsp. shortening
1 egg
⅔ cup milk
Butter, sugar, cinnamon

Sift together the flour, baking powder, salt and sugar. Mix the shortening into this. Beat egg, mix with milk and add to flour. Spread in a shallow baking pan, cover with softened butter, sprinkle quite thick with sugar and cinnamon (1 teaspoon of cinnamon to half cup of sugar) and bake in moderately hot oven.

FRUIT

BAKED HADDOCK WITH EGG SAUCE

GREEN CORN PATTIES

Baked Haddock—Egg Sauce

2 lbs. haddock
Salt, vinegar
Pepper

1½ cups white sauce
1 sliced hard cooked egg
Parsley

PLUNGE the haddock into boiling water to which has been added salt and a little vinegar. Let stand five minutes then add a little cold water to reduce temperature quickly. Simmer slowly until the flesh is tender and ready to fall from bones. Add the sliced hard cooked egg to the white sauce and pour over the fish when it has been removed to a platter. Garnish with parsley.

Green Corn Patties

Mix green corn shaved from the cob with one whole egg well beaten, a little milk and flour, season to taste, and drop into hot butter to fry on both sides. Proportion of ingredients according to need.

BLUEBERRIES—CREAM

POACHED EGGS—MUSHROOM SAUCE

SQUASH BUNS

Poached Eggs—Mushroom Sauce

6 eggs (or according to servings)
6 slices hot toast
½ lb. mushrooms

3 cups mushroom sauce
2 slices bacon
Salt, pepper
Paprika

COOK the stems of the mushrooms in a very little water and add white sauce to make 3 cups. Season with salt and pepper. Broil mushrooms, toast the bread, poach the eggs. Lay poached eggs in center of pieces of toast and broiled mushrooms around the edge. Cut bacon into coarse pieces and fry to light crisp. Pour mushroom sauce over toast, not touching the egg. Garnish with frizzled bacon and bits of parsley.

Squash Buns

1 cake yeast
1 cup water
Mashed potato
Flour
1 cup cooked mashed squash
1 cup sugar

1 cup milk
½ cup butter
1 tbsp. salt
1 cup raisins
Melted butter
Cinnamon, sugar

Dissolve the yeast in lukewarm water. Add a small amount of mashed potato and flour enough to make a soft batter. Let rise until light. Add remaining ingredients in order listed, with enough flour to make a stiff dough. Let rise again until light, roll out, and cut with biscuit cutter; brush with melted butter and sprinkle with sugar and cinnamon mixed. Leave space enough between buns so they will merely touch when done. Let rise and bake in moderate oven.

FRUIT

SCRAMBLED EGGS AND BACON

CORNMEAL ROLLS

Scrambled Eggs and Bacon

7 eggs well beaten
1 cup bacon shredded
1 tsp. grated onion
Salt, pepper

FRY the cupful of shredded bacon until nearly done. Drain off most of the fat, and in what is left sauté the onion. When this is tender, add the eggs and cook until the eggs are done. Stir constantly with a fork. Never stir scrambled eggs with a spoon, or add milk.

Cornmeal Rolls

2 cups flour
2 cups cornmeal
8 tsps. baking powder
1 tsp. salt
4 tbsp. shortening
1⅓ cups milk

Mix as biscuit. Roll the dough about one-third inch thick and cut with a round cutter. Brush with melted butter and fold over like a Parker House Roll. Bake in a hot oven 20 to 25 minutes.

SLICED ORANGES

SOUR MILK GRIDDLE CAKES

APPLE RINGS AND BACON

Sour Milk Griddle Cakes

2½ cups flour
¾ tsp. salt
1 egg
1 tbsp. sugar
2 cups sour milk
1¼ tsp. soda
1½ tbsp. butter melted

MIX and sift all dry ingredients together. Beat egg, add milk and melted butter. Add the sifted dry materials to this and beat thoroughly. Put the batter in a pitcher and pour onto hot griddle.

Apple Rings and Bacon

Cut bacon strips into squares and frizzle in hot frying pan. Do not cook to a crisp but just so the white part is transparent and the lean slightly brown. Remove the bacon from the fat and keep hot. Wash, wipe dry and core fine flavored large apples. Cut crossways into thick slices (without peeling). Fry these in the bacon fat until tender, but do not let them get mushy. Remove the apple rings to a platter and fill the centers with the frizzled bacon.

SALAD DRESSINGS

Salads and Salad Dressings

WHERE, not so many years ago, the cole slaw and wilted lettuce were the nearest approach to a salad that the average housewife knew, we now have a hundred different varieties universally served. Sometimes it is the main course, as at a luncheon or supper. Sometimes it is served as a separate course following the main dish, and often it is an appetizer served with the meal; again, it introduces the meal. Those most suitable to serve as the main dish of the meal are made of meat, fish or eggs. Lettuce is the commonest salad base, and oftenest used as garnish and background. This is reasonable because lettuce can be found in most markets the year round, and is reasonable in price. It is a vegetable of considerable nutritive value in itself and should be eaten as part of the salad. Only small, fresh leaves should be used as garnish. The coarser leaves may be shredded and used as salad. Lettuce can be kept fresh if washed when it first comes from market or garden, shaken, and then put into a closed vegetable dish in the refrigerator with only the dampness clinging to its leaves. Radishes, cucumbers, tomatoes and other vegetables, as well as parsley, celery, chicory and endive should be kept in the same way. It is sloppy housekeeping and poor economy to lay vegetables just as they come to the kitchen on an open shelf of the ice box.

Judgment should be shown in the selection of salads to accompany different kinds of meals. With a heavy meat dinner, only a light salad should be served, either a fruit salad which will also take the place of dessert, or a green, tart vegetable salad. Salads may be served on individual plates before coming to the table or served at the table. The latter is a pretty custom when the salad is a separate course. Even the salad dressing may be made at the table, if the guests are of not too restless a disposition. With a handsome cruet of oil, another of vinegar, a bucket of ice, a small caster of different seasonings before her (or him, for there are men who enjoy making a salad dressing) the manipulation is a pleasant sight. A "turned salad" is the best kind to make in this way. This allows the exhibition of a handsome salad bowl of wood, pottery, or the elegant cut glass bowl that was given your mother as a wedding present and which for twenty years has been packed away in the garret in a barrel. Now is the time to bring it out, and it may surprise you to find how your guests will be eaten up with envy.

The matter of what to eat with salads is sometimes a problem, although canny manufacturers have long since attempted to relieve the hostess of that difficulty. The following are some of the most appropriate. Salty crackers; these are good with either a tart or sweet salad. Cheese straws and cheese crackers; especially suitable with vegetable and aspic salads.

Toasted crackers: Spread any salted cracker with some such dressing as cream cheese mixtures of cheese and vegetable minced, minced ham and dozens of other combinations. Lay in a pan and toast in the oven.

Cheese straws: Pastry dough with cheese grated on it—rolled or cut into strips and baked.

Sandwiches: When the salad is the main dish as at a tea, then almost any kind of sandwich is suitable. These should be very thin, well seasoned and tasty.

Cheese: American cheese, Roquefort cheese, cream cheese, cottage cheese—especially cottage cheese, but for the matter of that, almost any cheese is in good company when traveling along with a salad, particularly one of vegetables or tart fruits.

Certain vegetables and fruit—and some meats—are the better for marinating (standing for an hour or longer in an oil and vinegar dressing) but lettuce should never be allowed to stand so, nor any vegetable or fruit that will wilt and be less appetizing.

Different kinds of salads require different dressings. A French Dressing with garlic in it is not suitable for fruit salad but is better for certain vegetable or meat salads than one without. A salad dressing made with fruit juice would not go well with a vegetable or fish salad.

Keep material for making different dressings on one particular shelf and in one particular place on it, for making dressings in a hurry.

Do not throw away the spiced or sweetened vinegar from pickles of any kind. This gives added and pleasant flavor to salad dressings and sauces. Experiment with it in French Dressings and in Mint Sauce.

Keep a bottle of vinegar with a garlic clove in it ready for use. Cut the clove in two and put in a new one when the vinegar is used up.

Extract of garlic as well as extract of onion are now to be had.

Amongst the staple requirements for making salad dressings are: olive oil, vegetable oil, mineral oil (for those on special diets), Worcestershire Sauce, Tabasco Sauce Chili Sauce, cider vinegar, tarragon vinegar (made by putting a tarragon leaf in cider vinegar), garlic, onion extract, capers, cayenne, paprika, horseradish. Parsley is easily grown in the smallest of gardens, as are also mint and chives. Parsley and chives may be grown in pots or boxes in the house during the winter. In using the garlic clove to rub the inside of a salad bowl, cut it in two and use the cut side.

All ingredients for making salad dressings should be very cold when used. All ingredients for vegetable salads should be fresh and crisp.

In making meat or poultry salads, cut the meat with a sharp knife or scissors in order not to leave jagged edges. Do *not* put such meat through a chopper, nor mince too fine in a bowl. Neither should meat be left in chunks.

Remember that lettuce is not the only green that can be used for garnishing salads. Chicory (the curly white center leaves), watercress, sorrell, young dandelions are amongst others.

Salad making is so important and frequent a part of the daily preparation of meals that suitable equipment should be provided as an economy of time and effort. Following are some of the most essential: Bowls for mixing and beating, preferably glass; electric mixer; rotary egg beaters; measuring cups and spoons; jar for mixing French Dressing: should have tightly fitting cover so that the dressing may be kept in refrigerator; suitable jar or bottle for use on table–for French Dressing; chopping bowl and knife, two sizes; large one for vegetables, smaller one for mincing parsley, chives, etc.; roller mincer for mincing parsley, etc.; scissors for cutting meats, poultry; should be strong and sharp; sharp knives, different sized; wooden spoons; purée sieve; colander; small sieve for fruit juices; vegetable cutters; lemon squeezer; egg slicer; can opener; bottle openers; cheese cloth for shaking lettuce; wooden bowl, spoon and fork for mixing salad, suitable for table service; double boiler –1 ½ quart; molds, individual and larger.

Additional ingredients for emergency shelf: mustard–dry and prepared; evaporated milk; packages of cheese; cans of fruit; tins of fish and vegetables; jars of pickles; catsup and chili sauce.

With such precautions as these, with a collection of good recipes and an adventurous disposition, the matter of making interesting, original and appetizing salads offers many pleasant and gratifying opportunities.

Mayonnaise

Suitable, plain, for fruit, vegetable, egg, or meat salad. Or as a base for many varieties of dressing. Should be highly seasoned

1½ cups salad oil	1 tsp. salt
2 tbps. vinegar	2 tsp. sugar
1 whole egg	1 tsp. paprika

Break egg in bowl and beat slightly; add salt, sugar and paprika and beat; now add salad oil a little at a time until dressing is thick. Add a little vinegar, then continue with oil and vinegar until all is used. One whole egg will really take two cups of oil, but if this amount is used, seasonings should be added accordingly. The above is a standard recipe but personal taste should dictate seasonings. Some may like more vinegar (or lemon juice), some more or less sugar. Two egg yolks will make a stiffer dressing than one whole egg. The main result desired, is a tasty, appetizing dressing, not too oily, not too sharp, and with enough paprika to give it color. Mayonnaise made in this manner should not curdle, but if it should, put half a teaspoonful of egg white in a fresh bowl and beat the curdled mixture into it a few drops at a time. Mayonnaise will keep almost indefinitely—certainly until any reasonable quantity is used up, if kept in a refrigerator.

Russian Dressing

Favorite with many people for hearts of lettuce or Romaine

1 cup mayonnaise	1 tbsp. lemon juice
½ cup chili sauce	1 tsp. Worcestershire sauce

Paprika

Stir all ingredients into the mayonnaise, mix thoroughly and chill.

Thousand Island Dressing

1 cup mayonnaise	3 tbsp. French dressing (with garlic)
2 hard cooked eggs	2 tbsp. chili sauce
2 tbsp. tomato ketchup	2 tbsp. chopped pickle
1 tsp. onion juice	

Mix all ingredients together and use very cold. Chop pickle fine.

French Dressing

Suitable for fruit or vegetable salad

¾ cup olive oil or salad oil	1 tsp. paprika
¼ cup tarragon vinegar	¾ tsp. salt
3 tsp. sugar	1 tsp. Worcestershire sauce

Put in bottle large enough to allow shaking. Mix thoroughly; keep cold and shake whenever used.

French Dressing No. 2

Rub yolks of 2 hard cooked eggs to a paste, add one-half cup of French Dressing, 1 teaspoonful of minced green pepper and a dash of paprika. Mix together and use on meat, poultry or vegetable salad.

Cooked Salad Dressing No. 1

Suitable for fruit salads, tomato, asparagus, cauliflower, etc.

6 tbsp. vinegar
3 eggs
2 tbsp. butter
1 tsp. salt
2 tbsp. sugar
1 tsp. paprika
Whipped cream

Heat vinegar in double boiler; when warm (not hot) stir in well beaten eggs. Cook, stirring constantly until thick and smooth. Remove from stove and add other ingredients. At the last, beat in whipped cream equal to the amount of dressing. Use at once. Makes about a pint.

Cooked Salad Dressing No. 2

3 tbsp. flour
3 tbsp. sugar
¾ tsp. salt
¾ tsp. mustard (dry)
Dash pepper
1 cup bottled or diluted evaporated milk
1 whole egg
2 tbsp. butter
⅓ cup lemon juice

Mix all dry ingredients and add milk. Cook in a double boiler ten minutes stirring until smooth. Pour over beaten egg. Return to double boiler and cook until thickened. Add butter and lemon juice. Beat smooth and remove from fire at once.

Sour Cream Dressing No. 1

1 cup sour cream
1 tbsp. sugar
1 tsp. salt
3 tbsp. lemon juice
1 tbsp. horseradish
1 tsp. chili powder
½ onion minced
1 tbsp. capers

Whip the cream, add sugar, salt and all other ingredients, lemon juice last. Chill. Sprinkle paprika over salad after it is mixed with dressing.

Sour Cream Dressing No. 2

Favorite for cucumbers, and tomatoes, or combination with onions

½ cup thick, sour cream
1 tsp. vinegar
½ tsp. dry mustard
Salt, pepper
Paprika
Sugar

Mix all ingredients together, seasoning to taste.

Honey Dressing

For use on fruit salads

1 pkg. cream cheese
½ cup strained honey
½ cup mayonnaise

Blend cheese and honey together; add mayonnaise; mix thoroughly and use on fruit salads.

Orange Salad Dressing No. 1

¼ cup sugar
4 tbsp. flour
½ tsp. salt
½ tsp. dry mustard
Dash paprika
1 cup orange juice
¼ cup lemon juice
2 tbsp. melted butter

Mix dry ingredients, add fruit juices and bring to the boiling point stirring constantly to avoid lumps or burning. Reduce the heat when the mixture begins to boil, cook slowly for three minutes, add butter and remove from fire. Stir until smooth and clear. Especially delicious for salads in which orange is used.

Orange Salad Dressing No. 2

2 cups salad oil
2 tbsp. lemon juice
3 tbsp. orange juice
¾ cup powdered sugar
½ cup tarragon vinegar
½ tbsp. Worcestershire sauce
½ tbsp. dry mustard
¾ tsp. paprika
¾ tsp. salt

Place all ingredients in a large bowl and beat well with rotary or electric beater. Will keep almost indefinitely.

Boiled Dressing for Cole Slaw

½ pt. vinegar
½ tsp. dry mustard
½ cup cream
Red pepper
Sugar
Small piece butter

Cook all ingredients together except cream until smooth and thick. Cool and add cream.

SAUCES

Notes on Sauces for Meats and Vegetables

WHETHER a meat, fish or vegetable will be improved by the use of a sauce is something that must be decided by the nature of the dish and the judgment of the cook. It seems to us that to drench a rich, juicy beefsteak with any kind of sauce is to insult the steak and defraud the user of the satisfaction he ought to find in the flavor of the meat itself, but there are many people, men especially, who think the addition of a piquant sauce enhances the flavor. That is merely a matter of taste—or prejudice, and the user should be allowed his preference. On the other hand a baked fish, the flesh of which is naturally dry, is greatly improved by a sauce. So is a hamburg loaf, a slice of baked ham, all game, or other meat that is likely to be dry in the cooking. Vegetables are more often than not benefited by the judicious use of a sauce, as cauliflower with cheese or cream sauce, peas and asparagus (in our opinion) by the addition of cream and butter, broccoli with Hollandaise and so on.

The making of sauces requires, first, a knowledge of the principles of such cookery, and, second, a sense of taste and an imagination. The general and well founded objection to white sauces in particular is that they are tasteless and pasty. Men sometimes cynically refer to them as "library paste gone wrong."

White sauce, in itself, is colorless—as the name implies, and lacking in personality until it has the addition of some colorful ingredient and good seasoning. A bit of that ubiquitous garden specialty forever popping up in recipes and known as parsley, or a dash of paprika the taste of which, unless an unreasonable quantity is used, will give character. Plenty of salt, pepper, and whatever particular seasoning is suitable and appetizing.

The good cook keeps certain standard sauces on hand as a basis for making whatever she wants. White Sauce, Brown Sauce, Tomato Sauce and Bechemel. These may be made up in reasonable quantity, and kept in a good refrigerator until ready for use. Liquid from chicken, veal and beef should be saved for making stock. Hot water and bouillon cubes can be used but meat stock is better. Tomato soup is used by a great many cooks–the commercially canned, but others prefer to make their own.

The usual method for making sauces is to melt the butter in a frying pan and when it is hot, to stir the flour into it. For white sauce neither the butter nor the flour is allowed to brown. For brown sauce, the butter is allowed to get smoking hot, the flour blended into it and cooked until brown.

A general rule for thickening is to allow two tablespoons each of butter and flour to one cup of liquid. Brown sauce requires a little more flour. When the sauce is put away, and after it has cooled, run a little melted butter over the top to keep from forming a crust.

To mix flour and milk, water or stock, put the ingredients into a tightly corked or covered large-mouthed bottle or glass can and shake. This gives a much evener consistency with less chance of lumping than when mixed by the usual method. The bottles in which certain kinds of pickles or chili sauce come are good for this purpose.

White Sauce

This is a basic rule to be made thicker or thinner by the use of more flour or milk, or less.

4 tbsp. butter
3 tbsp. flour
2 cups bottled or diluted evaporated milk
Salt, pepper

Melt butter and blend flour with it; cook until smooth, stirring constantly. Add cold or warmed milk a little at a time, stirring to blend. Continue to cook, in a double boiler, for ten or fifteen minutes, stirring often. Season with salt and pepper and a little paprika for color.

Cream Sauce

½ pt. cream
½ pt. white stock
1 tsp. salt
1 tbs. flour

Heat stock in double boiler; mix flour with a little cream, to paste. Add this to the stock and season. Chicken stock is preferable.

Cucumber Sauce No. 1

Especially good with Moulded Ham Salad

1 cup whipping cream
2 tbsp. sugar
2 tbsp. vinegar
1 cucumber chopped
Salt, pepper, paprika

Whip the cream, add sugar and vinegar; fold in chopped cucumber and add seasonings.

Cucumber Sauce No. 2

To serve with fish

½ cup mayonnaise
1 tsp. tarragon vinegar
1 chopped cucumber
Salt, pepper,
Dash of cayenne

Mix all together and serve very cold.

Currant Jelly and Mint Sauce

To serve with lamb

Melt one cup of currant jelly in double boiler, add 1 cup finely minced mint and ½ teaspoonful of tarragon vinegar. Do not cook. Serve warm with lamb.

Currant Jelly Sauce

To be used with game and wild fowl

To 2 cups of Brown Sauce add 4 tablespoonfuls of currant jelly, 4 tablespoonfuls of Madeira wine, and one-half teaspoonful of grated onion.

Egg Sauce

To serve with fish

To a medium white sauce add the yolks of 2 hard-cooked eggs chopped fine, 1 tablespoonful each of chopped parsley and capers, 1 tablespoonful melted butter, 1 tablespoonful of lemon juice, season with salt and white pepper, and heat in double boiler. Lastly, add whites of eggs cut in rounds. These can be cut around the yolks with a sharp knife before the yolks are chopped.

Caper Sauce

To serve with mutton or fish

Make a Drawn Butter Sauce and add 1½ tablespoonfuls of capers.

Creole Sauce

To serve with lobster

2 tbsp. butter
4 tbsp. minced green pepper
4 tbsp. minced onion
6 olives chopped
½ cup stewed tomatoes
¼ cup mushrooms cut in small pieces
1 cup brown sauce
Salt, pepper

Sauté green pepper and onion in hot butter until soft. Add tomato and cook for five minutes. Add mushrooms previously cooked in butter, chopped olives and Brown Sauce. Season and simmer for ten minutes.

Egg and Onion Sauce

To serve with fish

⅓ cup chopped onion
1 tbsp. butter
2 cups white sauce
2 hard cooked eggs
½ tsp. Worcestershire sauce

Sauté the chopped onion in butter until slightly browned and add to white sauce. Remove shells from eggs, cut in halves and take out yolks. Chop the whites and add to sauce; add Worcestershire. Put the yolks through a sieve and add to the sauce just before serving.

Cocktail Sauce

To use on sea food

1 cup ketchup
1 stalk celery chopped fine
1 tbsp. horseradish
Few drops Tabasco
Salt and pepper

Mix all together and use very cold.

Brown Sauce

To use with meats and as base for other sauces

4 tbsp. butter
3 tbsp. flour
2 cups brown stock
1 slice onion
Salt, pepper

Heat the butter and sauté the onion in it until slightly brown; remove the onion, stir butter and continue heating until it is quite brown; stir in flour which has been mixed with salt and pepper and brown together; add stock slowly, stirring continually. Bring to boiling point and cook for a minute or two.

Drawn Butter

For use on cauliflower, asparagus, broccoli or fish

2 tbsp. butter
1 tbsp. flour
½ pt. boiling water
½ tsp. salt

Blend butter and flour together in a double boiler; add the boiling water gradually, stirring until thick. Add salt. Take from fire and use at once.

Henry VI Sauce

To use on venison or other game

2 tbsp. lemon juice
1 tbsp. currant jelly
1 tbsp. orange juice
1 tbsp. brandy

Beat together until thoroughly mixed.

Bechemel Sauce

To use on fish, cutlets, sweetbreads

2 tbsp. butter
2 tbsp. flour
1 cup chicken stock
½ cup cream
1 egg yolk
1 tsp. lemon juice
Salt
Dash of nutmeg, cayenne

Heat butter in double boiler, add flour and blend; add seasonings and stock. Cook, continually stirring until thickened. Beat egg yolk, add cream to it and add to the first mixture. Remove from fire, strain and add lemon juice.

Tomato Sauce

2 cups cooked tomatoes
1 small onion, sliced
1 tsp. sugar
½ tsp. salt
2 cloves
Bay leaf
3 tbsp. butter
3 tbsp. flour

Simmer tomatoes and all seasonings for 10 minutes. Put through sieve and add gradually to the blended butter and flour. Cook until thickened, stirring constantly.

Hollandaise Sauce

For vegetables, fish, and meat

4 egg yolks
¼ cup cold water
¼ cup butter creamed
½ cup boiling water
1 tbsp. tarragon vinegar
1 tbsp. lemon juice
½ tbsp. grated onion
1 tsp. minced parsley
½ tsp. salt
¼ tsp. paprika
Small blade of mace

Beat egg yolks until thick; slowly add a fourth of a cup of cold water and cook in double boiler, stirring; add the creamed butter gradually. Cook the seasonings all together (including vinegar, lemon juice, onion, parsley) until reduced one-half. Strain and add boiling water. Then add this to egg and butter mixture. Serve hot on cauliflower, broccoli, artichoke, or fish.

Tartare Sauce

To serve with fish and sea food or cold meat

½ pt. mayonnaise
1 gherkin
1 tbsp. tarragon vinegar
3 green olives
1 tbsp. capers
½ tbsp. minced parsley
Paprika, salt

Chop olives, gherkins and capers very fine. Add to the mayonnaise and stir the vinegar in.

Mushroom Sauce

1 cup Brown Sauce using liquor from can
1 cup mushrooms
1 tsp. chopped parsley
Salt and pepper

Drain and chop mushrooms. Make a Brown Sauce using liquor from can. Heat the sauce, add the chopped mushrooms and season. Thin, if necessary, with cream.

INDEX

DESSERTS—*Continued:*

DESSERTS—*Continued:*